Financial Terms Dictionary - Trading Terminology E

Financial Terms Dictionary

Trading Terminology Explained

Published June 30, 2017

Revision 1.1

© 2014-2017 Evolving Wealth - Thomas Herold - All rights reserved

Financial Terms Dictionary

Copyright And Trademark Notices

This book is copyright 2017 Thomas Herold (the "Author"). All Rights Reserved. Published in the United States of America. The legal notices, disclosures, and disclaimers at the front of this eBook are Copyright (c) 2017 Thomas Herold and licensed for use by the Author.

All rights reserved.All trademarks and service marks are the properties of their respective owners. All references to these properties are made solely for editorial purposes. Except for marks actually owned by the Author, the Author (as both author and as publisher) does not make any commercial claims to their use, and is not affiliated with them in any way.

Unless otherwise expressly noted, none of the individuals or business entities mentioned herein have endorsed the contents of this book.

Limits of Liability and Disclaimer of Warranties

The materials in this book are provided "as is" and without warranties of any kind either express or implied. The Author disclaims all warranties, express or implied, including, but not limited to, implied warranties of merchantability and fitness for a particular purpose.

The Author does not warrant that defects will be corrected, or that that the site or the server that makes this eBook available are free of viruses or other harmful components. The Author does not warrant or make any representations regarding the use or the results of the use of the materials in this book in terms of their correctness, accuracy, reliability, or otherwise. Applicable law may not allow the exclusion of implied warranties, so the above exclusion may not apply to you.

Under no circumstances, including, but not limited to, negligence, shall the Author be liable for any special or consequential damages that result from the use of, or the inability to use this eBook, even if the Author or his authorised representative has been advised of the possibility of such damages.

Applicable law may not allow the limitation or exclusion of liability or incidental or consequential damages, so the above limitation or exclusion may not apply to you. In no event shall the Author's total liability to you for all damages, losses, and causes of action (whether in contract, tort, including but not limited to, negligence or otherwise) exceed the amount paid by you, if any, for this eBook.

Facts and information are believed to be accurate at the time they were placed in this book. All data provided in this book is to be used for information purposes only. The information contained within is not intended to provide specific legal, financial or tax advice, or any other advice whatsoever, for any individual or company and should not be relied upon in that regard. The services described are only offered in jurisdictions where they may be legally offered. Information provided is not all-inclusive, and is limited to information that is made available and such information should not be relied upon as all-inclusive or accurate.

Financial Terms Dictionary - Trading Terminology Explained

You are advised to do your own due diligence when it comes to making business decisions and should use caution and seek the advice of qualified professionals. You should check with your accountant, lawyer, or professional advisor, before acting on this or any information. You may not consider any examples, documents, or other content in this eBook or otherwise provided by the Author to be the equivalent of professional advice.

The Author assumes no responsibility for any losses or damages resulting from your use of any link, information, or opportunity contained in this book or within any other information disclosed by the author in any form whatsoever.

About the Author

Thomas Herold is a successful entrepreneur and personal development coach. After a career with one of the largest electronic companies in the world, he realised that a regular job would never fully satisfy his need for connection on a deep level. The only way to live his full potential was to start building his own business and find new ways to be in service to others.

For over 25 years he has helped many people - including himself - build their dream businesses. Toward that goal, he focuses on education, simplified and enhanced by modern technology. He is the author of 15 books with over 200,000 copies distributed worldwide.

Other than his passion for creating businesses, Thomas has spent over 20 years in the self-development field. Placing emphasis on the exploration of consciousness and building practical applications that allow people to express their purpose and passion in life, Thomas's work in this area has provided ample and happy proof that this approach works.

He believes that every person has at least one gift and that, when this gift is developed and nourished, it will serve as a fountainhead of personal happiness and help contribute to a better, more sustainable world.

For the past twelve years Thomas has studied the monetary system and has experienced some profound insights on how money and wealth are related. He has recently committed to sharing this financial knowledge in a new venture - the Financial Terms Dictionary, a hub of financial term descriptions designed to help people get started on their own money makeover and get a financial education in the process.

Thomas's ultimate vision for the Financial Terms Dictionary is to empower people to adopt a wealthy mindset and to create abundance for themselves and others. His ability to explain complex information in simple terms makes him an outstanding teacher and coach.

For more information please visit: Financial Terms Dictionary

Financial Terms Dictionary - Trading Terminology Explained

Financial Dictionary Series

There are 12 books in this financial dictionaries series available. Click the links below to see an overview and available formats. There is also a premium edition available, which covers over 900 financial terms!

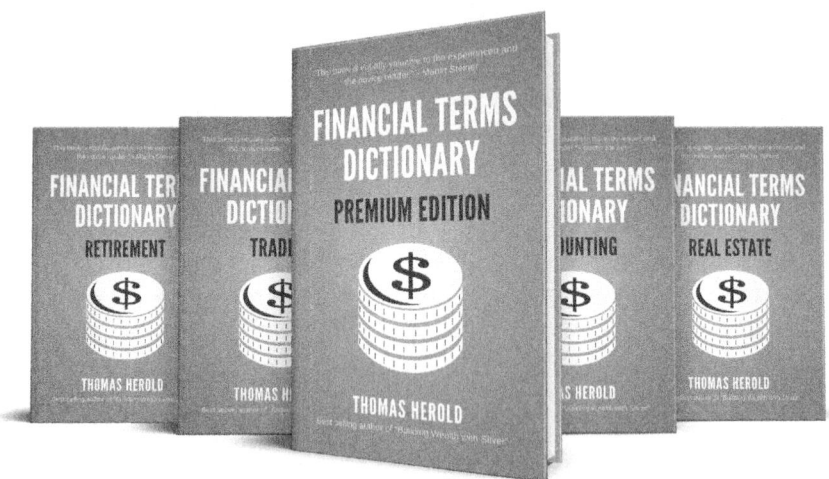

Standard Editions
Financial Terms Dictionary - Accounting Edition
Financial Terms Dictionary - Banking Edition
Financial Terms Dictionary - Corporate Finance Edition
Financial Terms Dictionary - Economics Edition
Financial Terms Dictionary - Investment Edition
Financial Terms Dictionary - Laws & Regulations Edition
Financial Terms Dictionary - Real Estate Edition
Financial Terms Dictionary - Retirement Edition
Financial Terms Dictionary - Trading Edition
Financial Terms Dictionary - Acronyms Edition

Basic & Premium Editions
Financial Terms Dictionary - Basic Edition
Financial Terms Dictionary - Premium Edition

Table Of Contents

Algorithmic Trading	11
Arbitrage	13
Australian Dollar	15
Bear Market	17
Benjamin Graham	19
Bernard Madoff	21
Binary Options	23
Bitcoin Currency	25
Black Monday	27
Black Thursday	29
Black Wednesday	31
Bond Market	33
Bonds	35
Brokers	37
Bubble	39
Carl Icahn	41
Closed End Funds	43
CME Group	45
Commodities	47
Commodity Broker	49
Commodity Exchange (COMEX)	51
Commodity Futures Modernization Act (CFMA)	53
Commodity Markets	55
Common Stock	57
Convertible Bond	59
Credit Default Swaps	61
Credit Derivatives	63
Currency	65
Currency Pairs	67
Currency Trading	69
Day Trading	71
Derivative	73
Digital Currency	75
Dividend Stocks	77
Dow Jones	79

Financial Terms Dictionary - Trading Terminology Explained

Dow Jones Industrial Average (DJIA) 81
Dow Theory 83
Earnings Per Share (EPS) 85
Efficient Market Hypothesis (EMH) 87
Energy Commodities 89
Equities 91
Equity Securities 93
EUREX Exchange 95
Euro Stoxx 50 Index 97
Exchange Rate Mechanism (ERM) 99
Expense Ratio 101
Federal Trade Commission (FTC) 103
Financial Times Stock Exchange (FTSE) 105
Fire Sale 107
Flash Crash 109
Foreign Exchange 111
Foreign Exchange Reserves 113
FOREX Markets 115
FTSE 100 Index 117
FTSE 250 119
Futures 122
Futures Contracts 124
Futures Exchange 126
George Soros 128
Government Bonds 130
Hard Currency 132
Hedge Account 134
Hedge Fund 136
Hedging 138
High Frequency Trading (HFT) 140
High Yield Bonds 142
High Yield Preferred Stocks 144
Holdings 146
Index Funds 148
Insider Trading 150
Intraday 152
Junk Bonds 154
Leverage 156

Financial Terms Dictionary - Trading Terminology Explained

Liquidity Preference	158
Margin Call	160
Margin Trading	162
Mortgage Broker	164
Moving Averages	166
Mt. Gox	168
Net Asset Value	170
New York Mercantile Exchange (NYMEX)	172
New York Stock Exchange (NYSE)	174
Nikkei 225	176
Option Spreads	178
Options	180
Over The Counter (OTC)	182
Penny Stocks	184
Pivotal Points	186
Preferred Stock	188
Prime Brokerage	190
Proprietary Trading	192
Put Option	194
Reserve Currency	196
Revenue Bonds	198
Reverse Split	200
Securities Markets	202
Selling Short	204
Shareholders	206
Special Drawing Rights (SDR)	208
Statistical Arbitrage	210
Stock Broker	212
Stock Split	214
Stocks	215
Straddle	217
Strangle	219
Swing Trading	221
Trade Credit	223
Trade Deficit	225
Trade Barriers	227
Trading Blocks	229
Turtle Trading System	231

Financial Terms Dictionary - Trading Terminology Explained

Unit Trust Fund 233
Wilshire 5000 Index 235
XAU Precious Metals Index 237
Xetra 239
Trade Balance 241
Trade Associations 243
Trade Agreement 245
Stock Buybacks 247
Stock Market Index 249
Short Squeeze 251
Treasury Bonds 253
Treasury Bills 255
Wall Street 257
iShares 259
Quota Effects 261
Repurchase Agreements 263
Risk Arbitrage 265
Russell 2000 Index 267
S&P 500 Index 269
Securities and Exchange Commission (SEC) 271

Financial Terms Dictionary - Trading Terminology Explained

Algorithmic Trading

Algorithmic trading has many names. Users also know it as black box trading and algo trading. This system of trading works with complicated and highly advanced mathematical formulas. It takes these models and engages in rapid decisions to execute transactions in various financial markets. This type of trading is only possible with super fast computers and programs. It combines these with the algorithms to come up with trading strategies that deliver the maximum returns.

There a variety of trading and investment strategies that can benefit from algorithmic trading. Some of these are inter-market spreads, speculation, market making, and arbitrage. Nowadays this style of trading is able to operate and automate trading and investment strategies by working on electronic platforms. This means that the programs themselves can carryout specific trading instructions. They can be set up to consider special scenarios like volume, price, and timing.

Bigger institutional investors who buy enormous amounts of shares are most likely to use algorithmic trading. These programs help them to gain the optimal price in the market without substantially impacting the price of the stock or making their buying costs higher.

Among the most popular types of algorithmic trading strategies are trading in advance of index fund re-balancing, scalping, arbitrage, and mean reversion. These are complex strategies that mostly require speed of discovery and instantaneous decision making to be effective.

Trading in advance of index fund re-balancing has to do with mutual funds. Pension funds and other retirement accounts are heavily invested in these vehicles. Because the underlying assets held in these funds constantly change, they must purchase or sell index funds to match. This algorithmic trading strategy looks for the points where the mutual funds are ready to re-balance. It then buys or sells first. In reality it makes money for the algorithmic traders at the expense of the mutual fund investors.

Scalpers look to make money on the bid versus ask spreads. If they trade the difference quickly enough repeatedly during the day, it can make them significant amounts of money. For it to work, the movement in the price of the stock has to be less than the spread of the security or stock in question. These kinds of movements happen anywhere from seconds to minutes. Only the quick decision making of the algorithm formulas is sufficient to maximize this strategy.

Arbitrage refers to finding the differences in pricing of two related entities. Global businesses utilize this effectively all the time. They can buy supplies for less or contract labor cheaper by getting it in different nations. It helps them to lower their expenses and boost their profits.

In algorithmic trading, arbitrage strategies work with examples like S&P 500 stocks versus S&P futures. These two markets for the securities or index will often encounter price differences. Stocks on NYSE or NASDAQ could move ahead of or behind the futures market for them. The powerful and fast algorithms are able to both track and trade such differences and profit as a result.

Mean reversion refers to coming up with the average for short term low and high prices on a security. The algorithms are able to compile such an average rapidly. When the price moves towards or away from this average mean, the programs can rapidly trade them as they move back towards it.

There are a few other strategies that algorithms are able to enhance. Some of these pertain to dark pools of capital and reducing their transaction costs. Dark pools are unregulated and off market trades created when institutional investors make their own private exchanges.

Arbitrage

Arbitrage refers to the practice of taking advantage of the price imbalances sometimes arising in two or even more markets. People who work in foreign money exchange run their whole businesses on this model. As an example, they look for tourists who require a rapid exchange of their cash for the local currency. Tourists agree to accept this local money for a lower amount than the actual market rate, and the money changer gets to keep the spread created by the higher rate that he charges them for the local currency. This spread that the different rates create becomes his profit.

Many different scenarios allow for investors or businessmen to become involved in the arbitrage practice. Sometimes, one market is not aware of the existence of the second market, or it simply can not access it. Arbitrageurs, persons who avail themselves of arbitrage, are also able to benefit from the different liquidities present in various markets.

Arbitrage is typically employed to discuss opportunities with investments and money rather than price imbalances for goods. Because of arbitrageurs operating in various markets whenever they spot opportunities, the prices found in the higher market will commonly drop while the prices in the lower market will usually rise so that they meet somewhere around the middle of the price difference. The phrase efficiency of the market then deals with the rate of speed at which these differing prices converge towards each other.

There are people who make arbitrage their livelihood. Working in arbitrage offers the possibilities of lucrative gains and profits. It does not come free of risk though. The greatest danger is that the prices may change rapidly between the varying markets. As an example, the spreads could rapidly fluctuate in only the tiny amount of time that is necessary for the two transactions to take place. In instances where these prices are moving quickly, arbitrageurs may not only find that they missed the chance to realize the profit between the differences in the prices, but that in fact they lost money on the deal.

Examples of arbitrage in the financial markets abound. Convertible arbitrage is working with convertible bonds to realize arbitrage. The bond can be converted into stock of the issuer of the bond. Sometimes, the amounts of shares that the bond will convert to are worth more than the price of the bond. In this case, an arbitrageur will be able to make a profit by purchasing the bond, converting it into the stock shares, and then selling the stock on the exchange to realize the difference.

Relative value arbitrage is using options to acquire the underlying shares of stock. It might be that the option is less expensive relative to the shares of stock that it will purchase. If a stock trades at $200, and the option that permits you to buy a share of the stock for $120 is trading at only $50, then you could buy the option, exercise it for the shares, and sell it for $200. You would only have spent $170 per share on the purchase, and then realize a $30 per share profit.

Australian Dollar

The Australian Dollar is the official national currency for the country of Australia. It is also considered to be one of the eight main trading and exchange currencies of the world, alongside the U.S. dollar, Eurozone euro, British pound sterling, Japanese Yen, Swiss franc, New Zealand Dollar, and Canadian Dollar. The most popular currency pair for the Australian dollars is the AUD/GBP Australian dollars to Great British pounds.

AUD is the official currency code for Australian dollars in the world of foreign exchange and Forex markets. The symbol of the Australian Dollar is $. Where currency cross pair and exchange rates are concerned, the most popular AUD pairs are as follows: AUD/GBP, AUD/EUR, AUD/USD, AUD/INR(Indian Rupee), AUD/NZD (New Zealand Dollar), AUD/THB (Thailand Baht), AUD/MYR (Malaysian Riggit), AUD/SGD (Singapore Dollar), and AUD/JPY (Japanese Yen).

The Australian Dollar is overseen and regulated tightly by the national central bank of Australia, called the Reserve Bank of Australia. It is the fifth most heavily traded currency on earth. Its nicknames are the buck, the Aussie, and dough. Because of the significant raw materials which the nation of Australia mines and exports, the Australian Dollars are called a leading commodity currency. This is why the AUD value is constantly impacted by the Asian import markets of such heavyweights as especially China.

The Australian currency consistently enjoys higher interest rates than the majority of its G8 currency peers. Thanks to this fact which is not lost on the world of global Forex traders, it is a favorite destination pair for carry trades, particularly with the Japanese yen as the one they borrow against. Carry trades prove to be strategies in Forex where traders sell a lower interest rate currency at the same time as they buy one of the higher interest rate currencies. They literally fund the purchase of the higher interest rate paying one with the proceeds from the sale of the lower interest rate paying currency. They then collect the spread difference between the two interest rates.

The history of the Australian dollar is an interesting one. The original colony of the "land down under" New South Wales became established in 1788.

At that time, the GBP Great British pound sterling was the formal currency of all dominions of the British Empire, even though Spanish silver dollars were also regularly utilized by the South Seas colony. The British authorities tackled this issue in 1813 in an effort to dissuade the locals from illegally utilizing the Spanish dollars. They cut the coins' centers out and these new defaced "holey dollars" and cores of the coins the "dumps" became the first type of coinage in Australia.

By 1825, the British government in Australia had imposed the Sterling standard. From this point on, British coinage started to be struck locally in Australia. The coins were bronze and silver pieces that were utilized all the way through 1910. At this point, a brand new national currency arose, the Australian pound. Because the Aussie pound was pegged in value against British Pound Sterling, it had a tangible gold standard backing it. Only three years later, the original Australian bank notes series became issued.

Australia abandoned the British pound linked currency in February of 1966. It was this year when the AUD Australian Dollar became formally introduced utilizing a decimal system of coinage. British types of pounds, shillings, and pence were eliminated in favor of simpler to utilize and understand dollars and cents.

The Australian banknotes were phased out in favor of a new technology called polymer in 1988. The Australians themselves developed this polymer technology in order to help fight counterfeiting of Australian bank notes.

Bear Market

Bear markets are periods in which stock markets drop for an extended amount of time. These pullbacks typically run to twenty percent or even greater amounts of the underlying stock values. Bear markets are the direct opposites of bull markets, when prices rise for extended amounts of time.

Bear markets and their accompanying drastic drops in stock share prices are commonly caused by declining corporate profits. They can also result from the correction of a too highly valued stock market, where stock prices prove to be overextended and decline to more historically fair values. Bear markets commonly begin when investors become frightened by lower earnings or too high values for their stocks and begin selling them. When many investors sell their holdings at a single time, the prices drop, sometimes substantially. Declining prices lead still other investors to fear that their money that they have invested in the stock market will be lost too. This motivates them to sell out through fear. In this way, the vicious cycle down progresses.

There have been many instances of bear markets in the United States since the country began over two hundred years ago. Perhaps the greatest example of an extended bear market is that found in the 1970's. During these years, stocks traded down and then sideways for more than a full decade. These kinds of encounters keep potential buyers out of the markets. This only fuels the fire of the bear market and keeps it going, since only a few buyers are purchasing stocks. In this way, the selling continues, as sellers consistently outnumber buyers in the stock exchanges.

For long term investors, bear markets present terrific opportunities. A person who is buying stocks with the plan to keep them for tens of years will find in a bear market the optimal sale price point and time to purchase stocks. Though many individual investors become frenzied and sell their stocks continuously during a bear market, this is exactly the wrong time to sell them.

Bear markets provide savvy investors with the chance to seek out solid companies and fundamentals that should still be strong ten to twenty years in the future. Good companies will still do well in the coming years, even if their share prices fall twenty or forty percent with the overall market. A company like Gillette that makes razors will still have a viable and dependable market going years down the road, even if the stock is unfairly punished by a bear market. Making money in a bear market requires investors to understand that a company's underlying core business has to be distinguished from its short term share price. In the near term, a company's fundamentals and stock prices do not always have much in common.

This means that a discounted price on a good company in a bear market is much like a periodic clearance sale at a person's favorite store. The time to buy the products heavily is while they are greatly discounted. The stock market is much the same. History has demonstrated on a number of different occasions that the stock prices of good companies will rebound to more realistic and fair valuations given some time.

Benjamin Graham

Benjamin Graham was born in 1894 in London, the then British Empire to an importer. When he was still young, his family moved to the United States to open up an import business. Despite his father dying shortly thereafter and his mother subsequently losing the family savings in 1907 to a financial crisis, Graham excelled in school and attended Columbia University afterward, which even offered him a teaching professorship after he graduated.

Rather than enter the world of academia full time, Benjamin Graham accepted a job with Newburger, Henderson, and Loeb on Wall Street as a chalker. He soon did fantastic financial research for the company and achieved the impressive status of partner before turning 25 years old. At this still young age, Graham was already earning more than half a million dollars per year, a vast fortune in the 1920s, equal to over $5 million per year in today's drastically devalued dollars.

Graham was not content with this incredible success. He started his own investment company partnership with a fellow broker Jerome Newman in 1926. This firm lasted thirty years through his retirement in 1956. Graham also began to lecture as a finance professor at Columbia in his free time at night.

Graham nearly suffered total financial destruction as a victim of the "Black Monday" Crash of 1929. His fledgling partnership managed to survive the national crisis thanks to the two partners selling most everything they owned and getting some aid from friends who had fared better during it. Graham's wife also returned to dance teaching to help pull the company through. Graham never forgot this most painful and humiliating of lessons once he got back on his proverbial feet with the partnership. It provided him with a number of valuable stop loss management lessons to share with his legions of readers in years to come.

By 1934, Benjamin Graham was writing and publishing his classic work *Security Analysis* with fellow Columbia academic David Dodd, a volume which remains in print to this day. The book featured countless valuable stories and instructions for how to invest in common stocks successfully using prudent investment practices. In this book, Graham and Dodd co-introduced the idea of the intrinsic value investment and their eternal wisdom on how to buy stocks at a discount to their true value.

Graham and Newman continued their legendary investment partnership all the way through 1956 and never again lost their clients any money. The earnings of the company were a difficult to replicate 20 percent returns annually at a time when the S&P 500 earned 12.2 percent per year.

Thanks to his moonlighting stint at Columbia as economics and investment professor, Graham met a young student named Warren Buffet and eventually consented to hire him after he graduated. Legendary billionaire investor Buffet has never forgotten either the education or the start his beloved mentor Graham gave him in the business, acknowledging Benjamin Graham as the investing master guru to this day.

Graham and Buffet combined their powers to pick out insurance company GEICO, a firm that has made both Buffet's Berkshire Hathaway group and Benjamin Graham's heirs a vast fortune. Graham and Newman bought the company outright in 1948 and then had to convert it to a public company and distribute shares to their partnerships' investors because of regulations that prohibited investment firms from owning insurance companies.

Benjamin Graham also wrote what is still called the Bible of Value Investing in 1949 a few years before he ultimately retired. This work *The Intelligent Investor: The Definitive Book on Value Investing. A Book of Practical Counsel*, has also never stopped being in print. In 1976 after 20 years in retirement, legendary investor, teacher, and writer Benjamin Graham finally died. He had justified his ongoing reputation as "Father of Security Analysis" for more than 80 years.

Bernard Madoff

Bernard Madoff used to be a nationally famous and admired stock broker and investment advisor. In the end, it turned out that he oversaw a multibillion dollar empire which he ran as an elaborate and far-flung Ponzi scheme. Madoff is presently serving out a 150 year prison sentence for his crimes in this endeavor.

Bernard Madoff was born in Queens, New York in 1938 on April 29th. After earning his Political Science bachelor's degree from Hofstra University in New York City in 1960, he pooled together $5,000 of his own money with another $50,000 which he borrowed from his wife Ruth's parents. The couple then founded Bernard L. Madoff Investment Securities, LLC.

Thanks to assistance from his father in law, a retired CPA, Bernard Madoff and his company were successful in attracting in wealthy and famous investors that gave him a prestigious client roster. Among his investor-clients were Steven Spielberg, Kyra Sedgwick, and Kevin Bacon. Word of mouth spread his consistent fame for delivering yearly returns amounting to ten percent or even higher. By the conclusion of the 1980s, the Bernard L. Madoff Investment Securities company handled over five percent of the entire daily trading volume of the NYSE New York Stock Exchange.

Not all of Madoff Securities' successes were mere mirages. He had been forward thinking in adapting his business to changing technologies and times. His company proved to be among the first to deploy computerized technologies in its trading. In this way, his firm actually became a key player in the rise of the famed NASDAQ stock market exchange, which is actually the National Association of Securities Dealers Automated Quotations. Madoff was such an important part in the NASDAQ operation that he eventually held the NASDAQ Chairmanship for three separate year-long terms.

Bernard Madoff loved to bring in his many family members to the family business. The company grew by leaps and bounds, prompting his younger sibling Peter to come aboard in 1970 as the company's Chief Compliance Officer. Afterwards, his two sons Mark and Andrew began to work for the firm as traders. Shana, Peter's daughter worked as rules compliance lawyer of the trading division. Peter's son Roger worked for the firm until he died in 2006.

It all seemed charmed and too good to ever end for Madoff's satisfied clients and colleagues. Yet the truth was that Madoff had been hiding a dark secret for over 30 years. On December 10th of 2008, he told his two sons he would award a few million dollars in company bonuses sooner than originally planned. When the two insisted on knowing where these funds would come from, he admitted that he had an arm of his company which actually ran as a massive and complex Ponzi scheme. The two sons went straight to the federal authorities with this information on their father. That next day December 11, 2008 saw the legendary Bernie Madoff arrested by the Feds under charges of securities fraud.

Bernard Madoff confessed to the federal investigators that his firm had actually lost an eye-watering $50 billion in investor money in recent years. March 12th in 2009 was the day he pleaded guilty on 11 different felony charges. These included investment adviser fraud, securities fraud, wire fraud, mail fraud, perjury, false statements, money laundering on three counts, theft from his employee benefit plan, and falsified filings before the U.S. SEC Securities Exchange Commission. He had moved an incredible $170 billion through his main accounts over decades of time. Yet at the time of his arrest, the statements of the firm only showed $65 billion in accounts, most of which had been lost in the markets. The judge sentenced the 71 year old Bernie Madoff to a 150 year long prison sentence without the possibility of parole.

Binary Options

Binary Options are a fairly new means of trading on the financial markets in the United States. They became a legal vehicle within the U.S. only back in 2008. Since then, they have rapidly evolved into what is now one of the quickest and simplest means of trading. These options are different from most other forms of trading since participants do not assume ownership of anything. Instead, they are simply trying to forecast the price direction of the asset that underlies the binary trade.

The most basic form of such binary options involves only two directions to potentially correctly predict. Will the underlying security go up or down is the only question traders must attempt to answer in this scenario. These are "all or nothing" trades without any confusing grey area in the middle. It makes them far easier to understand. Once traders arrive at their final conclusion on the price direction, they can punch in the security and see the percentage return on that given scenario if they are right before actually committing to the trade. It means traders know exactly how much time they have for the trade to work, what the maximum profit point is, and the maximum (total invested) loss amount could be. The simplicity of this idea appeals to countless traders.

Binary options permit trading on any of the significant cross currency pairs, stock market indices, many individual stocks, and commodities like gold and silver. This means that all of these various instruments, ranging from the British Pound Sterling currency versus the U.S. Dollar, to Apple stock, to gold futures can all be speculated on from a single unified and cohesive platform. It eliminates the need to switch back and forth between laptops or computer screens while trading internationally without having to switch from one broker to the next. This is especially true since a great number of the top binary options brokers have a wide range of stock market indices and individual stocks from the U.S., Europe, and Asia. This permits international traders to utilize their platforms without difficulties or hindrances. It makes these brokers a one-stop shop for binary options trades.

It is important to remember with these forms of option trades that every trade will entail a specific time line that the trader must pay careful attention to in order to profit. They may be set for shorter or longer time periods depending on the markets and the individual instrument involved. For those who resent having their funds committed for long, there are 5 minute options and even 60 second time frame trades available. Those who prefer to have more time for the trade to pan out are able to enter into trades with several hours and even days. These expirations can be changed as often as the trader wishes until the trade is executed. At this point, the time restriction becomes immutably set. Most binary options do not permit the traders to sell out early either at a partial profit or loss. Instead, they have to wait till the option expiration to realize their total gain or loss.

Three different kinds of binary options are available. These are the ones described above, as a basic straight call or put. Will the price be up or down at time of expiration? The second type is known as the one touch trade. In this binary option, traders select a target price before executing and committing to the trade. Should the underlying asset "touch" that price or surpass it at any point in the trade's life time, even just one time, then the investment is considered to be a profitable one. The final type is called a boundary trade. In this scenario trade, the broker supplies a range of prices to the traders. The traders have to decide if the price will fall within or without the provided range at expiration.

There are also several creative variations on these three kinds of trades along with a few exotic versions that feature higher payoffs of even 300 percent. Some of these are one touch trades with far-away target prices. While the odds of the underlying asset achieving such a price are considerably lower than with a closer target, the potential returns can be hundreds of percent if the traders are in fact correct in their prediction by expiration time.

Bitcoin Currency

Bitcoin is the name of a new electronic currency. An unknown individual who called himself Satoshi Nakamoto created this currency in 2009. This world's first widespread virtual currency appeals to many individuals because there are no banks or governments involved in issuing, trading, spending, or processing the transactions. There are also no transaction fees involved. Owners do not have to provide their actual identity to use them.

Bitcoin users like that they are able to purchase goods and services completely anonymously. They also enjoy the inexpensive and simple to use international payment system. This exists because this currency is not heavily regulated nor tied to any single bank or nation. Small businesses tend to like Bitcoin since they do not have to pay any credit card usage fees.

Many speculators have purchased Bitcoins for investment. Booms and busts in this currency are all too common. Those who bought in to the crypto currency early made spectacular returns as the value skyrocketed with growing demand. Others lost fortunes as the price of the Bitcoins subsequently crashed in value.

There are several ways to obtain these Bitcoins. Users buy them on open marketplaces known as Bitcoin exchanges. Those who wish to have them can buy and sell it with a variety of different currencies. Mt. Gox was the largest Bitcoin marketplace until it spectacularly collapsed and went bankrupt. Many clients who held their Bitcoins at Mt. Gox lost most of their money there at the time.

Individuals also buy and sell Bitcoins by transferring them to each other and by paying with them. They can do this with their computers or mobile apps. This is much like sending cash with a digital service like PayPal.

A last way to obtain Bitcoins is by mining them. Mining is the way that individuals create new Bitcoins. They do this by utilizing computers to solve complicated math problems or puzzles. When such a puzzle is solved, 25 Bitcoins are awarded to the group which solves them.

Owners keep their Bitcoins in a digital wallet. This can be stored on a personal computer or in the cloud. A virtual wallet is much like an electronic bank account which permits owners to receive or send Bitcoins, to save their money, or to pay for their goods and services. These wallets do not receive the protection of FDIC insurance as do traditional bank accounts.

To users, Bitcoins are simply computer programs or mobile apps which give the owners the Bitcoin wallet. The payment system is easier to utilize than is a credit card or debit card purchase. An individual does not require a merchant account in order to receive the currency. All an individual has to do to make a payment is to put the payment amount and address of the recipient then click send.

An important fact about Bitcoin is that no one owns the actual network. Bitcoin users control the Bitcoin currency. Various developers work on the software to improve it. Users are able to decide which version or software they use it on, which prohibits developers from forcefully changing the operation. For the software to work properly, all Bitcoin users have to work with programs that abide by the same rules.

As with most new currencies Bitcoin is not without problems. When digital wallets are left in the cloud, some servers have been hacked and coins stolen. Bitcoin exchanges like Mt. Gox have failed. Other companies have disappeared with their clients' Bitcoins. When the wallets stay on a person's computer, they can be destroyed by viruses or accidentally deleted.

Increasing government regulation appears to be in the future of Bitcoin and other crypto currencies. Because of the anonymous nature of the currency, they have evolved into the preferred payment method for illegal activities such as drugs and smuggling. Governments are concerned about being able to trace these types of activities back to the users. They are also worried about not being able to tax transactions made in Bitcoin currency.

Black Monday

Black Monday refers to three separate stock market crashes that coincidentally happened on Mondays. These were the crashes of October 19 in 1987, the one on October 28 in 1929, and the stock market correction crash of August 24 in 2015.

The Black Monday in 1987 proves to be the most common reference for the phrase. It was the biggest single day percentage drop in the markets in the history of the stock market. This dark day saw the Dow Jones Industrial Average plunge 22.61% on October 19, 1987 when the market cratered 508 points down to 1738.74. At the same time, the S&P 500 plummeted 57.64 points down to 225.06 for a 20.4% loss. The Dow did not recover this single day loss for two years.

The background to this crash started with a five year long bull market. The Dow Jones had run up 43% in just 1987. This brought it to a peak o 2,747.65 in the trading session of August 25, 1987. A little bit lower range held over a month until October 2. At this point, the markets began to decline precipitously. They declined 15% over the two weeks that led to Black Monday.

Various studies were done to determine what caused this nearly 37% drop in the markets in two weeks. The SEC Securities and Exchange Commission analysis decided that traders' nervousness about anti takeover legislation being reviewed in the House Ways and Means Committee led to it.

On Tuesday, October 13 they introduced this bill, and it passed October 15th. In only three days, stocks tumbled over 10%. This represented the biggest three day decline in markets in 50 years. The securities which declined the most steeply proved to be the corporations which would have suffered most from the legislation's impacts.

The bill had proposed to do away with a tax deduction on corporate takeover loans. Congress was attempting to better regulate the markets. Wall Street reacted with Black Monday. The upsetting tax deduction proposition was removed from the bill before it passed into law after the damage in the stock markets had already occurred.

More factors than this aggravated the crash. Stock trading programs were already computerized at this point. They caused the sell off to be worse than it should have. These programs were set up with sell stop loss orders that entered sell orders as the markets declined by a specific percentage. As the programs all began to react at the same time, the New York Stock Exchange dealers became overwhelmed. There simply were not enough buyers available on some of the stocks. This forced them to halt trading on the exchange.

Besides this, an October 16th announcement from then Treasury Secretary James Baker unsettled the markets. He stated the U.S. could permit the dollar's value to fall. This would have created lower stock prices for foreign investors. A great number of them decided to sell then to buy back in after the dollar declined. Baker was only attempting to lower the worrisome increase in the U.S. trade deficit.

Numerous investors, economists, and observers feared that the devastating crash would lead to recession. The Federal Reserve managed to hold it off by forcing money into banks. This stabilized the markets and led to a partial recovery. At the conclusion of October, the Dow was back up by 15%. The rest of the year saw the Dow confined to a narrower trading range. It stayed between 1,776 and 2,014 until 1988. Though there was no direct recession resulting from Black Monday, it did serve as a precursor to the Savings and Loan Crisis of 1989 and the recession of 1990-1991.

Black Thursday

Black Thursday began the stock market crash of 1929. That Thursday saw the markets decline steeply by 11%. The following Black Monday of 1929 a few days later proved to be worse. Stocks crashed another 13% that Monday, October 28th. The following day became known as Black Tuesday as all of the remaining gains for the whole year were wiped out in that continuing stock market rout. This comprised the worst markets crash in American history. Black Thursday and the subsequent few days of crashes eventually led to the Great Depression.

The day before Black Thursday, investors had already taken significant losses and were feeling nervous. That prior Wednesday the markets declined by a steep 4.6%. The Washington Post made matters worse with their Thursday morning headline that roared, "Huge Selling Wave Creates Near Panic as Stocks Collapse." The market opened at 305.85 on Thursday morning and proceeded to drop 11% throughout the day. The losses of this first crash day proved to be greater than a typically lengthy stock market correction.

Wall Street bankers became worried as they observed that stocks had already retraced almost 20% from the record close of September 3, 1929 at 381.2. The Black Thursday volume turned out to be three times as high as the daily average at 12.9 million shares. This made matters worse. After the three stock market crashes of Black Thursday, Black Monday, and Black Tuesday, the three foremost banks attempted to restore market confidence by purchasing stocks. This intervention seemed to work for a time, but it proved to have only a temporary effect.

These crashes alone did not begin the Great Depression of 1929. They did set the scene in destroying business investing confidence. Next individuals understood that the banks had taken their savings and invested them in stocks on Wall Street. They raced to be the first to withdraw their deposits. Banks closed down for the weekend then only disbursed ten cents for every dollar.

A great number of individuals who had never participated in the stock markets similarly lost all of their life time savings. The banks that no longer had deposits were forced into bankruptcy. This meant that businesses could no longer access loans and individuals were unable to purchase houses.

Wall Street sought safety in gold and pushed up the prices of the precious metal. At the time the dollar was on the gold standard. People traded in their dollars in exchange for gold which dangerously reduced gold reserves. This forced the Federal Reserve to increase interest rates to safeguard the dollar's threatened value. It was this contractionary monetary policy that severely worsened the self destructive economic down spiral.

The irrational exuberance of the Roaring Twenties led to the black week of 1929. Stock market investing grew to become a national hobby. Stock market values roared up by 218% in the years from 1922 up to just before the crash. These returns amounted to more than 20% per year.

The financial situation became aggravated as people with no cash to invest could simply buy stocks on margin from their stock brokers with as little as 10% or 20% down. Banks began investing their depositor's money without letting them know.

The resulting misappropriation of funds caused the run on the banks that came to characterize the Great Depression. Because of these all too common events, President Roosevelt came up with the Federal Deposit Insurance Corporation as part of his New Deal in order to restore confidence in the banks and to safeguard future depositors' money.

Financial Terms Dictionary - Trading Terminology Explained

Black Wednesday

Black Wednesday refers to September 16, 1992. This proved to be the day that Britain was forced to withdraw from the European Exchange Rate Mechanism system of currency band pegs. The same day it had to allow the pound to be devalued by 15%. The catastrophe for the Bank of England and British government occurred only two years after British sterling had become a member of the long running EU ERM in 1990.

From the beginning of becoming a member of the Exchange Rate Mechanism, British Prime Minister John Major had struggled to keep the pound within its designated floating band. The weekend following Wednesday September 16 was to be a French referendum on the Maastricht Treaty. Polls showed 58% of the French were against closer economic and political union with the rest of the EU. This had put markets on edge and increased the pressure on the pound, considered to be the weakest member of the fledgling monetary union.

The European ERM system mandated that governments keep their participating currencies within a band pegged to other currencies in the system. In order to hold these values steady compared to each other, countries with the more valuable currencies were supposed to sell their own currency and purchase the weakest ones.

In September of 1992, the British pound turned out to be the weakest in its band while the German Deutschmark remained the most powerful currency. In fact it was not only the British pound struggling ahead of the French referendum. The Spanish peseta and Italian lira were also falling under intense pressure. The pound had the misfortune of getting the most media attention.

The antagonist in the day's bloodbath turned out to be currency hedge fund speculator George Soros. He and his Quantum Fund took on the Bank of England directly in the currency markets. He accomplished this by borrowing UK gilts bonds and selling them. He then purchased them back moments later for lower prices. Soros and other speculators following his lead were able to repeat this action every couple of minutes and turn a profit with every trade. Soros later explained how he had earned £1 billion (British pounds) by selling the pound sterling he never even owned.

The pressure grew throughout the day as the Bank of England kept purchasing British pounds in an effort to support their price within the band. At middle of the morning, Bank of England officials had to purchase £2 billion every hour in order to defend against the global speculators' selling pressure.

They also pushed interest rates up to 12% in an effort to support the pound. Prime Minister Major refused to accept defeat easily and later that day raised British interest rates higher to 15%. By the time currency markets closed in London, the pound still remained outside of its required currency band.

At 7:40 pm that night, the government announced Britain had suspended membership in the ERM. It was never to re-enter it. The entire European Exchange Rate Mechanism came close to the edge of collapse over the shock announcement and sudden withdrawal.

The EC monetary committee entered crisis talks to keep the system together. It later emerged that the German Bundesbank had failed to keep up its end of the ERM agreement by selling marks and buying pounds on the critical day. Britain had spent nearly £10 billion, roughly a quarter of their reserves, in efforts to defeat the currency speculators.

Thirteen years after Black Wednesday, the Treasury released papers that proved the Bank of England lost £3.3 billion in the day from the continuously declining value of their own currency they kept purchasing.

Bond Market

A bond market is a financial market where investors buy and sell bonds. In practice this is mostly handled electronically over computers nowadays. There are two principal types of bond markets. These are primary markets where companies are able to sell new debt and secondary markets where investors are able to purchase and resell these debt securities. Companies generally issues such debt as bonds. These markets also trade bills, notes, and commercial paper.

The goal of the bond markets is to help private companies and public entities obtain funding of a long term nature. This market has generally been the domain of the United States that dominates it. The U.S. comprises as much as 44% of this bond market on a global basis.

There are five primary bond markets according to SIFMA the Securities Industry and Financial Markets Association. These include the municipal, corporate, mortgage or asset backed, funding, and government or agency markets. The government bond market comprises a significant component of this market thanks to its massive liquidity and enormous size. Because of the stability of U.S. and some international government bonds, other bonds are often contrasted with them to help determine the amount of credit risk.

This is because government bond yields from countries with little risk like the U.S., Britain, or Germany are traditionally considered to be free of default risk. Other bonds denominated in these various currencies provide greater yields as the borrowers are more likely to default than these central governments.

Bond markets often serve a useful secondary function to reveal interest rate changes. This is because the values of bonds are inversely related to the interest rates which they pay. This helps investors to measure what the true cost of obtaining funding really is. Companies which are perceived to be riskier will have to pay higher interest rates on their bonds than companies believed to have strong and stable credit and repayment abilities. When companies or government entities are unable to make a partial or full payment on their bonds, this becomes a default.

When a company or a government needs to raise money and does not want to issue stock, it can sell bonds. These are contracts the issuers who are the borrowers make with investors who function as lenders. When investors purchase such instruments, they lend money to the issuing organization (company or government). The issuer of the bond promises to repay the original investment back along with interest in the future.

Bonds traded on these markets have many elements in common, whichever type of market they represent. All bonds have a face value. This is the amount of money which a bond would be valued at when it matures and the amount on which interest payments are based. They also have coupon rates that represent the interest rate which the issuer of the bond pays in its interest payments.

The coupon dates turn out to be the times when the issuer will pay its interest payments. Issue prices are the amounts for which the issuer sells the bond in the first place. The maturity date proves to be the exact date when the bond would be repaid. At this time, the issuer of the bond would pay the bond's face value to the bond holder.

Though a holder of a bond might keep it until maturity, this is often not the case. Many investors buy and sell them on the bond markets as their needs dictate. It is possible to sell a bond at a premium when the market value becomes greater than the original face value. Investors could also sell them at a discount to their original face value as the market price declines.

Bonds

Bonds are also known as debt instruments, fixed income securities, and credit securities. A bond is actually an IOU contract where the terms of the bond, interest rate, and date of repayment are all particularly defined in a legal document. If you buy a bond at original issue, then you are literally loaning the issuer money that will be repaid to you at a certain time, along with periodic interest payments.

Bonds are all classified under one of three categories in the United States. The first of these are the highest rated, safest category of Federal Government debt and its associated agencies. Treasury bills and treasury bonds fall under this first category. The second types of bonds are bonds deemed to be safe that are issued by companies, states, and cities. These first two categories of bonds are referred to as investment grade. The third category of bonds involves riskier types of bonds that are offered by companies, states, and cities. Such below investment grade bonds are commonly referred to as simply junk bonds.

Bonds' values rise and fall in directly opposite correlation to the movement of interest rates. As interest rates fall, bonds rise. When interest rates are rising, bonds prices fall. These swings up and down in interest rates and bond prices are not important to you if you buy a bond and hold it until the pay back, or maturity, date. If you choose to sell a bond before maturity, the price that it realizes will be mostly dependent on what the interest rates prove to be like at the time.

Bonds' investment statuses are rated by the credit rating agencies. These are Standard & Poor's, Moody's, and Fitch Ratings. All bond debt issues are awarded easy to understand grades, such as A+ or B. In the last few years of the financial crisis, these credit rating agencies were reprimanded for having awarded some companies bonds' too high grades considering the risks that the companies undertook. This was especially the case with the bonds of banks, investment companies, and some insurance outfits.

Understanding the bond markets is a function of comprehending the yield curves. Yield curves turn out to be pictorial representations of a bond's interest rate and the date that it reaches maturity, rendered on a graph. Learning to understand and read these curves, and to figure out the spread between such curves, will allow you to make educated comparisons between various issues of bonds.

Some bonds are tax free. These are those bonds that are offered by states and cities. Such municipal bonds, also known as munis, help to raise funds that are utilized to pay for roads, schools, dams, and various other projects. Interest payments made on these municipal bonds are not subject to Federal taxes. This makes them attractive to some investors.

Brokers

Brokers are professional intermediaries that work on behalf of both a seller and a buyer. When brokers function as agents on behalf of only a buyer or seller, they become representatives and principal parties in any deal. Brokers should not be confused with agents, who instead work on the behalf of a single principal. In the financial world, there are stock brokers, commodity brokers, and option brokers.

Stock brokers are highly regulated broker professionals that sell and buy stock shares and related securities. They work on the part of investors who purchase and sell such securities. Stock brokers transact through either Agency Only Firms or market makers in a given security. These types of brokers are commonly employees of brokerage firms, such as Morgan Stanley, Prudential, or UBS.

Stock brokers are essential in stock transactions, since these exchanges of stocks can only occur between two individuals who are actual members of the exchange in question. A regular investor can not simply enter a stock exchange like the NASDAQ and ask to buy or sell a stock. This is the role that brokers fulfill.

Within the stock broker realm, three different kinds of broker services exist. One of these is advisory dealing, in which a broker makes recommendations to the client of what types of shares to purchase and sell, yet allows the investor to enact the ultimate decision. A second type is an execution only broker, who will simply transact the customer's specific buying and selling instructions. Finally, discretionary dealing involves brokers who learn all about the customer's goals in investing then carry out trades for the customer based on his or her interests.

These same functions are carried out by other financial market brokers as well. Commodities brokers deal in commodities contracts for clients in commodities such as gold, silver, wheat, and oil. Commodities contracts are comprised of options, futures, and financial derivatives. These commodities brokers act as middle men to an investor to transact buy and sell orders on such commodities exchanges as the New York Mercantile Exchange, Commodities Mercantile Exchange, and New York Board of Trade.

Options brokers deal in options on stocks, commodities, or currencies, depending on what their area of specialty proves to be. They specialize in providing research, trading, and education on options to individual investor clients. Besides handling the main options that include straddles, option spreads, and covered calls, a number of options brokers facilitate trade in related fields that include ETF's, stocks, bonds, and mutual funds.

Brokers in the financial world are typically regulated by one oversight group or another. Stock brokers, for example, are licensed and overseen by the Securities Exchange Commission. They must pass an exam called the Series 7 in order to practice their trade as a stock broker. Commodities brokers, on the other hand, must obtain a Series 3 license from the Financial Industry Regulatory Authority. They are closely monitored by the Commodities Futures Trading Commission. Options brokers are monitored by the regulatory agency associated with the area of options that they trade.

Bubble

In economic terms, a bubble is high volume levels of trade at prices that are significantly out of line with actual intrinsic values. A simpler definition is the trading of assets that have over inflated values. Bubbles are also called market bubbles, speculative bubbles, balloons, financial bubbles, and speculation mania. Prices within bubbles can vary wildly. At times, they are no longer predictable using the traditional market determining forces of only supply and demand.

There are countless explanations offered for the reasons that bubbles occur even when there is no speculation, uncertainty, or limited rationality in the market. Some have theorized that bubbles could be caused in the end by prices coordinating against each other and by changing social scenarios. Bubbles are generally identified with certainty after they have burst, in the light of drastic drops in prices. This results from the difficulty of ascertaining real intrinsic values in actual trading markets. Bubbles burst, sometimes violently, in what is known as a crash or a bursting bubble.

Mainstream economics holds that you can not predict or call bubbles before they happen or while they are forming. It argues that you can not stop bubbles from developing, and that attempting to gently prick the bubbles leads to financial crises. This school of economic thought favors authorities waiting vigilantly for bubbles to burst by themselves, so that they can handle the aftermath of the bursting bubble with fiscal and monetary policy tools.

The Austrian school of economics argues that such economic bubbles are most always negative in their impacts on economies. This is because bubbles lead to misappropriation of economic resources to inefficient and wasteful uses. The Austrian business cycle theory is based on this argument concerning bubbles.

Examples of economic bubbles abound within the U.S. economy. In the 1970's, as the United States departed from the gold standard, American monetary expansion led to enormous bubbles in commodities. Such bubbles finally ended after the Federal Reserve tightened up massively on the excess money supply by increasing the interest rates to in excess of 14%. This led to the bursting of the commodities bubble that caused gold and oil to fall down to more historically normal levels.

Another example of price bubbles proved to be the rising housing and stock market bubbles created by the extended period of low interest rates that the Federal Reserve enacted from 2001 to 2004. These bubbles burst once the interest rates returned to more normal levels.

An enormous amount of dislocation occurred in the following years as this bubble burst rippled over to the financial system and the entire economy in 2007 and 2008. The Great Recession and financial collapse were created in the wake of this bursting bubble. This example demonstrates how the larger bubbles grow before they finally pop, the more dangerous and damaging they become when they finally do burst.

Carl Icahn

Carl Icahn is a billionaire corporate raider, investor, hedge fund manager, and philanthropist. He earned a vast fortune operating as one of the infamous corporate raiders of Wall Street back in the 1980s. He is consistently ranked in the top 100 richest men, and he secured the spot of 43 on the Forbes' billionaire list for 2016.

Carl Icahn was born in 1936 in New York City. He started a financial career in 1961 working for Dreyfus & Co. as a broker. By 1968, he had been successful enough to get his uncle's financial help to secure a New York Stock Exchange seat. With this, he opened his own securities firm Icahn & Co. dedicated to options trading and arbitrage plays.

By the late 1970s, Carl Icahn had moved his efforts on to taking over a family owned appliance company Tappan. Once he was the majority share holder, he started a proxy battle to sell the company. His first successful corporate raid allowed him to sell the outfit to Electrolux for double the share prices. This was to be his first of many ventures that earned him a leading reputation among the corporate raiders throughout he 1980s.

Icahn would do this via a process called greenmail. He would threaten to gain control of major corporations like Viacom, Phillips Petroleum, RJR Nabisco, Texaco, and Marshall Field. He later sold his stocks and exited with substantial gains for he and his partners. His defenders say that he also made regular shareholders major money in the process. He became so good at this that his real life endeavors inspired the Wall Street 1987 blockbuster movie main character Gordon Gekko.

Not all of Carl Icahn's efforts succeeded. He tried to run some companies that he purchased. He met with success with American Car & Foundry Company, but lost money with the TWA (Trans World Airlines) bankruptcy and the failure with Time Warner. Though other Wall Street raiders such as Michael Milken and Ivan Boesky fell victim to scandal, Icahn avoided their mistakes and managed to carry his activist investing successfully through the 1990s and early 2000s. Even when he failed to take over RJR Nabisco, he still earned over $600 million in the battle.

Carl Icahn opened his first hedge fund in 2004. This failed to break up Time

Warner or to gain control of Blockbuster. He had more success in selling companies such as Kerr-McGee and Mylan Laboratories. He took on the role of CEO of Icahn Capital LP, subsidiary company to his Icahn Enterprises in 2007. His fund closed to investments from outsiders in 2011. The year 2012 saw him acquire a major stake in Netflix. Though over 80 years old, he continues to capture headlines in dealings with Apple and eBay and a feud he went though publicly with Bill Ackman of Pershing Square Capital Management. In 2016, he held majority stakes in firms Tropicana Entertainment, XO Communications, and CVR Energy.

Besides being a tough negotiator and ruthless investor, Carl Icahn has also shown a more humanitarian side to the world. He has given substantially to medical research and education. Genomics has been a specialty interest of his. In 2012, he provided a $200 million donation to Mount Sinai School of Medicine. He also set up the Icahn Scholars Program to help bring over the top physician scientists to the school. He has also founded a number of homeless shelters and charter schools throughout the Bronx and New York City.

Financial Terms Dictionary - Trading Terminology Explained

Closed End Funds

Closed end funds refer to those investment companies which are publicly traded and regulated by the SEC Securities and Exchange Commission. They are similar to mutual funds in some ways. Both represent investment funds which are pooled and overseen by a portfolio manager. The closed end varieties raise fixed amounts of capital. They do this in IPO initial public offerings. Such funds will then be established and structured, listed on a stock exchange, and finally then traded, bought, and sold as a stock is on one of the exchanges.

Other names for these closed end funds are closed end mutual funds or closed end investments. These funds have things in common with the open end funds as well as characteristics which are unique to them and which set them apart from such ETF exchange traded funds and mutual funds.

Closed end funds are only able to raise their capital in a single instance by utilizing an IPO and issuing a set quantity of shares. Investors in this closed end operation will then buy the shares like stock. They do have an important difference from typical stocks. Their shares are actually a certain interest within a given portfolio of securities that an investment advisor will actively manage. Usually they focus on a chosen and particular sector, geographic area and market, or industry.

Stock prices of these closed end funds vary with the market supply and demand forces. They also fluctuate based on the changes in the values of the underlying assets or securities which the fund contains. While there are many of these particular closed end funds, among the biggest in the fund universe is the Eaton Vance Tax-Managed Global Diversified Equity Income Fund.

There are a number of important characteristics which the closed end and open end funds share in common. Management teams run their investment portfolios in the two cases. The two types similarly assess and collect their annual expense ratio. They also may both provide capital gains and income distributions to their stakeholders.

The differences between the two types of funds in this universe are important. While open ended funds have their own particulars of trading, the closed end funds will trade exactly like stocks on their respective exchanges. The open ended variants receive a value and pricing only one time per day at the end of trading. The closed end variety will be both priced and traded repeatedly all through the market trading days. The closed end funds need a broker service to sell or buy them. In marked contrast to this, investors in the open ended funds many times may buy and sell their relevant shares directly with the provider of the fund.

A closed end fund also has some unique characteristics in the ways that its shares become priced. There is a difference between the funds NAV net asset value and the trading price. The NAV will be figured up at regular intervals throughout the day by computers. The actual price for which they trade on exchanges becomes set only by demand and supply forces interacting on the exchange. The end-result of this unique set of features is that the closed end fund might actually trade at a discount or premium to the net asset value.

This might occur for several different reasons. Those funds which are closed ended might be concentrating on a sector in the markets which happens to be more popular, such as biotechnology or alternative energy sources and technology. This would allow sufficient interest from investors to bid up the price of the fund to a premium over its actual NAV. When such funds are run by a stock picker with a successful track record, they can trade for a premium. At the same time, when investor interest is insufficient or there is a negative profile of risk and return perceived on the fund, it will often trade for a discount to net asset value.

CME Group

The CME Group is the Chicago Mercantile Exchange group of futures market companies. It calls itself the most diverse and global leading marketplace for futures and derivatives. The group itself is made up of four different DCM Designated Contract Markets. These include the Chicago Mercantile Exchange (CME), Chicago Board of Trade (CBOT), New York Mercantile Exchange (NYMEX), and the Commodity Exchange (COMEX). All four exchanges have their own commodities which they trade as well as different historical beginnings.

The world comes to the CME Group to manage its risk. The group provides the greatest variety of worldwide benchmark products in every significant class of assets. Through these offerings they assist businesses around the globe in compensating for the many risks they face in the uncertain global economy of today. Chicago Mercantile Exchange received the honors of Exchange of the Year and Risk Awards Winner for 2016.

Beyond their various trading products they offer an educational Futures Institute with a Futures Challenge competition to try to help potential investors learn how to trade these markets. This program takes six days and allows participants to learn interactively and simulate their own trading while they compete against others for cash awards. First place offers $1,000, second place $500, and third place a $250 reward. In order to compete, participants must complete six training modules, lay out their trade plan, and pass a quiz. This gives them a good understanding of the basic operations of futures trading.

The Chicago Mercantile Exchange represents the largest futures and options on futures exchange in the United States and the second largest one in the world. The commodities available to trade on this exchange center on currencies, interest rates, stock indices, equities, and a few agricultural products. CME was established in 1898 as a non profit company. In its early days investors knew the exchange as the Chicago Butter and Egg Board all the way till 1919. CME proved to be the first financial exchange in the U.S. to demutualize so that it could become a company owned by stockholders in November of 2000.

The CBOT's roots go back to 1848. In its initial days it allowed for trading of agricultural products like soybeans, corn, and wheat. Today it offers trading in agricultural as well as financial contracts. Futures contracts and options today are available on a number of additional products such as energy, U.S. Treasury bonds, gold, and silver.

For many decades the exchange functioned solely as an open auction market. Traders would get together in a trading pit and utilize hand signals to buy and sell. Now the CBOT also offers futures contracts that are electronically traded. The entity became a for profit company via an IPO on the New York Stock Exchange in October of 2005.

NYMEX is the largest futures exchange for physical commodities in the world. The trading done here occurs through the two divisions of NYMEX and COMEX. On NYMEX, traders can participate with platinum, palladium, and energy markets. In COMEX they are able to trade precious and industrial metals such as silver, gold, and copper. COMEX also offers index options on the FTSE 100 exchange in London.

During the day, NYMEX and COMEX utilize a system of open outcry on the floor. After regular trading hours, all trading is done on an electronic trading system. Dairy merchants originally founded the NYMEX as the Butter and Cheese Exchange of New York. NYMEX and COMEX merged together in 1994. Today the exchanges specialize in precious metals and energy products.

Commodities

Commodities turn out to be items that are taken from the earth, such as orange juice, cattle, wheat, oil, and gold. Companies buy commodities to turn them into usable products like bread, gasoline, and jewelry to sell to other businesses and consumers. Individual investors purchase and sell them for the purposes of speculation, in an attempt to make a profit.

Commodities are traded through commodities brokers on one of several different commodities exchanges, such as COMEX, or the Commodities Mercantile Exchange, NYMEX, or the New York Mercantile Exchange, and NYBOT, or the New York Board of Trade, among others.

Commodities are traded with contracts using a great amount of leverage. This means that with a small amount of money, a great quantity of the commodity in question can be controlled and traded. For example, with only a few thousand dollars, you as an investor are able to control a contract of one thousand barrels of heating oil or one hundred ounces of gold.

As a result of this high leverage that you obtain, the amounts of money made or lost can be significant with only relatively small moves in the price of the underlying commodity. This leverage results from the fact that commodities are nearly always traded using margin accounts that lead to significant risks for the capital invested. For example, with gold contracts, each ten cent minimum price move represents a $10 per contract gain or loss.

Commodity trading strategies center around speculation on factors that will affect the production of a commodity. These could be related to weather, natural disasters, strikes, or other events. If you believed that severe hurricanes would damage a great portion of the Latin American coffee crop, then you would call your commodity broker and instruct them to buy as many coffee contracts as they had money in the account to cover.

If the hurricanes took place and coffee did see significant damage in the region, then the prices of coffee would rise dramatically as a result of the negative weather, causing the coffee harvest to be more valuable. Your coffee contracts would similarly rise in value, probably significantly.

Financial Terms Dictionary - Trading Terminology Explained

A variety of commodities can be traded on the commodities exchanges. These include grains, metals, energy, livestock, and softs. Grains consistently prove to be among the most popular of commodities available to trade. Grain commodities are usually most active in the spring and summer. Grains include soybeans, corn, oats, wheat, and rough rice.

Metals commodities offer you the opportunity to take positions on precious metals such as gold and silver. Changes in the underlying prices of base metals may also be traded in this category. Metals include copper, silver, and gold.

Energy commodities that you can trade are those used for heating homes and fueling vehicles for the nation. With the energy complex you can trade on supply disruptions around the world or higher gas prices that you anticipate. Energy commodities available to you are crude oil, unleaded gas, heating oil, and natural gas.

Livestock includes animals that provide pork and beef. Because these are staple foods in most American diets, they provide among the more reliable pattern trends for trading. Pork bellies, lean hogs, and live cattle are all examples of tradable livestock commodities.

Softs are comprised of both food and fiber types of commodities. Many of these are deemed to be exotic since they are grown in other countries and parts of the earth. Among the soft markets that you can trade are sugar, coffee, cocoa, cotton, orange juice, and lumber.

Commodity Broker

A commodity broker commonly is an individual who makes commodity trades for his or her customers. The term also refers to the brokerage company that manages the trades for whom this broker works. This is an oversimplification as there are several different kinds of brokers. Where the CFTC Commodities and Futures Trading Commission is concerned, there are FCM Futures Commission Merchants, IB Introducing Brokers, and AP Associated Persons who are the individuals at the various commodity broker firms.

Commodity brokers do interesting jobs. They are involved in facilitating trades done in the commodity markets on behalf of the typical investor. The main other way to place such trades is by having one's own seat on the commodities exchange or by trading in the open outcry commodity pits. For the majority of people interested in trading these markets, they will be required to utilize the broker in some fashion to place their trades.

The commodity brokers themselves have one of two ways they can route their clients' trades through to the exchanges. They may have their company's floor traders who can place the trade literally on the exchange floor. Otherwise they will possess a special direct link trading platform that will allow them to place and then execute the trades via the electronic system on the various exchanges.

The commodity exchanges depend on these commodity brokers to gather in the business and clients for them. This is because they are unable to do so directly thanks to the governing rules on the way brokers carry out their business. The exchanges find it much simpler to carry out trade with only several dozens of brokerage firms than they do with literally hundreds of thousands of different customers trying to place their particular trades at the exchange directly.

Besides this valuable introducing service which the commodity broker provides, a great number of individual investors and traders need the brokers to offer them both recommendations and general position trading advice. This is because the commodities markets are often hard to comprehend in the beginning. Without the services and assistance of a good commodity broker, many investors would simply never engage in commodities trading ultimately.

Until the 1990s, the realm of commodities trading was limited to only the commodity pits at the various exchanges. The majority of the different orders came in from what was called a full-service commodity broker. The customers would first call their introducing brokers to make them aware of a trade they wished to enter. Next this broker would write up the order and place a timestamp on it. They immediately called their FCM clearing firm which takes their orders. The broker would articulate the exact trade from the ticket which their customer had phoned in to them.

The clearing firm was receiving calls at a special phone bank directly on the floor of the relevant exchange. A clerk would be taking down the order. The clerk would then write up a ticket to hand off to one of the floor brokers. These individuals stood in the trading pits and physically filled the order. The floor broker would then hand back the ticket to a runner who would run it back to the clerk. Finally the clerk would phone the introducing broker back and provide the trade confirmation and fill price. After the broker received his confirmation information, he would contact the original client back to provide the fill price and other information.

This form of manual trading via the telephone has all but disappeared in the past two decades. Now clients simply log on to the trading platform which their broker provided. They enter the trade information and hit buy or sell using their mouse. Such orders instantly route and match up at the relevant exchange's trading platform so that the confirmation on a market order is no more than one to two seconds away. This has made the trading process far more efficient, less expensive, and faster. Other traders insist on working with the full-service broker model still so they have a professional with whom they can talk about the various trading strategies and possibilities.

Commodity Exchange (COMEX)

The COMEX Commodity Exchange is the wholly owned subsidiary of the Chicago Mercantile Group that is responsible for both precious metals and base metals futures and options on futures trading. This once independent exchange is where the speculators, hedging companies, and traders all come to participate in trading FTSE 100 London exchange index options, along with precious metals silver and gold futures and options on futures, and industrial metals futures such as copper, aluminum, lead, and zinc futures.

For the first more than half a century of its existence, the Commodity Exchange proved to be an individually owned and run commodities futures exchange. COMEX arose in New York back in 1933 in the depths of the Great Depression. Through ups and downs in the markets, this exchange endured.

On December 31st of 1974, the Commodity Exchange launched its gold futures contract. This was the date when Americans regained the right to own gold again after a more than 40 year hiatus. This made it the biggest and most important center around the globe for gold futures and options. COMEX next launched options trading based on their gold futures in 1982 to cement their place in the world futures market and history. Silver has also been traded on the exchange since the 1970s.

COMEX merged with rival exchange NYMEX in 1994 to form the two still separately run exchanges under the listing of NYMEX Holdings, Inc. They did not obtain their publicly traded listing on the New York Stock Exchange until November 17th of 2006 when it began to trade under the ticker symbol of NMX. This new entity did not maintain its independence for long.

By March of 2008 the Chicago Mercantile Exchange Group of Chicago had conclusively committed to an agreement to purchase all of NYMEX holdings at a combined stock and cash offering that totaled $11.2 billion. The deal successfully completed in August of 2008.

From this point forward, the once independent and then jointly held NYMEX and COMEX exchanges continued their existence as Designated Contract Markets of the CME Group. As such, they joined the two sister exchanges of the organization, the Chicago Mercantile Exchange and the Chicago Board of Trade. All four of these exchanges together make up the DCMs of the CME Group.

COMEX still maintains its separate identity under the CME Group. The precious metals trade is what it is best known for today. This precious metals complex volume that it transacts both monthly and annually is so large that it is greater than the volume of all competing futures exchanges in the world combined.

Commodities Exchange brings in participation from around the globe. A substantial number of the traders from East Asia, Europe, and the Middle East remain at their offices until the daily closure of COMEX.

This fact provides the Commodities Exchange with unparalleled liquidity almost around the clock. This more or less explains why it has been so very successful for the past near century despite intense competition in a constantly changing global trading environment. The hours that it trades continue to reflect the global participation. This is why the Commodities Exchange has opened ever earlier in order to meet the needs of the Asian, Middle Eastern, and European overseas trading clientele base.

Electronic trading on COMEX starts from the night previously from 4pm until the following morning at 7am. The regular trading session occurs from 8:20am through to 2:30pm. This means that COMEX is open for 21 hours per trading day from Monday to Thursday. Sunday electronic hours begin from 7pm EST. The group publishes both exchange open interest and volume every trading day.

Financial Terms Dictionary - Trading Terminology Explained

Commodity Futures Modernization Act (CFMA)

In the year 2000, the U.S. Government passed the Commodity Futures Modernization Act. The act did several things. First it reaffirmed the regulatory authority of the Commodity Futures Trading Commission over all American futures markets. This authority became extended for a period of five years with this act.

A second and more significant result of the act came about as the government allowed Single Stock Futures to be traded for the first time in the United States. Other countries already allowed their investors to trade these particular types of futures when Congress passed this act. In America up to this point where the CFMA passed, it was illegal for investors to participate. Yet investors were eager to gain the leverage that these futures delivered.

Single Stock Futures are popular precisely because they do allow significant exposure to equity markets. A single stock future is a special kind of futures contract. The instrument allows a buyer to trade a certain number of shares in a single company at a price that they agree on now for a particular date in the future. The price is known as the strike price or futures price. The future date that the two parties set is the delivery date.

Buyers of these contracts are long the future in the stock. Sellers of the contract are short the stock in question. The buyer makes money if the price of the underlying stock increases, while the seller makes money if the value of the underlying stock declines. There is no cost to open the contract besides commissions and fees.

Single Stock Futures trade typically in contracts of 100 shares. Buying the contract does not cause any dividend or voting rights to transfer from the seller to the buyer. Futures trade using margin and provide tremendous leverage. There are no short selling rules applied to them as there are to stocks themselves.

Other countries adopted the Single Stock Futures trading ahead of the United States. The American market was not allowed to trade them before the passage of the Commodity Futures Modernization Act of 2000. This was because there was conflict between the two regulatory agencies the

U.S. Securities and Exchange Commission and the Commodity Futures Trading Commission. The two could not work out which agency would regulate these new Single Stock Futures products and trading.

When the government passed the CFMA of 2000 into law, they agreed to a compromise. Both of these agencies decided to share the jurisdiction under a plan that allowed the Single Stock Futures to finally start trading on November 8 of 2002. This allowed the United States based traders to catch up with other countries who were already trading these instruments.

The Commodity Futures Modernization Act brought the United States into a global market of the Single Stock Futures that included Great Britain, Spain, South Africa, India, and other countries. The South African market has traditionally been the largest of the single stock futures marketplaces. Their average numbers of contracts amount to 700,000 each day.

Though the CFMA allowed single stock futures to be traded, this did not establish a marketplace for them on which they could be traded in the U.S. Two different companies began trading them initially. One of these closed. The remaining company trading these types of futures in the U.S. is now known as the One Chicago. This is a joint venture of the main Chicago commodities and futures exchanges the Chicago Mercantile Exchange, the Chicago Board Options Exchange, and the Chicago Board of Trade.

Commodity Markets

Commodity Markets refer to exchanges where individuals and businesses can trade, buy, or sell primary inputs and raw materials either in person or virtually (over the Internet or phones). These days there exist around 50 important commodities markets around the globe. Each of these works in some way to make trade and investment possible in around 100 different main commodities.

Commodities can be subdivided into two principal types. These are soft and hard commodities which entities trade on the commodities markets. Soft commodities refer to livestock and agricultural produce. This includes wheat, corn, sugar, coffee, cattle, pork bellies, and soybeans. Hard commodities are generally the kinds of natural resources which have to be extracted or mined. This includes such famous commodities as silver, gold, oil, and rubber.

A wide range of means exist for investing in such commodities. Investors have the ability to buy stocks in companies whose enterprises are based upon commodities prices. They might also buy them indirectly through ETF exchange traded funds, index funds, or mutual funds which specialize in them. There is a much more direct way to invest in these commodities though. This is through purchasing futures contracts on the commodities themselves from the commodity markets on one of the various commodities exchanges. Such a contract will contractually obligate the owner of the instrument to sell or buy the commodity for a preset price level on a future delivery date.

There are two cities in the United States which host the most important commodities markets and exchanges domestically. These are New York City and Chicago. A few less important exchanges are based in other cities of America. The biggest of them by far is the CME Chicago Mercantile Exchange which became so wealthy and powerful (as the CME Group) that it bought out a host of other rival exchanges. On the CME, investors and traders can buy, sell, and trade such well-known commodities as pork bellies and lean hogs, lumber, cattle, feeder cattle, butter, and milk.

Another exchange is the CBOT Chicago Board of Trade, which dates back to 1848 in Chicago. On this exchange, contracts include gold, ethanol, rice, oats, wheat, corn and soybeans.

On the NYBOT New York Board of Trade, there are a wide range of commodities. Chief among these are the standards of the commodities world orange juice, sugar, cocoa, ethanol, and coffee. On the NYMEX New York Mercantile Exchange investors can trade such commodities as gold, oil, copper, silver, platinum, palladium, aluminum, propane, heating oil, and even electricity.

There are also a few regional American commodity markets. These include the MGE Minneapolis Grain Exchange and the KCBT Kansas City Board of Trade. Both mostly concentrate their commodities offerings on agriculture. Among the biggest and most important international commodity markets are the LME London Metals Exchange and the Tokyo Commodity Exchange.

Nowadays, these commodity markets mostly trade on cutting-edged and state of the art electronic systems. There are a few of the United States' exchanges which still utilize the in-person, open outcry method. Commodities' trading which takes place outside the operating hours and locations of the exchanges is called the OTC over the counter market.

Commodity markets are highly regulated in the United States. It is the responsibility of the CFTC Commodity Futures Trading Commission to regulate the options and futures on commodities markets. Their primary goal is to ensure efficient, competitive, and transparent marketplaces which assist consumers by protecting the clients from manipulation, fraud, and unethical practices.

Once upon a time, the regular investors could not invest at all in commodity markets. This was because it took major amounts of money, time, and know-how to do it successfully. Thanks to the various numerous routes to the different commodities markets today, even those traders who are not professionals can take part in the excitement and opportunity that are the commodity markets.

Common Stock

Common stocks are shares in an underlying company that represent equity ownership in the corporation. They are also known as ordinary shares. These are securities in which individuals invest their capital. Common stock is the opposite of preferred stock.

While common stock and preferred stock both represent ownership in the company, there are many important differences between the two. Should a company go bankrupt, common stock holders are only given their money after preferred stock owners, bond owners, and creditors. Yet, common stock performs well, typically seeing greater levels of price appreciation than does preferred stock.

Common stock typically comes with voting rights, another feature that preferred stock does not have. These votes are used in electing the board of directors at the company's annual meeting, as well as in determining such things as company strategy, stock splits, policies, mergers and acquisitions, and the sale of the company. Preemptive rights in common stocks refer to owners with these rights being allowed to keep the same proportion of ownership in the company' stock, even if it issues additional stock.

Common stocks do not always pay dividends to share holders, as preferred stocks typically do. The dividends of common stocks are not pre-set or fixed. This means that the dividend returns are not completely predictable. Instead, they are based on a company's reinvestment policies, earnings results, and practices of the market in the valuing of the stock shares themselves.

Common shares have various other benefits. They are typically less expensive than are preferred stock shares. They are more heavily traded and readily available as well. The spreads between the buying and selling prices on them tend to be tighter as a result. Common stocks generally provide capital appreciation as the price of the shares rises over time, assuming that the company continues to do well and meet or exceed expectations. Dividends are often paid to common share holders when these things prove to be the case.

Common stocks can be purchased in any denominated amount. Round lots of common stocks are sold by even one hundred share amounts. This means that five hundred shares of common stock would be considered to be five lots of common stock.

Common stocks represent principally capital gains types of investments, as an investor is looking to buy them low and sell them at a higher price. This leads to a capital gain when the stock is sold at this greater level. The capital gain is the difference between the selling price and the purchasing price. Common stocks can also be cash flow types of investments when they pay a reliable stream of dividends every quarter. These income amounts are typically smaller than the one time amounts realized in capital gains, though they are obtained four times per year on a quarterly basis, or occasionally more often on a monthly basis.

Convertible Bond

A convertible bond is like a hybrid between a stock and a bond. Corporations issue these bonds which the bondholders may choose to convert into shares of the underlying company stock whenever they decide. Such a bond usually pays better yields than do shares of common stocks. Their yields are also typically less than regular corporate bonds pay.

Convertible bonds provide income to their investors just as traditional corporate bonds do. These convertibles also possess the unique ability to gain in price if the stock of the issuing company does well. The reasoning behind this is straightforward. Because the bond has the ability to be directly converted into stock shares, the security's value will only gain as the stock shares themselves actually rise on the market.

When the stock performs poorly, the investors do not have the ability to convert the convertible bond into shares. They only gain the yield as a return on the investment in this case. The advantage these bonds have over the company stock in these deteriorating conditions is significant.

The value of the convertible instrument will only drop to its par value as long as the company that issues it does not go bankrupt. This is because on the specified maturity date, investors will obtain back their original principal. It is quite correct to say that these types of bonds typically have far less downside potential than do shares of common stocks.

There are disadvantages as well as advantages to these convertible bonds. Should the issuer of the bond file for bankruptcy, investors in these kinds of bonds possess a lower priority claim on the assets of the corporation than do those who invested in debt which was not convertible. Should the issuer default or not make an interest or principal payment according to schedule, the convertibles will likely suffer more than a regular corporate bond would. This is the flip side to the higher potential to appreciate which convertibles famously possess. It is a good reason that individuals who choose to invest in single convertible securities should engage in significant and extended research on the issuer's credit.

It is also important to note that the majority of these convertible bonds can be called. This gives the issuer the right to call away the bonds at a set share price. It limits the maximum gain an investor can realize even if the stock significantly outperforms. This means that a convertible security will rarely offer the identical unlimited gain possibilities which common stocks can.

If investors are determined to do the necessary research on an individual company, they can purchase a convertible bond from a broker. For better convertible diversification, there are numerous mutual funds which invest in only convertible securities. These funds are provided by a variety of major mutual fund companies.

Some of the biggest are Franklin Convertible Securities, Vanguard Convertible Securities, Fidelity Convertible Securities, and Calamos Convertible A. Several ETF exchange traded funds provide a similar convertible diversification with lower service charges. Among these are the SPDR Barclays Capital Convertible Bond ETF and the PowerShares Convertible Securities Portfolio.

It is important to know that the bigger convertible securities portfolios such as the ETFs track have a tendency to match the performance of the stock market quite closely in time. This makes them similar to a high dividend equity fund. Such investments do offer possible upside and diversification when measured against typical holdings of bonds. They do not really offer much in the way of diversification for individuals who already keep most of their investment dollars in stocks.

Credit Default Swaps

A credit default swap, or CDS, is a contract exchange that transfers between two parties the exposure of credit to fixed income products. Two parties are involved in this exchange. The purchaser of a credit default swap obtains protection for credit. The seller of this credit default swap actually guarantees the product's credit worthiness. In this process, the default risk moves from the owner of the fixed income security over to the party that sells the swap.

In these CDS transfers, the purchaser of the protection gives a series of fees or payments to the seller. This is also known as the spread of the Credit Default Swap. The party selling the protection gets paid off in exchange for this, assuming that a loan or bond type of credit instrument suffers from a negative credit event.

In the most basic forms, Credit Default Swaps prove to be two party contracts arranged between sellers and buyers of credit protection. These Credit Default Swaps will address a reference obligor or reference entity. These are typically governments or companies. The party being referenced is not involved in the contract as a party or even necessarily aware of its existence. The purchaser of such protection then pays pre defined quarterly premiums, or the spread, to the party who is selling the protection.

Should the entity that is referenced then default, the seller of the protection pays the face value of the instrument to the buyer of the protection against a physical transfer of the bond. Such settlements can also be accomplished by auction or in cash. Defaults in Credit Default Swaps are called credit events. These defaults might include a bankruptcy, restructuring of the referenced entity, or a failure to make payment.

Credit Default Swaps are much like insurance on credit. The difference between them and such insurance lies in the fact that a CDS is not regulated like life insurance or casualty insurance is. Besides this, investors are capable of purchasing or selling this type of protection without having any such debt of the entity that is referenced. Resulting naked credit default swaps permit investors to engage in speculation on issues of debt and credit worthiness of entities that are referenced. These naked Credit Default Swaps actually make up the majority of the CDS market.

The majority of Credit Default Swaps prove to be in the ten to twenty million dollar range. They typically have maturities ranging from one to ten years. The Credit Default Swap market is mostly unregulated and turns out to be the largest financial market on earth.

These CDS products were actually created in the early part of the 1990's. The market for them grew dramatically beginning in 2003. By the conclusion of 2007, the total amount of them in existence proved to be an astonishing $62.2 trillion dollars. This amount declined to $38.6 trillion in the wake of the financial crisis at the conclusion of 2008. Since then, it has been growing alarmingly again. Critics of Credit Default Swaps have consistently referred to them as financial weapons of mass destruction, capable of blowing up the financial system and world economies in the process.

Credit Derivatives

Credit derivatives refer to bilateral contracts which are privately held. These contracts permit the holders to manage their credit risk exposure. Such derivatives turn out to be financial assets. Examples of the better-known ones in the derivatives universe are swaps, forward contracts, and options. The price of these is necessarily based upon the credit risk of economic entities like governments, companies, or private investors. This means that banks which are worried about one of their customers not being capable of repaying their loan are able to purchase protection against such a potential loss in default. They do this by keeping the loan on their books at the same time as they transfer the credit risk off to a third party more commonly referred to as the "counter party."

Such credit derivatives are only one of numerous different kinds of financial instruments available to investors and financial institutions today. With these derivatives, they are merely instruments whose existence derives from underlying financial instruments. The value which underlies them comes from a stock or other asset.

Two different principal forms of derivatives exist. These are calls and puts. Calls provide the right but not obligation to purchase a stock for a pre-set price called the strike price. Puts deliver the right but not obligation to sell particular stocks for pre-arranged strike prices. With either calls or puts, investors are obtaining insurance in case a stock price rises or falls. This makes every form of derivative product an insurance vehicle and particularly these credit derivative examples.

Numerous credit derivatives exist on the markets today. Among these are CDO Collateralized Debt Obligations, CDS Credit Default Swamps, credit default swap options, total return swaps, and credit spread forwards. Banks are allowed to utilize these complicated instruments in order to completely take away their default risk from even an entire loan portfolio. The financial institutions or banks pay a premium, or upfront fee, for this accommodation.

Considering a concrete example helps to make the credit derivatives concept clearer. Plants R Us borrows $200,000 off of a bank with a ten year repayment term. Because Plants R Us shows a poor credit history, they are forced to buy the bank a credit derivative in order to be able to receive the loan. The bank accepts this product which will permit them to transfer all of the default risk to a third counter party. This means that the counter party would be forced to deliver all unpaid interest and principal on the loan in the event that Plants R Us defaults on the said loan. For this guarantee, Plants R Us pays an annual fee to the counter party for their assumed risk. Should the Plants R Us not default on the loan, then the counterparty firm keeps the entire fee. This makes it a win-win-win situation for all three parties. The bank is protected against a default by Plants R Us, which gets to have its loan. The counter party collects the yearly fee. All parties gain and benefit from the arrangement.

Credit derivatives' values vary widely depending on several factors. These include the borrower's credit quality as well as the counter party's credit quality. The biggest concern comes down to the credit quality of the third party - counter party. If the counter party defaults or is otherwise unable to honor their commitments specified in the derivatives contract, then the financial institution will not get its payment for the loan principal and interest. The counter party would naturally no longer receive its annual premium payments any longer either. This is why the quality of credit for the counter party is so much more critical than is the credit quality of the borrower (Plants R Us in the example).

Currency

Currency is also known as money that is accepted by businesses, the public, and the government as payment for goods and services. This includes paper notes and coins that a government issues and that circulate around a country and its economy.

Internationally, currency can be used to pay for imports in the balance of payments. Since ancient times currency has always formed the medium of exchange for trade. Currency has evolved over the years from gold and silver coins to bills that represent them to paper money that is today backed only by faith and trust in the government that issues it.

The U.S. currency has become the most heavily used reserve currency and medium for exchange around the globe. In the U.S., the BEP Bureau of Engraving and Printing creates currency in the form of the U.S. dollar. They produce literally billions of dollars of this currency every year and deliver them to the Federal Reserve System. These bills are known as Federal Reserve notes but are more commonly called dollars. The Federal Reserve states that there are around $1.4 trillion in these bills in circulation.

Keeping up with this incredible demand for dollars currency is not easy. The BEP proves to be among the biggest such operations for printing currency in the globe. They maintain operations in both Washington, D.C. and Forth Worth, Texas. Times have changed considerably at the BEP from its humble origins in 1862. In those days, they produced this currency on a machine that the small group of operators cranked by hand. They did this in the Treasury building basement.

Nowadays they utilize impressive technology that involves a cutting edged manufacturing process to produce the American paper money. The personnel doing this work are craftsmen who are extremely well trained and very skilled. They work with specific equipment and state of the art technology that utilizes the time tested historic techniques for printing. The production process involves a number of specific steps.

Counterfeiting has created a challenge for the BEP. They redesigned the U.S. currency to defeat the criminals who counterfeit the dollar bills. Special background colors have been added to these new notes that ensures it is harder to counterfeit their more secure safeguards. Such improved designs are used on the $100, $50, $20, $10, and $5 bills. These were rolled out in stages, with the new $20s brought out in 2003. New $50s followed for 2004, $10s for 2006, $5s for 2008, and the all new $100s for 2013.

The newly improved currency notes are the identical size as the prior issued notes. The images are historical with similar pictures to ensure that the bills appear and feel like other American dollars. Old security features are still utilized as well. This includes the watermark on the portraits that can be seen against a light, $5 special two number watermarks, a special security thread that can only be seen when placed to glow beneath an ultraviolet light, and better color shifting ink that shows different colors as notes are shifted.

$100 notes still have the raised printing and 3 dimensions security ribbons as in the last re-design. Counterfeit notes are still a tiny percentage of the circulating currency in the U.S. Technology advances have made it easier for computers to create realistic looking counterfeit notes.

Treasury has seen more of these computer generated fakes in recent years. This is why they chose to redesign the American paper currency so they could keep ahead of the technology empowered counterfeiters and their expanding methods for designing and printing the various dollar notes.

Currency Pairs

Currency pairs are two currencies expressed in terms of each other. They are price quoted in the forex market. One currency's value is always expressed against another currency, such as with GBP/USD. This creates the values of currency comparisons against other currencies. In a currency pair, the first one listed is referred to as the base currency. Forex market brokers call the second currency in the pair the quote currency. The pairing explains the numbers of units of the quote currency investors need to buy a base currency unit.

Forex trades always concern two of these pairs. When investors purchase a currency in the forex market they are buying the one and selling another at the same time. This does not change the fact that the currency pair is still one unit whether the trader buys it or sell it. When they buy the pair, they are actually purchasing the base currency by selling the quote currency. When they sell the pair, they are instead selling the base currency by buying the quote currency.

Currency pair values are expressed by bid and ask prices. The bid is how much it will cost to buy a single unit of base currency in quote currency. The ask price is the selling price to obtain a single unit of the quote currency in terms of the base currency.

As an example, consider the EUR/USD. When this pair is quoted as EUR/USD = 1.12, a buyer who purchases it receives one euro for $1.12 US. A seller of this pair would be trading 1 euro to obtain $1.12 US. These pairs can be quoted in reverse as well, as in USD/EUR. For example in this configuration the pair might list for .8975. Buying a single dollar would cost .8975 Euros with this example. Generally the more expensive currency is listed as the base currency for the pairs in forex markets.

In fact the most commonly traded of the pairs is the EUR/USD. This pairing receives not only interest from people who wish to change dollars for Euros and vice versa. There is additional interest generated by other Euro cross pairs, such as with EUR/CHF against the Swiss Franc, EUR/GBP against the British Pound, and EUR/JPY against the Japanese Yen.

The interest in these pairs is typically opposite the direction of the U.S.

dollar. This means that when the market is negative on the U.S. dollar, the Euro will receive bids because of the general selling of USD. The other pairs against the dollar which are less liquid as in USD/CHF also are sold using the more liquid pairings. This would also create bids for Euros in the EUR/USD pair and market.

The second most active pair of forex currencies is the USD/JPY. This pair has a history of having the greatest correlation to political relations between the U.S. and Japan. Many U.S. administrations have employed this currency pair in an attempt to influence trade with Japan. The Chinese have taken over the top trade tension place for the U.S. in Asia. USD/JPY still functions in its role as Chinese regional currency proxy.

There are other major currency pairs that occupy the majority of trades in the Forex markets. The pairs that are considered among the major are the ones that trade against the other majors. Besides the Euro, the U.S. Dollar, and the Japanese Yen, these majors include the British pound, the Canadian Dollar, the Swiss Franc, the New Zealand Dollar, and the Australian Dollar.

Currency Trading

Currency trading is speculating on the largest financial market on earth. Despite the fact that this is the world's largest, most liquid, and most impressive market, many individual traders do not know much about it. This is mostly because until Internet trading became popular, access to these markets was limited.

Only the large banks, multinational businesses, and shadowy hedge funds were able to trade them. Today the currency markets trade 24 hours per day, 6 days per week. This several trillion dollar market trades on every continent. Trillions of dollars per day change hands in the foreign exchange marketplace. All of this combines to make currency trading markets the most easily accessed on earth.

This speculative currency trading is not the main reason that the Forex, or Foreign Exchange, markets exist. They were set up to help big international companies change currencies from one kind to another. Many of these corporations need to trade currency constantly to pay for such costs as international goods and services payments, payroll, and acquisitions overseas.

Despite the origins of these currency markets, only around 20% of the total market volume comes from these company trades. An incredible 80% of the daily trades in the currency markets are from speculative currency trading hedge funds, large banks, and individual investors who want to take a position on one of the major currency pairs.

Currency traders are able to engage in these markets without many of the constraints that plague the stock markets. If individuals believe that the GBP/USD pair will drop dramatically, they are able to short sell as much of the currency pair as they desire. There are no uptick rules with currency trading. There are similarly no position size limits in currency trading.

Traders could buy tens of billions of any currency pair if they had the money to cover the trade. There are also no rules on insider trading with this type of currency trading. It does not exist. Economic data in Europe is routinely leaked several days ahead of the official release date.

Another way that currency markets are different from stock markets is that there are no commissions in foreign exchange markets. All currency companies are dealers. These dealers take on the counterparty currency in any trade. They earn their money with the spreads between the bid, the cost to buy the currency pair, and the ask, the cost to sell it.

Currency trading is always done in pairs. When a trader enters such a trade, the person is long one currency in the pair and short the other currency. Selling 100,000 GBP/USD means that the trader has sold the British Pounds and bought the U.S. dollars. This means that the trader is long dollars and short pounds.

Currency valuations are expressed in pips, or percentages in point. These pips prove to be the littlest trade increment in the foreign exchange pairs. This makes one pip equal to one-one hundredth of a percent. In all pairs except the Japanese Yen, these prices are quoted out to the fourth decimal point. This means that EUR/USD would be quoted in terms of 1.1595.

There are many different minor currency pairs on the market. The majority of foreign exchange dealers only allow individuals to trade the most seven widely traded and liquid pairs. These include the four major pairs of Euro/Dollar, British Pound/Dollar, Dollar/Swiss Franc, and Dollar Japanese Yen. The other three pairs allowed are the three commodity currency pairs of New Zealand Dollar/Dollar, Australian Dollar/Dollar, and Dollar/Canadian Dollar.

Currency trading is typically done in margin type accounts. The leverage is typically 100:1 on most of the major currency pairs. This means that currency traders are able to control 100,000 of a currency pair with only $1,000 of the base unit currency.

Financial Terms Dictionary - Trading Terminology Explained

Day Trading

Day Trading is the stock market strategy of purchasing and selling a given stock all in the say day. This form of trading is completely different from long term investing or even momentum or swing trading, which involves time frames of several days to several weeks. Day traders often try to make money on small movements in the stock price. In these cases they are attempting to leverage bigger amounts of investment capital to capture these lesser price movements in indexes or stocks that are extremely liquid.

Day trading can provide profits that allow individuals to make a living at it. It also can be an easy way for traders to lose money if they do not stick to a carefully designed strategy or if they have no experience in it. There are a variety of strategies that these day traders follow. These include selection, entry, and exit policies.

Entry strategies are critical for day traders. These traders first have to find a stock which works well for the day trading concept. Stocks with both liquidity and volatility are the best candidates. When a stock has liquidity, it is easy to get in and get out of the stock with small spreads and little slippage. Spreads represent the distance between a stock's bid and ask price. Slippage is the variance between a stock's actual trading price and the anticipated trading price.

Volatility proves to be the best way to measure the range of the daily price movements. It is in this daily volatility range that day traders work. For day traders, greater volatility can mean the chance to make higher profits or lose more money.

After day traders pick out the right kind of stock, they have to learn the best ways to find good entry points into the stock. Three tools that they utilize in this task are Level II quotes, daily candlestick charts, and actual time news services. Level II quotes show the orders as they occur. Daily candlestick charts give traders price action analysis. Actual time news service is critical since these companies release it directly as the news happens. This kind of news makes stocks move.

Daily and intraday candlestick charts provide a variety of useful information to day traders. They are able to see the volume of the stock and whether it is decreasing or increasing in picture form. The candlesticks can also form patterns like dojis and engulfing patterns that provide insight to these traders. Candlestick patterns may also provide useful elements of technical analysis such as triangle shapes and trend lines of a stock.

The entry strategies that day traders utilize are based on the identical tools that longer term traders employ. A key difference surrounds the proper time to exit the trade. Day traders are looking for the point where the interest in the stock in question decreases. They see this using their Level II volume tools.

Exit strategies are the other main component of a day trading policy. Traders using leverage trade on margin. Margin is borrowed money from the stock broker that multiplies potential gains and losses. Using margin means that a trader has a greater vulnerability to dramatic price movements in the stock than would a longer term trader not using margin. This is why day traders must use stop losses. These exit orders allow traders to sell out of a stock position and limit the losses.

The two different types of stop losses that day traders employ are physical and mental. Physical stop losses are more precise and disciplined. Traders program them to sell the stock at a particular price level that fits the loss the trader is prepared to take.

Mental stop losses are those points where the trader feels his or her reasons for entering have been invalidated. The trader would simply give a sell order at market price to close out of the position immediately. The problem with mental stop losses is that it is too easy for emotions to get involved and for the trader to continue to hold on to the position hoping that it will turn around. This can magnify losses when traders fall into this trap. Day traders should never risk more in a single than they can afford to lose both mentally and financially.

Derivative

In the financial world, derivatives are agreements between two different parties that contain values that are dependent on the price movements of an asset, as anticipated in the future, to which they are linked.

This asset, which might be a currency, stock price, or other element is referred to as the underlying. Derivatives are also alternative investments and financial instruments, of which they are numerous kinds. The most common forms of derivatives are futures, swaps, and options.

Investors use derivatives for many different activities. These include for gaining leverage on an investment so that when a small movement occurs in the value of the underlying, they can realize a great gain in the derivative value.

They may also be employed for speculation to profit from, assuming that the underlying asset value goes in the direction that they anticipate. Businesses might similarly hedge their risks in an underlying through opening a derivative contract that moves conversely to their position in the underlying, canceling all or part of the risk in the process. Investors similarly are capable of gaining exposure to an underlying that does not have a tradable instrument associated with it, like with a weather derivative.

Investors can also utilize derivatives to give themselves the ability to create options in which the derivative value is associated with a particular event or condition being met.

Derivatives principally remain a means of offering hedging insurance, allowing one party to lessen their risk exposure while the other reduces a different kind of risk exposure. Derivatives examples of transferring risk are helpful to consider. Millers and wheat farmers might create a derivative by signing a futures contract. This could specify a certain dollar value of money in exchange for a particular quantity of wheat to be exchanged at a future time. In this case, the two parties have actually diminished their risk for the future. The miller is not exposed to possible shortages of wheat, while the farmer is saved from the possible variances in price.

Risk is not completely eliminated in this example since the derivative contract will not cover events that the contract does not mention in particular, like weather conditions. There is similarly a danger that one of the parties will default on their part of the contract. To mitigate these problems, clearing houses insure many futures contracts, although not every such derivative is insured for the risk of counter party default.

Another way of looking at derivatives in this example is that while they reduce one form of risk, they actually present another one. The miller and farmer both pick up another risk by signing off on this contract. For the farmer, the danger lies in the fact that although he is saved from declines in the price of wheat, he is also exposed to the possibility that wheat prices will rise above the set amount in the contract, costing him extra income that he might have obtained. The miller also picks up a risk that the cost of wheat will drop below the amount that he has locked in with this contract.

Digital Currency

A digital currency refers to an asset which possesses numerous interesting and groundbreaking characteristics. On the one hand, they are much like traditional forms of money that people spend and keep, such as cash and coins. On the other hand, such currencies are not physical. This means that they do not have literal physical representations or the associated physical limitations. This currency is kept in a digital wallet, which can have physical characteristics if it is a cold storage type of digital wallet.

Digital currency in particular and electronic money in general is gradually becoming more significant as the world continuously evolves into a society that is more and more cashless. The amount of money supply which is expressed in digital format is constantly growing. Thanks to the rising popularity of such crypto-currencies as especially Bitcoin, there now exists the distinct possibility of migrating entirely away from traditional paper bills and coins at some point in the future.

Such digital currency only can exist and function when secure transactions are guaranteed online. This makes these currencies both an occupant and hostage of digital environments. They are generally represented and depicted in the form of information. Bitcoin has become so popular that numerous companies currently accept this form of digital currency. PayPal even allows for the utilization of Bitcoin now.

It is interesting to note that Bitcoin is not the only digital currency option available to individuals and businesses for transactions. A range of such currencies exist which can be used to pay for transactions. The next five most important after Bitcoin are Litecoin, Darkcoin, Peercoin, Dogecoin, and Primecoin. They have many advantages over traditional money.

The first of these is the instant transfer ability. Individuals are no longer required to wait on a central clearinghouse somewhere to handle the transaction. The days of from one to five business days waits for transfers are long gone thanks to these digital currencies. Crypto-currencies are so popular precisely because the effect of such a transfer is instantaneous.

The majority of these digital currencies also come with no fees. Whatever something costs in Bitcoin or another such digital currency, people simply pay with it at transaction cost and no hidden fees are applied. This is a stark difference from many credit card or even PayPal transactions.

Individuals and businesses especially love the fact that these digital currencies come completely without borders. This means that a seller or buyer does not have to be concerned with exchange rates or foreign transaction fees (which are often exorbitant). Cross border transactions are simple and effective to put through, though people must still watch the exchange rate at which they are offered in the local currency into which they are paying.

For the majority of applications and scenarios, these crypto-currencies also prove to be extremely secure. It is the digital wallet where the danger lies. The money is not being stored in a bank vault or even on a bank computer. The wallet must be backed up on a daily basis to prevent it from being lost. In order to ensure that it is secure, the only way to guarantee this is by utilizing cold storage.

Cold storage takes the digital wallet completely offline and off network. It means that the "pin code" like authorization element will be stored on a small device that resembles a USB miniature drive device. The nature of these devices is that they do not accept software. This means that Trojan Horses and viruses which steal information can not be imprinted on them. They also are never online long enough to be hacked, as users only connect them to a computer long enough to digitally sign the transaction.

These digital currencies have convincingly changed the rules of the financial transaction game. Their limits are two fold. The first is that a business must be willing to accept Bitcoin or rival currencies in order for a consumer to pay with it. The second is that digital currency regulation is inevitable. Central banks are jealous animals. They are already suspicious of their monopolized currency-printing functions being assumed in a non-regulated and more difficult to track environment by a non-centralized form of money.

Dividend Stocks

Dividend Stocks refer to stocks that pay especially generous and predictable shares of the corporate earnings out to their share holders. They are especially important for those investors who require dependable continuous streams of income off of their investment portfolios, such as retirees. This is why the optimal stock portfolio for those who are officially retired includes a strong and diverse mixture of industry-leading corporations which provide consistent, generous dividend yields.

These Dividend Stocks are famous for paying out significant stock dividends as a distribution on their earnings. They may pay this in the form of additional shares or as cash, depending on the wishes of the share holder in question. Sometimes the company will declare a stock dividend instead of a cash dividend, removing the ability of the shareholder to choose the form in which the dividend actually pays. When dividends become payable strictly as more stock, they are also known as stock splits.

For the companies that declare regular cash dividends of these Dividend Stocks, with each share stake holders have, they receive a set portion of the earnings from the corporation. This is literally being paid for simply owning the stock shares.

Consider a real world example to better understand how these Dividend Stocks work out in practice. Gillette, the world famous market leader in the shaving razors industry, may pay a dividend of $4 on an annual basis. Typically these dividends will be paid practically on a quarterly basis. This means four times each year Gillette would provide a $1 payout for each share of stock which the stake holders possess. If an investor owned 100 shares, he or she would receive four checks per year of $100 each check at approximately the conclusion of each quarter.

Most dividends from these Dividend Stocks come out in cash. Investors have the option to have them reinvested into additional company stock shares. Sometimes the corporation will provide a more advantageous reinvestment price than the current market prices to encourage such reinvesting of dividends in the company stock. These plans are called DRIPS (Dividend Re Investment Plans).

There are also occasional special dividends offered on an only one-time basis. They could be provided if the company wins a large and lucrative lawsuit, liquidates its share of an investment and receives a windfall payout, or sells part of the business to another firm for cash. These dividends can be made in cash, property, or stock share dividends.

There are several important dates with which Dividend Stocks' investors need to be familiar. These are declaration date, date of record, ex-dividend date, and payment date. Declaration date is the calendar day when the company's Board of Directors announces a dividend payout. This is the point where the firm adds a liability for the dividend payout to its company books. This means that it owes money (or shares) to the stake holders. This date will be the one when they announce both the date of record as well as the dividend payment date.

The date of record is the one where the corporation will review the appropriate records to determine who is holding the shares and is thus eligible for the dividends. Only holders of record will receive the dividend payment. The ex-dividend date is the day after which any investors who wish to receive dividends must own the shares. Only stake holders who possess shares on the day before the ex-dividend date get paid. Finally dividends are literally doled out on the payment date.

While most stock companies will pay out dividends on either a quarterly or half yearly basis, real estate investment trusts are structured differently. They pay out their dividends on an every-month basis as they receive monthly income from their various commercial, industrial, and/or residential properties.

Dow Jones

Dow Jones is an international and American news company based in the United States. Wall Street Journal co-editor Charles Dow and Edward Jones co-founded the company with fellow reporter Charles Bergstresser back in 1882. The independent history of Dow Jones & Company continued under the Bancroft Family from the 1920s all the way until 2007. At this point, an extensive takeover struggle ensued. In the end, News Corp. took over the company which it has owned and run as a subsidiary since 2007.

The company had been most famous for its continuous publication of stock market indices such as the Dow Jones Industrial Average and the Dow Jones Transportation Average. Besides this, it publishes a number of important financial publications such as its flagship product The Wall Street Journal along with Market Watch, Barron's, Financial News, and Factiva. It has run the Dow Jones Newswire service for decades. This is one of the biggest and most prestigious newswire services in the world.

The Wall Street Journal continues to be a leading daily newspaper that the company publishes in both print and online editions. It covers financial, business, international, and national news and topics throughout the world. They started publishing this gold standard of newspapers on July 8th, 1889.

Today there are 12 different versions of it they produce in nine separate languages. These include English, Japanese, Chinese, Spanish, German, Portuguese, Turkish, Korean, and Bahasa. The Journal has won 35 Pulitzer Prizes for its excellent and world leading journalism.

In 2010, News Corp. sold off the Dow Jones Indexes subsidiary. The CME Group bought it and continues running it. Since then, the company has concentrated its efforts on its publications of financial news and on delivering information and financial news and tools to companies involved in finance.

The company continues its efforts in the arena of publishing and data provision today. It calls itself the ultimate source for business data and news. The company boasts journalism that continues to be award winning, cutting edged technology, and sophisticated data capabilities. They combine these in order to provide news and financial tools and insights that move the world financial markets. Their efforts also help key players to make crucial decisions and major companies and individuals to run their businesses.

The company has expanded from its humble roots as niche news agency provider in a basement on Wall Street to become the global powerhouse of information and news that it is now. It claims that the reason for its success and long lasting appeal comes from a combination of factors. These include their constant commitment to accuracy, innovation and depth, and years of experience. It helps them to keep their efforts firmly focused on their future endeavors.

Dow Jones today calls itself the modern day portal to intelligence. They have state of the art data and information feeds. Their research is performed by experts in the field. The firm utilizes leading and creative technologies and solutions that are fully integrated. Their staff reporters practice journalism that consistently wins awards.

The company's delivery systems and apps can be fully customized to work on a variety of platforms. This helps them to get the important financial and news information gathered, written, and published. Thanks to their leading technologies, they can get it to their customers wherever they are and whenever they require it.

The Dow indices continue to be benchmarks for the overall stock market as a whole. The DJIA includes the thirty leading companies that represent the major U.S. based enterprises. These are no longer primarily industrial in nature as they were when Charles Dow and Edward Jones put their names on them.

Dow Jones Industrial Average (DJIA)

The Dow Jones Industrial Average, commonly referred to by its acronym DJIA, is also many times called the Dow 30, the Dow Jones, the Dow, or even just the Industrial Average. It proves to be the second oldest stock market index in the Untied States after the Dow Jones Transportation Average. The Dow Jones Industrial Average came into being when Charles Dow, the co founder of Dow Jones and Company worked with a business colleague Edward Jones, a statistician, to come up with an index that monitors the industrial sector. This index demonstrates the daily stock market trading session progress of thirty of the largest companies that are publicly traded within the U.S.

Ironically, most of the present day thirty companies listed in this index no longer have much or even anything to do with the historical definition of heavy industry. The components in the average are weighted by price and scaled in order to adjust for the impacts of stock splits and varying other forms of adjustments. This means that the total value that you see in the daily representation of the Dow Jones does not prove to be the true average of the different company stock prices.

Instead, it is the total of such company prices that are added up and then divided by a special divisor. This divisor is a number that is adjusted any time one of the company stocks underlying it pays a dividend or engages in a stock split. In this way, the index presents a constant value that is not altered by the external factors of the component stocks.

The Dow Jones Industrial Average remains one of the most heavily followed and carefully watched indices in the American stock market, along with peers the S&P 500 Index, the NASDAQ composite, and the Russell 2000 Index. The founder Dow intended for the index to monitor the American industrial sector's actual performance. Even so, the index is constantly affected by much more than simply the economic and corporate reports issued. It responds to both foreign and domestic incidents and political episodes like terrorism and war, as well as any natural disasters that might cause economic damage.

The Dow Jones Industrial Average's thirty components simultaneously trade on either the New York Stock Exchange Euronext or the NASDAQ

OMX, which are the two largest American stock market outfits. Derivatives based on Dow components trade via the Chicago Board Options Exchange, as well as with the Chicago Mercantile Exchange Group. The latter is the largest futures exchange outfit on earth, and it presently owns fully ninety percent of the Dow Jones founded indexing business, along with this Industrial Average.

Investors who are interested in gaining the ability to track the progress of the Dow Jones Industrial average have several choices. There are index funds that buy the components of the index so that you do not have to own all thirty companies yourself. You might also invest in the Dow 30 by purchasing shares of the Exchange Traded Fund known as the Diamonds ETF. This trades under the AMEX exchange via the symbol DIA. Finally, you could by options and futures contracts based on the performance of the Dow Jones Average on the Chicago Board of Trade.

Dow Theory

Dow Theory is a method for picking successful stock trades. At over a hundred years old, it may be the oldest system for selecting stocks that is still utilized. This is why investors often refer to it as the grandfather of stock selection theory.

Charles Dow created his Dow Theory in a series of Wall Street Journal editorials he wrote from 1900 to 1902. He laid down the basic fundamentals of his theory in these articles. They explained how the stock markets worked. Charles Dow also created two of the main indexes for the stock markets that the markets still use today. These are the Dow Jones Industrial Average and the precursor to the Dow Jones Transportation Index (the Dow Jones Rail Index). Charles died in 1902. His death left this work to be completed by other followers who published several books on the subject over the next sixty years.

Dow Theory is still important to markets and investors today. People study the theory to understand how several of the main indexes work. Investors also have created a number of systems based on Dow Theory over the years as well. The principles of technical analysis are rooted in Dow Theory ideas. Technical analysis centers on reading charts. These technicians use information in the charts to predict future stock prices.

Six basic ideas underpin Dow Theory. Some investors have attempted to discount these concepts over the years. Over time they generally prove to be true despite the skeptics.

The first one states that the market considers all information with its price levels. This means that stock prices reflect past, present, and even future information. The market takes everything into account including inflation, interest rates, soon to be released earnings announcements, the emotions of investors, and even future event risk.

The second idea says that three trends make up the market actions. These include primary trends, secondary trends, and minor trends. The primary trends usually last over a year. Secondary trends hold for several weeks to several months. They run counter to primary trends. Minor trends occupy less than three weeks.

The third Dow Theory concept claims that three main phases make up the primary trends. The accumulate phase starts the market prices moving up. The mass participation phase is where average investors buy into the market and drive prices significantly higher. This is the longest lasting phase in any market. The excess phase is where the market becomes overbought. Bigger, more knowledgeable investors begin to sell their shares to new investors ahead of a downturn in this phase.

A fourth idea states that two market indexes must agree on the trend change. It is not just any two indexes that have to concur. Bull markets and bear markets only switch when the Dow Industrial average and Dow Transports average agree together on the change in the trend.

Dow Theory's fifth tenet is that volume confirms the trend. Volume represents the number of shares that change hands. Without major volume appearing on any significant move against a trend, the trend is usually still intact. Volume should be greater when price is moving in the direction of the trend. When price goes against the trend, volume should be less.

The final idea of Dow Theory claims that a trend continues until there is a clear reversal. It requires overwhelming evidence to convincingly reverse the trend. Trading against the trend will usually hurt investors. This makes the popular statement "the trend is your friend" more than just a catchy stock market slogan. It also proves to be a significant philosophy behind Dow Theory.

Earnings Per Share (EPS)

Earnings per share refer to the given total of earnings that a company has for every share of the firm's stock that is outstanding. There are several formulas for calculating earnings per share. These depend on which segment of earnings are being considered. The FASB, or Financial Accounting Standards Board, makes corporations report such earnings per share on their income statement for all of the major components of such statements including discontinued operations, continuing operations, extraordinary items, and net income.

To figure up the basic net earnings per share formula, you only have to divide the profit for the year by the average number of common shares of stock. With discontinued operations, it is only a matter of taking the discontinued operations income and dividing it by the average number of common stock shares outstanding. Continuing operations earnings per share equal the continuing operations income over the average number of common shares. Extraordinary items works with the income from extraordinary items and divides it by the weighted average number of common shares.

Besides the basic earnings per share numbers, there are three different types of earnings per share. Last year's earning per share are the Trailing EPS. These are the only completely known earnings for a company. The Current earnings per share are the ones for this year. These are partially projections in the end until the last quarterly numbers are released. Finally, Forward earnings per share are earnings numbers for the future. These are entirely based on predictions.

Earnings per share calculations do not take into account preferred dividends on categories besides net income and continued operations. Such continuing operations and even net income earnings per share calculations turn out to be more complex as preferred share dividends are taken off of the top of net income before the earnings per share is actually calculated. Since preferred stock shares have the right to income payments ahead of common stock payments, any money that is given out as preferred dividends is cash which can not be considered to be potentially available for giving out to every share of the commonly held stock.

Financial Terms Dictionary - Trading Terminology Explained

Preferred dividends for the present year are generally the only ones that are taken off of such income. There is a prevalent exception to this. If preferred shares prove to be cumulative then this means that dividends for the entire year are taken off, regardless of if they have been declared yet or not. Dividends that the company is behind on paying are not contemplated when the earnings per share is calculated.

Earnings per share as a financial measuring stick for a company are extremely important. In theory, this forms the underlying basis for the value of the stock in question. Another critical measurement of stock price is price to earnings value, also known as the PE ratio. This PE ratio is determined by taking the earnings per share and dividing them into the price of the stock. Earnings per share are useful in measuring up one corporation against another one, if they are involved in the same business segment or industry. They do not tell you if the stock is a good buy or not. They also do not reveal what the overall market thinks about the company. This is where the PE ratio is more useful.

Efficient Market Hypothesis (EMH)

The efficient market hypothesis is also known by its acronym EMH. It refers to an investment theory which claims that investors can not outperform the stock markets practically on a consistent basis. This is because the efficiencies created by the inner workings of the stock market mean present day share prices will always reflect and incorporate all relevant and practical information.

The idea states that stocks will practically always sell for their true fair value on the various stock exchanges. This infers that the typical investor can not efficiently buy undervalued shares or sell them at overly high prices. This is why it is theoretically impossible for investors to better the ultimate return of the stock markets no matter how expertly they select stocks or how well they time the markets. Efficient market hypothesis claims that the only means of outperforming the markets is through buying investments with higher risk and therefore coming with accompanying better returns.

Despite the fact that this efficient market hypothesis remains a foundation of modern day financial theories, it is still regarded with suspicion and controversy. Many investors and especially stock picking fund managers consistently defy it and try to select their own stocks. Those who concur with the EMH theory state that stock pickers are wasting their time in an effort to track down undervalued shares, or in predicting market trends, using either technical or fundamental analysis.

Clearly the economists and other scholarly individuals can hold up a significant amount of evidence that supports the efficient market hypothesis. Despite this, a broad range and variety of arguments against it still exist. Legendary investing stock pickers like Warren Buffet have managed to outperform the markets year in and year out over many decades. This should not be consistently possible at all by the arguments and logic of the EMH.

Other critics of the efficient market hypothesis hold up such Black Swan Events as the Black Monday 1987 crash in the stock markets. On this particular occasion, the DJIA Dow Jones Industrial Average plunged by in excess of 20 percent in only one day. This does raise a valid point about stock prices and how efficiently they are always valued when they can suddenly fall by a fifth of their value in only hours.

Believers in this efficient market hypothesis argue that markets are both efficient and random. This means that investors should be able to make their best consistent returns by choosing to invest in low fee, unmanaged, broadly representative portfolios. Morningstar Inc., the famous market research firm has compiled a great amount of data to support this assertion. They compiled the returns of active fund managers in every category. Then they held these up versus an index of relevant funds or ETF exchange traded funds. The study concluded that for any year to year period, there were merely two different groups of active fund managers who managed to consistently outperform the passively held funds over half the time. The two that outperformed were the diversified emerging markets funds and the small growth funds.

As far as all of the remaining categories such as U.S. large value, U.S. large blend, and U.S large growth (and most others), those who invested in either ETFs or lower cost index funds would have made higher returns. It is true that a small percentage of the active fund managers do manage to realize superior performances versus the passively managed funds at times and points. The problem that this presents for individual investors lies in predicting which fund managers will do this. Fewer than a quarter of the best performing active fund managers can outperform their passive manager benchmark funds consistently. Certainly Warren Buffet counts as one of those most successful few. It helps to explain his enduring popularity and success with investors for decades now.

Financial Terms Dictionary - Trading Terminology Explained

Energy Commodities

The term energy commodities refers to a variety of coal, oil, and gasoline derived products. These include such energy sources as coal, Brent Sea Oil, gasoline, heating oil, and natural gas. These energy resources prove to be essential in daily life. This makes consumers most aware of such commodities. Besides being among the most heavily used, they are also typically among those which are most widely traded.

These energy commodities find use in so many industrial applications that they maintain a strong investment appeal. Their prices have the ability to rise substantially over shorter time frames when demand picks up or supply drops. Energy is also a major component in inflation indices around the world, which makes investments in energy an effective hedge against rising prices. Higher oil and gasoline costs translate to higher prices in general throughout the U.S. and world economies.

Investors who are interested in investing in these different types of energy commodities have a variety of choices of investment vehicle and commodities. There are Exchange Traded Funds and Notes (ETFs and ETNs), futures and options contracts, and energy sector company stocks from which to choose.

Brent Sea Oil turns out to be the major oil benchmark in the world. It is the one to which around two-third of worldwide oil trade is tied and is especially relied upon in the EMEA region (Europe, Middle East, and Africa). This indicator represents a sweet form of crude oil, though it is not as sweet as the American benchmark WTI (West Texas Intermediate) crude oil. Brent oil is used to produce gasoline and mid purity distillates like diesel and kerosene. Crude oil finds applications in a wide range or consumer products that underpin modern day life, including plastics. Crude must first be refined in order to be turned into most useful products like gasoline or heating oil.

Coal is responsible for providing the energy for half of all the electricity generated on earth. It is usually obtained through open pit mining or via underground shaft mining. Major coal deposits exist in the Midwestern and Eastern United States as well as regions of Russia and China. Coal is principally utilized in generating electricity. Almost 40% of all energy production in the world comes from coal. In the last few years, coal has become less important in developed countries and more critical in developing nations like China who need cheap fuel. It is also useful for steel production because of the incredibly hot temperatures it produces which are critical for creating the purest steel.

Gasoline proves to be among the most critical of the energy commodities, especially for the American transportation industry. The American market makes up over 40% of all demand for gasoline. Emerging markets are utilizing an increasingly larger share of this energy resource.

Heating Oil finds its main uses in boilers and furnaces as the fuel source for warming businesses and homes. It is most heavily employed in places in the Northeastern United States and the United Kingdom and Ireland. Natural gas can be hard to access in some of these markets or too expensive to use in places where it is very cold.

Natural Gas is among the most important fuels for generating power. It is particularly popular in the cooling and heating systems throughout the United States. Natural gas powers either steam or gas turbines to create electricity. It is increasingly preferred over oil and coal as it is a much cleaner energy source that produces fewer greenhouse gas emissions. It has been made more practical for transporting thanks to LNG Liquid Natural Gas terminals that work with a CNG Compressed Natural Gas form.

Equities

Equities are another name for stocks and similar types of investments. Stocks turn out to be financial instruments that represent ownership, or equity position, within a given corporation. As such, they give an owner a stake in a representative share of the company's profits and assets. Such ownership in a given firm is determined by taking the total numbers of shares in the company's equities that the individual owns, and dividing it by the actual number of shares that exist.

The majority of these equities similarly give voting rights that provide representative votes in some decisions that the company makes. Not every company issues equities; only corporations engage in the practice, while limited partnerships and sole proprietorships do not. Equities can be further divided into smaller categories based on the market capitalization, or size, of the company in question.

Because they often yield greater returns over significant periods of time, they are typically characterized by higher amounts of risk than are bonds and money market funds. Because of these unique potential returns and associated risks, equities are generally considered to be their own class of assets that are utilized to a degree in putting together investment portfolios with proper diversification. Many different kinds of equities exist, including domestic equities, emerging market equities, developed market equities, and Real Estate Investment Trusts.

Domestic Equities prove to be those stocks for the publicly traded corporations that principally conduct their business in the same country in which the investor lives. When a person holds such equities, they receive their share of dividends that the corporation pays. Equities come with a higher degree of risk than do bonds, as bond holders have a greater claim on a corporation's assets should liquidation follow bankruptcy. Equity holders are commonly wiped out in such liquidation.

Emerging Market Equities are equities in corporations that are based in countries that are still developing their economies. Included in these are China, Brazil, and India. These nations feature economies that are commonly volatile and lack many protections for investors, like auditing and laws or monitoring of securities that are found in the industrialized countries.

Developed Market Equities are equities in firms that work primarily outside of an investor's home country but still in an industrialized country. For Americans, this mostly translates to European country companies, as well as those in places such as Japan, Australia, and New Zealand. Such companies and economies in these nations prove to be more stable than those in developing countries.

Real Estate Investment Trusts, also known as REIT's, are equity funds that invest in residential and commercial real estate. Because they receive lease and rent payments off of their investments, these typically pay greater percentage returns in dividends. These higher distributions mean that REIT's are much like a combination of fixed income and typical equity investments. This means that they commonly feature greater risk along with better anticipated returns than do the majority of fixed income investments.

Equity Securities

Equity securities prove to be those asset classes which feature shares of stock in a given corporation. Investors hold these as reported by a company's official balance sheet. Corporations issue such securities in an effort to raise business capital via the financial markets. They use this money for significant company life events, such as for product development, merger and acquisition activity, or internal expansion. The funds are seldom for daily operating needs.

When investors buy equity securities, they gain a partial stake in the underlying firm. This is a primary alternative to turning to the bond markets to borrow money in taking on debt via the publicly traded bond markets. When a company first issues such equity securities, this is called an IPO initial public offering. Companies often raise enormous amounts of cash in this means, since investors are always hunting for new stock issues that will enable them to possess a part of a new and exciting opportunity.

The total number of shares that an IPO released varies wildly. It comes down to the amounts which the companies obtain permission to issue in their financial documents which they file with the regulatory overseer for their area. Corporations are allowed to sell a specific amount of stock shares in a given price range on the actual IPO day. After these shares have been dealt out to the public via the financial markets, the price of their equity will go up and down on the stock markets every trading day. This movement all depends on the perception of investors and the accompanying demand for the shares on any given day.

It is not common for such a firm to issue its entire inventory of available stock shares in a single offering. Rather than do this, they commonly reserve a certain quantity of shares to be issued at a later date in a second offering. This is called a follow on offering or secondary offering. The management of a company would elect to do this as they know they will likely need to raise fresh additional capital in the future in order to pay for hoped for expansionary plans.

When corporations continue to issue out their equity securities via the financial exchanges there is a downside for the existing shareholders and company investors. As additional shares are available to be bought, the pre-

Financial Terms Dictionary - Trading Terminology Explained

existing stake holders have their equity stake diluted as a percentage of the total. As an example, a major share holder could possess a huge quantity of shares that equate to fully 10 percent of all outstanding company shares which can be traded. Should the company choose to boost the total number of shares which are tradable, the equity of the shareholders will immediately drop in terms of the percentage ownership of all available shares.

The main alternative to issuing equity securities lies in issuing debt securities These publicly issued bonds offered via the bond markets by a company (or even government) raise money by taking on debt which must be repaid one day, known as the maturity date. Investors who buy debt instruments like these become de facto creditors of the bond issuing entities. The main disadvantage to such issuance in debt is that the company issuing has to provide continuous interest payments to the bond holders throughout the life of the bond contract. The company is able to maintain its ownership in itself in exchange for this trade off of interest payments.

Financial Terms Dictionary - Trading Terminology Explained

EUREX Exchange

EUREX is a state of the art options and futures exchange which Deutsche Borse of Germany jointly operated with SWX the Swiss Exchange until 2012. At this point, Deutsche Borse acquired the remaining shares of the EUREX exchange from SWX. The exchange operates offices in nine global locations including in Frankfurt, London, Chicago, Zurich, and Paris.

This international exchange specializes in providing trading on derivatives based in Europe. As such, it turns out to be the biggest European options and futures market. Products across nine asset classes trade on the exchange. These range from Swiss and German debt instruments to individual stock and stock indexes of European companies and exchanges.

EUREX clearing handles the clearing of every transaction carried out on the exchange. In this way, it serves as a multi asset class clearing central counterparty for the considerable product range. It also clears products that trade over the counter.

The exchange itself has become enormous. The Futures Industry Association said in its 2015 annual survey that the EUREX exchange holds the position of third biggest derivatives exchange based on the volume of contracts it trades. Its headquarters is located in Eschborn, Germany near Frankfurt, the financial capital of Germany. The operators of the exchange are the EUREX Frankfurt AG and EUREX Zürich AG. Both publicly traded companies are now entirely owned by Deutsche Börse, the German stock exchange operator.

The EUREX Exchange offered something almost unique when it began functioning in 1998. In both the United States and Great Britain, open outcry trading still dominated markets. EUREX came along as among the first exchanges in the world to provide a trading platform which was completely electronic instead of the more traditional pit or open outcry trading so prevalent at that time. Using this method of trading, buyers and sellers perform transactions via remote locations that are connected by the electronic network and trading platform.

The exchange launched its present day platform the T7 trading architecture in 2013. This system advanced the electronic trading of derivatives significantly. Deutsche Börse Group developed it. Using this dependable system, over 7,700 different traders operating in more than 35 countries are connected so that they can trade in excess of seven million contracts each market day.

The EUREX Exchange won several major impressive awards for 2016. *Global Capital* presented it with the "European Exchange of the Year" honor for the second year in a row. It received this nod for its broad range of products that hedge risk throughout nine alternative and traditional asset classes, as well as for its impressive offerings of equity index products and volatility derivatives. *Financial News* also honored EUREX with the 2016 Best Derivatives Trading Platform. This is also its second consecutive year to win this award.

EUREX gradually enabled Deutsche Börse to wrest control of the Bund German bonds futures trading away from London. Up till the late 1990s, the London Financial Futures Exchange dominated trading in this segment. This back and forth struggle for control of this important market became known as the "Battle of the Bund."

Euro Stoxx 50 Index

The Euro Stoxx 50 Index proves to be the leading European Blue-chip like index that comprises securities of mega companies from the Euro Zone. This index offers investors and financial institutions a vehicle for following and investing in the Blue chip type of sector leaders for the zone. It includes 50 stocks (as the name implies) drawn from 11 different Euro Zone member nations. These are economically important zone nations Spain, Portugal, the Netherlands, Luxembourg, Italy, Ireland, Germany, France, Finland, Belgium, and Austria.

This Euro Stoxx 50 Index has been licensed out to a wide range of financial institutions to be the basis of a great variety of investment products like ETF Exchange Traded Funds, Options on futures, Futures contracts, and structured products around the globe. Besides this master index of the Euro Stoxx 50 Index, it is subdivided into other indices. These include the following: Euro Stoxx 50 Subindex France, Euro Stoxx 50 Subindex Italy, and Euro Stoxx 50 subindex Spain which covers the national big 50 companies by market capitalization in each off the economic powerhouse countries of France, Italy, and Spain, respectively.

The operator of this important pan-Euro Zone Euro Stoxx 50 Index and business is the company STOXX Limited on behalf of Deutsche Boerse Group. They also offer international tradable and creative index concepts on other indices to numerous countries throughout the world. As of the end of June 2016, STOXX 50 and DAX have worked with iShares to create and offer two new exchange traded funds traded in Hong Kong. iShares exchange traded funds family are both managed and marketed by the BlackRock investment firm. They started trading these two new Euro STOXX 50 Index ETFs on the Hong Kong Stock Exchange at the conclusion of June 2016.

The components in the Euro Stoxx 50 Index are updated several times a year as appropriate to changing market capitalizations. As of the end of December 2016, the components included French firms oil and gas producer Total, health care and pharmaceuticals maker Sanofi, European and Global banking giant BNP Paribas, international insurance titan AXA, luxury personal household goods maker LVMH Moet, cosmetics international leader L'Oreal, chemical maker Air Liquide, industrial goods and services maker Schneider Electric, banking giant GRP Societe Generale, food and largest yogurt maker Danone Group, aircraft maker Airbus, construction materials producer Vinci, telecommunications provider Orange, industrial goods and services producer Safran, health care company Essilor International, construction and materials producer Saint Gobain, Real Estate company Unibail-Rodamco, Utilties giant Engie, and international media conglomerate Vivendi.

German components of the index were electronics and industrial goods giant Siemens, chemicals and pharmaceutical titan Bayer, leading technology firm SAP, chemicals international leader BASF, re-insurance leader Allianz, luxury car maker Daimler, telecommunications leader Deutsche Telekom, industrial goods and services provider Deutsche Post, healthcare leader Fresenius, luxury car maker BMW, insurance firm Muenchener Rueck, internationally known shoe and clothing manufacturer Adidas, utilities giant E.On, world's largest auto maker Volkswagen, and largest German financial institution Deutsche Bank.

Spanish components in the index were international banking conglomerates BCO Santander and BCO Bilbao Vizcaya Argentaria, telecommunications international behemoth Telefonica, utilities leader Iberdrola, and retailer Industria de Diseno Textil SA.

Dutch companies in the index include electronics and industrial goods maker Philips, Anglo-Dutch consumer products giant UniLever, financial services investment leader ING, technology leader ASML Holdings, and retailer Ahold Delhaize.

Italian components of the index were oil and gas producer and distributor ENI, largest Italian bank Intesa SanPaolo, and national utility company ENEL. The Irish component is construction and materials maker CRH. The Belgian component is alcohol and food giant Anheuser-Busch InBev. The Finish component is technology and cell phone maker manufacturer Nokia.

Exchange Rate Mechanism (ERM)

Exchange Rate Mechanisms are systems that were established to maintain a certain range of exchange for currencies as measured against other currencies. These ERMs can be run in three different ways. On one extreme they can float freely. This permits the systems to trade without the central banks and governments intervening.

The fixed Exchange rate mechanisms will do whatever it takes to maintain rates pegged at a specific value. In between these two extremes are the managed ERMs. The best known example of one of these is the European Exchange Rate Mechanism known as ERM II. It is in use today for those countries who wish to become a part of the EU monetary union.

The European Economic Community formally introduced the European ERM system to the world on March 13, 1979. It was a part of the EMS European Monetary System. The goal of this new system centered on attaining monetary stability throughout Europe by reducing the variable exchange rates. This was set up to prepare the way for the Economic and Monetary Union. It also paved the way for the Euro single currency introduction that formally occurred on January 1, 1999.

The Europeans changed their system once the Euro became adopted. They introduced ERM II as a way to link together those EU countries who were not a part of the eurozone with the euro. They did this to boost extra eurozone currencies' stability. A second goal was to create a means of evaluating the countries who wished to join the eurozone. In 2016 only a single currency uses the ERM II. This is the Danish krone.

The European ERM ceased to exist in 1999. This was the point after the eurozone country European Currency Units exchange rates became frozen and the Euro began trading against them. ERM II then replaced the initial ERM. At first the Greek drachma remained in the ERM II alongside the Danish currency. This changed when Greece adopted the Euro in 2001. Currencies within the newer system may float in a fairly tight range of plus or minus 15% of their central exchange rate versus the euro. Denmark does better than this. Its Danmarks Nationalbank maintains a 2.25% range versus the central rate of DKK 7.46038.

In order for other countries that wish to join the Euro to participate, they are required to be a part of the ERM II system for minimally two years before they can become members of the eurozone. This means that at some point, a number of currencies for member states that joined the EU will have to be in the system. This includes the Swedish krona, Polish zloty, Hungarian forint, Czech Republic koruna, the Romanian leu, Bulgarian lev, and Croatian kuna. Each of these is supposed to join the system according to their individual treaties of accession.

In the case of Sweden, the situation is more complicated. The country held a referendum on becoming a part of the mechanism to which the citizens voted no. The European Central Bank still expects that Sweden will join the system and eventually adopt the euro. This is because they did not negotiate for an opt out of the currency as did the U.K. and Denmark. The Maastricht Treaty requires that EU member states all eventually join the exchange rate mechanism.

Britain participated in the mechanism from 1990 until September of 1992. On September 16, 1992 the British famously crashed out of the system on what became known as Black Wednesday because of manipulation of the pound by currency speculators led by Hedge Fund Billionaire George Soros.

Expense Ratio

Expense ratio relates to the costs that a mutual fund incurs as it trades and does normal business. Typical mutual fund expense ratios include a number of different costs. Among these are management fees, transaction costs, custody costs, marketing fees, legal expenses, and transfer agent fees.

Management fees comprise those charges that the fund pays to the company which handles the portfolio management. They invest the fund's money as per the direction of the mutual fund board of directors. Management costs are typically the largest single portion of the mutual fund's expenses.

These fees commonly range from as little as .5% to as much as 2%. Lower fees are usually more advantageous for investors. This is because every dollar that goes to the management of the fund is not increasing the share holders' wealth. Some mutual fund types charge a higher amount in fees. International or global mutual funds will usually cost more than simple domestic market mutual funds. They justify these greater charges by the difficulty of managing an international portfolio.

Transaction costs include the fees that the fund pays to stock brokers. These are negotiated to extremely low rates such as a penny per share or even lower thanks to the enormous volumes that mutual funds trade. Those funds that are constantly purchasing and selling investments create significantly greater transacting costs for themselves and their investors. Higher turnover rates like this also can lead to larger capital gains taxes and other costs.

The investment holdings of a mutual fund must be kept by a custodian bank. This creates custody costs where these banks register the bonds, stocks, and other investments for the fund. Some of the banks do this electronically and others keep actual stock certificates in their vault storage.

Custodian banks also collect interest and dividend payments, maintain accounting for the various positions so gain/loss info is readily available to management, and handle stock splits and other transaction issues. These custodian costs prove to be a less significant percentage of expense ratios for the mutual funds.

Marketing fees for mutual funds come out of the money that the investors pool. This money is utilized to advertise the fund so they can raise additional investment dollars. More money in the fund means more management fees for the portfolio managers. These 12b-1 marketing fees are money that does not benefit an investor after the fund exceeds $100 million in net assets. A very small number of brokers actually refund such fees to their investors.

There are some legal expenses that mutual funds must incur in the course of normal operating business. These include for paperwork they are required by law to file for regulators like the SEC, specific licenses, incorporation, and other legal procedures. The majority of funds count such costs as a small amount of their overall expense ratio.

Transfer agent costs cover the expenses that arise when a shareholder cashes out or buys into the fund. Transfer agents must handle various account statements, paperwork, and money in the process. These agents take care of all the mundane daily paperwork for purchases, redemptions, and processing which keep the fund and other capital markets working.

There are various other costs that are not included in the mutual fund expense ratio but many experts feel should be. These include mutual fund sales loads. These fees are simply commissions that go into the pocket of the institution, company, or stockbroker that persuaded you to buy the mutual fund in the first place. Because of these and other high costs of many mutual fund expense ratios, some people prefer low cost index funds that involve very low management costs.

Federal Trade Commission (FTC)

The FTC Federal Trade Commission proves to be the agency responsible for protecting the American consumers. They strive to stop tricky, fraudulent, and unfair practices in business in the nation's marketplaces. They also disburse valuable information to consumers that helps them to recognize, stop, and sidestep these frauds.

The FTC accepts consumer complaints by phone, email, their website, and through the mail. They take these complaints and enter them into a database that is called the Consumer Sentinel Network. This secure online tool is utilized for investigation purposes by literally hundreds of criminal and civil agencies for law enforcement throughout the United States and overseas.

What the FTC would like to do is to stop these types of deceptive and non-competitive business dealings before they hurt consumers. They are also attempting to improve consumer opportunities so that they are better informed about and comprehend the nature of competition. The agency attempts to perform all of these tasks without putting too many burdens and restrictions on businesses activities that are legitimate.

Congress created the FTC back in 1914. Originally its mandate lay in stopping unfair means of competition in trade and business caused by the trusts. They were a part of the government's stated goal to bust up these trusts. Congress has given them more authority to monitor and fight practices that were against fair competition over the years by passing other laws.

The government enacted another law in 1938 that was broadly addressed to stop any deceptive or unfair practices and acts. They have continued to receive direction and discretion to govern a number of other laws that protect consumers over the subsequent years. Among these are the Pay Per Call Rule, the Telemarketing Sales Rule, and the Equal Credit Opportunity Act. Congress passed another law in 1975 that gave the Federal Trade Commission the ability to come up with rules that regulated trade throughout the industries.

The FTC has a vision for the American economy. They want to see one that has healthy competition between producers. They also desire to see consumers able to obtain correct information. Ultimately the government agency looks for all of this to create low priced and superior quality goods. They encourage innovation, efficiency in business, and choice for consumers.

This agency carries out its vision with three strategic goals. It starts with them protecting consumers by heading off trickery and deception in the business and consumer marketplace. They desire to keep competition going strong. In this role, they stop mergers and business dealings that they believe are against competition. They also work to increase their own performance with consistently improving and excellent managerial, individual, and organizational efforts.

All of these goals and efforts combine to make the FTC one of the government agencies that most impacts each American citizen's economic and personal life. They are the only government entity that possesses a mandate for both competition jurisdiction and consumer protection in large segments of the U.S. economy. They go after aggressive and effectual enforcement of the laws.

The FTC shares its knowledge with international, state, and federal groups and agencies. The group creates research tools at a variety of conferences, workshops, and hearings every year. They also develop and distribute easy to understand educational materials for business and consumer needs in the transforming technological and global market.

The FTC carries out its work through its Bureaus of Economics, Competition, and Consumer Protection. They receive assistance from the Office of General Counsel. Seven regional offices around the country help them to carry out their mandate.

Financial Times Stock Exchange (FTSE)

The Financial Times Stock Exchange represents an enormous group of indices owned by the London Stock Exchange. The acronym originated in the days when it was half owned by the Financial Times newspaper and the LSE. Now this group is an entirely owned subsidiary of only the London Stock Exchange.

When individuals use the word FTSE, they are most commonly referring to the most important benchmark index of the group the FTSE 100. These 100 companies are the hundred largest British companies which the London Stock Exchange lists. As such the Blue Chip companies of the British economy represent the biggest companies by market capitalization in the U.K. Besides this FTSE 100 index, the group produces the FTSE 250, the 350, the Small Cap, and the All-Share.

The FTSE 250 companies are those next 250 largest companies after the FTSE 100. Combining the 250 and the 100 yields the 350 index. Merging the 350 and Small Cap provides the All Share Index.

London Stock Exchange launched the FTSE 100 on January 3, 1984. The companies in the index are calculated for size based on their market capitalization, or number of existing shares times the price per share. The group recalculates the indices every quarter to adjust for any of the companies in the 250 index that have moved up to the 100 index and those in the 100 group that have dropped to the 250 group.

Besides this, they have to remove companies that have been taken over or merged with others. The index must also be updated for name changes, as happened with British Gas becoming BG Group and Centrica, Midland Bank becoming HSBC, and Commercial Union Assurance becoming Aviva. Name changes, mergers, and takeovers are changed as soon as they become effective.

FTSE 100 updates its composite companies based on those which rise to a position in the top 90 largest companies on the London Stock Exchange. Those which fall to the 111th position or lower are dropped. They maintain this overlapping band so that there will not be too much change in the index in any given quarter. The group is concerned about the stability of the index and the rate of change because it forces investment companies and funds to rebalance when the benchmark 100 index changes. This is an expensive process for the large investors that the group tries to mitigate.

The 100 index and other benchmark indices are calculated up every 15 seconds throughout the trading days. The values are published in real time all day. The indices are open from 8am to 4:30pm on all weekdays that are not market holidays.

FTSE 100 is considered to be a good barometer for geopolitical and economic events throughout the world. When the major global markets soar, it does as well. When they plummet, it falls in sympathy. The largest single point drop for the 100 index happened on the day following Black Monday in the U.S. on October 20th of 1987. On this occasion, the 100 index fell 12.22% in a single trading session.

FTSE is not only a series of British stock indices. The group also produces and compiles every day more than 100,000 additional indices around the globe. Among these are the Global Equity, Italy's MIB, the China A50 and 50, the Portugal 20, and the TWSE Taiwan. In 2015 the group merged with Russell to become the FTSE Russell Group. This gave it reach into a number of American stock market indices like the Russell 2000.

Fire Sale

A fire sale is a phrase with a variety of interesting meanings. The term originated in reference to the reduced sales price for goods which were damaged in a fire of a shop or business. Since then, it has come to refer to any event which forces a business to move its assets or inventory goods for prices that are substantially discounted. The reason the business would be forced to engage in such a practice is because they are in a bind through some type of serious and often-times fatal financial distress.

Where financial markets are concerned, the phrase fire sale also refers to any securities (stocks, bonds, or other financial instruments and investments) which trade at a deep discount to their intrinsic value. This could occur in extended and painful bear market phases in the equities markets.

There are a number of examples which help to clarify the several different meanings of this concept of a fire sale. Take a department store as a prime example. When the department store company has to close its doors because of a bankruptcy event, the store might offer such a sale. In this specific scenario, the department store will offer its inventory of goods at what would normally be considered ridiculously low prices.

They do this so that they can liquidate the entirety of their in stock inventory. Since the store is closing up for good, they must be rid of each item in the store's inventory. The only means of effectively accomplishing this lies in providing prices so drastically reduced that bargain hunters will be lured in to purchase the stock. When the prices offered on the merchandise are so good as to be irresistible, then this qualifies as a fire sale.

Where securities are concerned, there are always examples of a fire sale of a given stock issue. Any time a particular equity security sells for far less than the value it is perceived to be worth, this qualifies as such a sale. Look at a clear example to consider. When the Dow Jones Industrial Average cratered by a full thousand points within the day, Proctor and Gamble (ticker symbol PG) crashed and burned by a quarter of its value on a temporary basis. This led investors and analysts to declare that there had been a real fire sale on the share of Proctor and Gamble that particular day.

In this particular scenario, the phrase for this kind of a sale signifies that the asset in question possesses significantly greater value than the price for which its owner is suddenly willing to sell it.

These stock or bond securities which appear to be offered for this dramatic sale often provide an appealing risk to reward payoff possibility for the types of buyers known as value investors. This is because the asset is not likely to experience significantly further deterioration in valuation, yet the profit potential to the upside could possible prove to be impressive. The truth is that there is no single set of metrics for valuing whether or not a particular stock is actually selling for a ridiculously low price. One factor that many analysts can agree on is that if a stock is being valued at multiple year lows in the price, then it is generally considered to be a huge bargain.

As an example, stocks which are trading continuously for 14 times earning multiples would likely be fire sales when they trade for a far lower multiple of earnings of a mere seven. For this to be true in all scenarios though, the fundamentals for the given company and its stock must remain more or less unchanged. In other words, they can not simply have deteriorated appreciably in the meanwhile.

Flash Crash

The Flash Crash has also been called the 2010 Flash Crash and the Crash of 2:45. It occurred on May 6 in 2010. This stock market collapse occurred in the United States and caused a trillion dollars of equity to be temporarily wiped out. It began officially at 2:32 EST. The crash happened over only the next 36 minutes.

During this crash, major stock indices including the Dow Jones Industrial Average, the S&P 500, and the NASDAQ composite fell apart and then rebounded with unparalleled speed and volatility. At one moment, the DJIA set its largest point drop within a single day to that time. It fell 998.5 points representing over 9% of its value.

Most of this drop happened in only minutes. The index then went on to recover a substantial portion of the drop a little later. Up to this point, this represented the second biggest point swing in a single day at 1010 points.

Trading volume exploded briefly as volatility increased. The prices of stock indices, individual stocks, futures on the indices, options, and ETF exchange traded funds were all over the board. In 2014, the CFTC Commodities Futures Trading Commission released a report that called this just over thirty minute crash among the most chaotic points in all of the history of global financial markets.

The government responded by putting a number of new regulations into play after the 2010 Flash Crash. Despite this fact, they were insufficient to stop another such rapid crash on August 24, 2015. During this second episode, bids on literally dozens of stocks and ETFs plunged to as little as a single penny per share as ETFs decoupled from their underlying value, per the Wall Street Journal article of December 6, 2015. As a result of this second incident, regulators placed ETFs under additional scrutiny. This also led to the analysts at Morningstar stating that legislation from the Depression era was governing the digital age technology of ETFs.

It took the Department of Justice almost five years to charge an individual with criminal misconduct that contributed massively to the original flash crash. They charged the trader Navinder Singh Sarao with 22 counts of market manipulation and fraud. Apparently he had utilized spoofing algorithms to trick the exchanges.

Immediately before the crash unfolded, Sarao had put in orders for thousands of the stock index futures contracts known as E-mini S&P 500 contracts. These orders constituted $200 million in bets that the markets would then decline. Before the orders were cancelled by his algorithm, it modified or replaced them 19,000 times. Thanks to this individual action, the government and regulators banned front running, layering, and the spoofing of orders.

In the investigation that the CFTC conducted, they came to the conclusion that Sarao bore substantial responsibility for the imbalances of the orders in derivatives markets. These impacted the stock markets and made the crash so much more severe. The small time trader Sarao was operating from his parent's house in the suburban part of west London when he carried out these actions. He had started manipulating the markets back in 2009 when he purchased and modified trading software that would permit him to quickly and automatically place and cancel his orders.

A later CFTC report in May 2014 determined that the high frequency traders who were assigned much of the blame for the flash crash did not cause it themselves. They did contribute to the severity of it as their orders were taken before those of other participants in the market.

Foreign Exchange

Foreign exchange involves converting the currency of one nation into another nation's currency. Foreign exchange rates can be set in several different ways determined by the country's government. Free market economies allow their currency to float freely most of the time. The value of the money is determined by the markets according to supply and demand factors.

Other nations choose to peg the value of their money to a stronger and more stable currency like the U.S. dollar or the Euro. They might also choose to use a basket of currencies for such a peg. A third alternative is for a country's government to fix the value of their money at a set rate. The majority of nations choose to allow their foreign exchange rates to float freely versus the ones of other nations. This causes them to fluctuate up and down constantly throughout the day.

Sometimes nations which allow the value of their money to float freely will choose to intervene in foreign exchange markets to devalue their exchange rate. They might feel that their money's value has risen too fast and is hurting the competitiveness of their exports. As their exchange rate rises, the cost of their goods becomes more expensive to customers in foreign markets. In such a case, the country may announce that they are buying their own money at a lower rate or they may sell it off in Forex markets. Interventions like this tend to be less common except in volatile exchange environments.

Currency values are usually set by the forces of the market and are based on a number of national and international elements. These include trade and investment, flows of tourism, and geo political event risk. Trade and investment requires that the companies or nations purchase the host nation's money for the transaction. Investors may also want to purchase investments in another country. They would need that nation's money in order to make such investments.

When tourists come to visit a nation, they require the local money. They will exchange their own country's money for that of the one which they are visiting. Every one of these transactions constantly requires foreign exchange. This explains why the forex markets are the largest financial marketplaces in the world by far.

Banks handle this foreign exchange between each other on an international level. This creates a forex market that operates 24 hours per day and six days a week. The major centers of foreign exchange are disbursed around the world. These trades and transactions mostly occur in eight major forex centers. These are London, New York City, Tokyo, Singapore, Switzerland (Zurich and Geneva), Hong Kong, Sydney, and Paris. Each of the transactions comes under the regulation of the Bank of International Settlements.

Floating exchange rates are set by the supply and demand of all of these trades. More demand for a currency against a stable supply will increase the value of it against another. The rates are also impacted by numerous economic reports and geopolitical events. Some of the better known and followed ones are unemployment rates, interest rate levels and decisions, manufacturing data, gross domestic product changes, and inflation reports.

For countries that choose to go the route of pegged exchange, their governments must artificially set and maintain their exchange rates. These rates do not change up and down throughout the day. Instead the government will reset its value on reevaluation dates. Emerging market countries often find this a useful means of managing their foreign exchange rates in order to ensure that they are stable. They will be required to maintain large reserves of their pegged currency so that they can manage the inevitable supply and demand changes that affect their own foreign exchange.

Financial Terms Dictionary - Trading Terminology Explained

Foreign Exchange Reserves

Foreign exchange reserves are comprised of any currency which is foreign to the central bank holding it. If the American Federal Reserve held British pounds, this would be an example of such reserves. These exchange reserves can include bank deposits, foreign banknotes, bonds, treasury bills, and various other kinds of government securities. The phrase also includes IMF SDR special drawing rights' units and gold reserves.

Such foreign exchange reserves can be utilized for a range of purposes. The main one is to provide the central government with necessary resilience and flexibility in any sort of currency crisis. If several currencies were to crash or become severely undervalued, these central bank vaults contain assets in other currencies which they can fall back on in order to outlast temporary market fluctuations and currency crises.

Practically every nation on earth, irrespective of their economy's relative size and strength, chooses to inventory substantial foreign exchange reserves. Over half of all such foreign reserves in the globe exist in the form of U.S. dollars. This is because dollars represent the most heavily traded global currency in the world. Other commonly found forms of foreign exchange currency reserves include the Euro zone's euro (EUR), the British pound sterling (GBP), the Japanese yen (JPY), the Swiss Franc (CHF), and ever increasingly the Chinese yuan (CNY). The euro is hands down the second largest form of such international exchange reserves. The yuan is the fastest growing component of foreign reserves today.

A number of economists and currency analysts concur that it makes the most sense to keep significant foreign exchange reserves in currencies which are not closely related to the ones of the nation in question. This helps to hedge the central bank from possible currency shocks and devaluations. It has become an increasingly Herculaneum task to do so since the majority of currencies are now closely correlated.

These days the People's Republic of China contains the most impressive array of international exchange reserves. This is due to their over 3.5 trillion dollars in foreign assets denominated in foreign currencies. The majority of these are based in the dollar and treasury securities proffered overseas by the U.S. Treasury.

Foreign exchange reserves serve the most common purpose of backing up the domestic currency of any country. This is necessary as currency by itself is inherently of no value. It is only an IOU from the government which issued it in the first place. The only assurance a receiver of this currency has that the currency value itself will be maintained is the good faith, trust in, and credit of the government and nation. This gives such foreign reserves great importance as a form of concretely backing up such assurance. Liquidity and security are critically important in defining what makes a reliable currency reserve investment.

Foreign exchange reserves are also utilized as an instrument in the tool kit of monetary policy these days. This is especially important for any country that is determined to use a fixed exchange rate. This helps a central bank to exercise control over its own currency value on the open market when they have other currencies to push into the markets against their own. Nations have opted to build up larger storehouses of foreign reserves since the untimely demise of the Bretton Woods system in 1971 over 45 years ago.

For example, China maintains simply enormous foreign exchange reserves so that it can control the exchange rates of its own currency the yuan. This helps it to foster beneficial international trading arrangements for its country and economy. They also keep such large dollar reserves because of the requirements of international trade which still mostly settles in U.S. dollars exclusively. Nations such as Saudi Arabia choose to keep huge foreign reserves because their entire economy depends on the one production and resource of oil to which their economy is almost entirely addicted. When oil prices plunge, their economy benefits at least temporarily from the flexibility provided by their heavy buildup of foreign exchange holdings.

FOREX Markets

FOREX markets are the world wide foreign exchange markets. They are called FX markets as well. FOREX markets are different from all of the other major financial markets in that they are over the counter and decentralized. They exist for the purpose of trading currencies.

Unlike with other markets, the FOREX markets are also open twenty-four hours a day during the week and on Sunday, since the different financial centers around the globe serve as trading bases for a variety of buyers and sellers. This foreign exchange market is the place where supply and demand mostly decides the different currencies' values for nations around the world.

The main point and reason for the FOREX markets are to help out investment and trade internationally through permitting businesses to easily change one currency to the other one that they require. In practice, individuals or businesses actually buy one amount of foreign currency through paying for it with a given amount of a different currency.

As an example, Canadian businesses may import British goods by paying for them in British Pounds, even though their income and base currency are Canadian dollars. The foreign exchange markets allow for investors to speculate on the rising and falling values of various currencies as well. It also makes the infamous carry trade possible, where investors are able to borrow currencies with low yields or interest rates and use them to purchase higher interest rate yielding currencies. Critics have said that the FOREX markets also hurt some countries' competitiveness against other countries.

This market is extremely popular and unique for a variety of reasons. It possesses the greatest trading volume on earth, managing in the three to four trillion dollar range every single trading day. This gives it enormous liquidity. It is also geographically centered all over the world, from Wellington in New Zealand to London in Great Britain to New York in the United States. Traders love that the market runs fully twenty-four hours per day except for on the weekends, when it reopens Sunday afternoon.

Finally, an enormous degree of leverage, that can be as much as two hundred to one, allows for even people with small accounts to make potentially enormous gains. Because of all of these factors and its world wide trading base, the FOREX markets have been called the ones where perfect competition is most evident. This is the case even though central banks sometimes intervene directly in these markets to increase or decrease the value of their currency relative to a trading partners' or trading competitors' currency value.

FTSE 100 Index

The FTSE 100 Index proves to be the trading world designation for the largest index managed by the FTSE Group out of London in the United Kingdom. FTSE is actually jointly owned by parent companies the Financial Times and the London Stock Exchange. This mash up of FT from Financial Times and SE from London Stock Exchange is how they arrive at the acronym FTSE. In general when analysts refer to the FTSE, they mean the FTSE 100 Index itself. This is actually a misnomer, since there are literally thousands of different FTSE indices the company owns and operates around the globe on numerous different national stock exchanges on every continent.

This FTSE 100 Index has been called the globe's most heavily referenced and most popular stock market index throughout the world. In practice, it represents around 80 percent of the entire market capitalization of the heavily multinational London Stock Exchange. The weighting system the FTSE company utilizes means that the bigger a corporation is, the larger a share of the index it occupies, thanks to it being a market capitalization-weighted index. This index is real time calculated all trading day long. The firm updates and publishes it continuously throughout the open market hours on an every 15 seconds basis.

Many analysts and investors rely on the FTSE 100 Index as some sort of prosperity indicator for British companies and the United Kingdom economy in general. This is actually a misnomer. It is all thanks to a significant constituency of the representative firms from the index being headquartered in other nations throughout the globe. It means that the index's daily movements do not truly reflect the strength of the British economy and corporations. Instead, the secondary index of the group, the FTSE 250 is more accurate a bell weather for British businesses and the economy. This is because a far smaller representation of international corporations populates the 250 index. It makes it a much better indicator for Great Britain generally speaking.

FTSE the company decides every quarter which are the 100 largest member companies on the LSE. Their tradition is to calculate this on the Wednesday after the first Friday of the month for March, June, September, and December, respectively. They utilize the business day close values from the night before to decide if any constituents should be replaced.

It is no exaggeration to call the FTSE 100 Index the Blue Chip index of the London Stock Exchange. These are the largest and most economically powerful and far-reaching corporations from Great Britain and around the world (ex the United States) in many cases.

The constituent members of the FTSE 100 as of time of publication were as follows: 3I Group, Associated British Foods, Admiral Group, Anglo American, Antofagasta, Ashtead Group, AstraZeneca, Aviva, Babcock International, BAE Systems, Barclays, Barratt Development, BHP Billiton, BP, British American Tobacco, British Land, BT Group, Bunzl, Burberry Group, Carnival, Centrica, Coca Cola HBC AG, Compass Group, Convatec, CRH, Croda International, DCC, Diageo, Direct Line, Easy Jet, Experian, Fresnillo, GKN, GlaxoSmithKline, Glencore, Hammerson, Hargreaves Lans, Hikma, HSBC Bank Holdings, Imperial Brands, Informa, Intercontinental Hotels, Intertek Group, International Consolidated Airlines, INTU Properties, ITV, Johnson Matthey, Kingfisher, Land Securities, Legal & General, Lloyds Group, London Stock Exchange, Marks & Spencer, Medi clinic, Merlin, Micro Focus, Mondi, William Morrison, National Grid, Next, Old Mutual, Paddy Power Betting, Pearson, Persimmon, Provident Financial, Prudential, Randgold Res., RDS A Shares, RDS B Shares, Reckitt Benison Group, RELX, Rentokil International, Rio Tinto, Rolls Royce Holdings, Royal Bank of Scotland, Royal Mail, RSA Insurance, Sage Group, J. Sainsbury, Schroders, Scottish Mort, Severn Trent, Shire Pharmaceuticals, Sky PLC, Smith & Nephew, Smiths Group, Smurfit Kap., SSE, St. James's Place, Standard Chartered, Standard Life, Taylor Wimpey, Tesco, TUI AG, Unilever, United Utilities, Vodafone Group, Whitbread, Wolseley, Worldpay Group, and WPP Group (the world's leading advertising company giant).

FTSE 250

FTSE 250 is a broad-based stock index maintained by the FTSE company. This company is much like Standard and Poor's in that they both concentrate their efforts on calculating indices. The FTSE is not made up of any stock exchange, though among its co-owners is the famed and historic London Stock Exchange (LSE). The other co-owner of the company is its namesake the Financial Times newspaper publishing empire.

Easily the best known of the FTSE indices is the FTSE 100. There are many thousands of indices owned, produced, and calculated by FTSE, but only one is the blue chip index of all British and international company and economy stocks based on the LSE. The second most important and widely cited index from the company is this FTSE 250. This one is made up of the 101st to 351st largest companies in the U.K. As these firms tend to be much more British and far less international than those making up the FTSE 100, they are gauged to be a superior measurement of how the British economy and U.K. based firms are actually performing.

The FTSE 250 index list is altered four times a year on a quarterly basis. This occurs reliably every March, June, September, and December month. The index itself is continuously calculated instantly in real time. The owner of the index publishes it every minute accordingly online and through financial news and media outlet feeds.

As of November 7, 2016, the 350 different constituent companies which comprise the FTSE 250 are as follows: 3i Infrastructure, AA, Aberdeen Asset Management, Aberforth Smaller Companies Trust, Acacia Mining, Aggreko, Aldermore Group, Alliance Trust, Allied Minds, Amec Foster Wheeler, AO World, Ascential, Ashmore Group, Assura, WS Atkins, Auto Trader Group, Aveva, Balfour Beatty, Bankers Investment Trust, Barr, A.G., BBA Aviation, Beazley Group, Bellway, Berendsen, Berkeley Group Holdings, Bank of Georgia Holdings, BH Macro, Big Yellow Group, B & M European Retail Value, Bodycote, Booker Group, Bovis Homes Group, Brewin Dolphin Holdings, British Empire Trust, Britvic, Brown N, BTG, Cairn Energy, Caledonia Investments, Capital & Counties Properties, Card Factory, Carillion, Centamin, Cineworld, City of London Investment Trust, Clarkson, Close Brothers Group, CLS Holdings, CMC Markets, Cobham, Computacenter, Countryside Properties, Countrywide, Cranswick, Crest

Financial Terms Dictionary - Trading Terminology Explained

Nicholson, CYBG, Daejan Holdings, Dairy Crest, Debenhams, Dechra Pharmaceuticals, Derwent London, DFS, Dignity, Diploma, Domino's Pizza, Drax Group, Dunelm Group, Edinburgh Investment Trust, Electra Private Equity, Electrocomponents, Elementis, Entertainment One, Essentra, Esure, Euromoney Institutional Investor, Evraz, F&C Commercial Property Trust, Fidelity China Special Situations, Fidelity European Values, Fidessa Group, Finsbury Growth & Income Trust, FirstGroup, Fisher, James & Sons, Foreign & Colonial Investment Trust, G4S, Galliford Try, GCP Infrastructure Investments, Genesis Emerging Markets Fund, Genus, Go-Ahead Group, Grafton Group, Grainger, Great Portland Estates, Greencoat UK Wind, Greencore, Greene King, Greggs, GVC Holdings, Halfords Group, Halma, Hansteen Holdings, HarbourVest Global Private Equity, Hastings Group, Hays, Henderson Group, HICL Infrastructure Company, Hill & Smith, Hiscox, Hochschild Mining, Homeserve, Howden Joinery, Hunting, Ibstock, ICAP, IG Group Holdings, IMI, Inchcape, Indivior, Inmarsat, Intermediate Capital Group, International Personal Finance, International Public Partnerships, Investec, IP Group, Jardine Lloyd Thompson, JD Sports, John Laing Group, John Laing Infrastructure Fund, JPMorgan American Investment Trust, JPMorgan Emerging Markets Investment Trust, JPMorgan Indian Investment Trust, JRP Group, Jupiter Fund Management, Just Eat, KAZ Minerals, Keller, Kennedy Wilson Europe Real Estate, Kier Group, Ladbrokes Coral, Laird, Lancashire Holdings, LondonMetric Property, Man Group, Marshalls, Marston's, McCarthy & Stone, Meggitt, Mercantile Investment Trust, Metro Bank, Millennium & Copthorne Hotels, Mitchells & Butlers, Mitie, Moneysupermarket.com Group, Monks Investment Trust, Morgan Advanced Materials, Murray International Trust, National Express Group, NB Global, NCC Group, NMC Health, Ocado Group, OneSavings Bank, P2P Global Investments, PageGroup, Paragon Group of Companies, PayPoint, Paysafe, Pennon Group, Perpetual Income & Growth Investment Trust, Personal Assets Trust, Petra Diamonds, Petrofac, Pets at Home, Phoenix Group Holdings, Playtech, Polar Capital Technology Trust, Polypipe, PZ Cussons, QinetiQ, Rank Group, Rathbone Brothers, Redefine International, Redrow, Regus, Renewables Infrastructure Group, Renishaw, Rentokil Initial, Restaurant Group, Rightmove, RIT Capital Partners, Riverstone Energy, Rotork, RPC Group, Safestore, Saga, Savills, Scottish Investment Trust, Scottish Mortgage Investment Trust, Segro, Senior, Serco, Shaftesbury, Shawbrook Bank, SIG plc, Smith (DS), Smurfit Kappa Group, Softcat, Sophos, Spectris, Spirax-Sarco Engineering, Spire Healthcare, Sports Direct, SSP

Financial Terms Dictionary - Trading Terminology Explained

Group, Stagecoach Group, St. Modwen Properties, SuperGroup, SVG Capital, Synthomer, TalkTalk Group, Tate & Lyle, Ted Baker, Telecom Plus, Temple Bar Investment Trust, Templeton Emerging Markets Investment Trust, Thomas Cook Group, Tritax Big Box REIT, TR Property Investment Trust (two listings, both ordinary & sigma shares), Tullett Prebon, Tullow Oil, UBM, UDG Healthcare, UK Commercial Property Trust, Ultra Electronics Holdings, Unite Group, Vectura Group, Vedanta Resources, Vesuvius, Victrex, Virgin Money, Weir Group, Wetherspoon (J D), W H Smith, William Hill, Witan Investment Trust, Wizz Air, Woodford Patient Capital Trust, Wood Group, Workspace Group, Worldwide Healthcare Trust, and Zoopla.

Futures

Futures prove to be financial derivatives that are also called forward contracts. Such a futures contract gives a seller the obligation to deliver an asset, such as a commodity, to the buyer at a pre set date. These contracts are heavily traded on major produced commodities like wheat, gold, oil, coffee, and sugar. They also exist for underlying financial instruments that include government bonds, stock market indexes, and foreign currencies.

The history of futures goes back to Ancient Greece where the first recorded example is detailed about an olive press arrangement that philosopher Thales entered into. Futures contracts become commonplace at trade fairs throughout Europe by the 1100's. Merchants did not feel secure traveling with significant amounts of goods, so they would only bring display samples along and then sell merchandise that they would deliver in greater quantities at future dates.

Futures contracts created an enormous bubble in the 1600's with the Dutch Tulip Mania that caused tulip bulbs to skyrocket to unthinkable levels. In this speculative bubble, the majority of money that was exchanged turned out to be for tulip futures and not the tulips themselves. The first futures exchange in the United States opened in 1868 as the Chicago Board of Trade, where copper, pork bellies, and wheat were traded in futures contracts.

In the early years of the 1970's, futures trading grew explosively in volume. Pricing models created by Myron Scholes and Fischer Black permitted the quick pricing of futures and options on them. Investors could easily speculate on commodities prices through these futures. As the demand for the futures skyrocketed, additional significant futures exchanges opened and expanded around the world, especially in Chicago, London, and New York.

Futures trading could not happen effectively without the exchanges. Futures contracts are spelled out in terms of the asset that underlies them, the date of delivery, the last day of contract trading, transaction currency, and size of ticks or minimum permissible price changes. Exchanges have developed into major and predictable markets through their standardizing of all of these various factors for many different kinds of futures contracts.

Financial Terms Dictionary - Trading Terminology Explained

Trading futures contracts involves major leverage. This means that they carry tremendous opportunities as well as risks. Futures, with their ability to control enormous quantities of commodities and financials, have been the root causes for many collapses. Enron and Barings Bank were both brought down by financial futures. Perhaps the most famous futures meltdown involved the Long Term Capital Management group.

Even though this company had the inventors of the futures pricing models Scholes and Black working for them, the company lost money in the futures markets so quickly that the Federal Reserve Bank had to become involved and bail out the company to stop the whole financial system of the Untied States from collapsing.

Futures Contracts

Futures contracts are legally binding agreements which two parties usually enter into on a futures exchange trading floor or electronic platform. They spell out the particulars for selling or buying specific financial instruments or commodities for a pre-set price at an exact moment in the future. Such contracts have become standardized to make it easy to trade them on the various futures exchanges. They provide information on the quantity and quality of the commodity, though this depends on the nature of the underlying asset.

Futures contracts can be settled in two ways. Some of them require actual physical delivery of the commodity specified. Others simply settle between the two parties in cash. These contracts specify all important characteristics for the item which the parties are trading. This makes them different from the word "futures" that more generally refers to the markets in which these commodities and instruments trade.

There are two actual types of participants in the futures markets who utilize such futures contracts. These are speculators and hedgers. Individual traders and managers of portfolios can use them to place speculative bets on the direction of price movements for the given asset that underlies the contracts. Hedgers involve buyers or producers of the contact asset itself attempting to lock in the price for which they will later buy or sell their commodity.

There are many different commodities and assets for which futures contracts exist. The most obvious of these are hard assets such as precious metals, industrial metals, natural gas, crude oil and other energy products, grains, seeds, livestock, oils, and carbon credits. Literally dozens of the more significant stock market indices around the globe have these contracts available to trade. Some major individual stocks have their own futures contract on their shares as well. The major interest rates and most important currency pairs also have such contracts and markets to trade.

Futures contracts which require physical delivery do not often result in such physical delivery. Many investors in these contracts trade them and sell them before the date of delivery. They can roll them forward by selling the imminent to expire contract and buying a further month out to replace them.

For producers of a good, these contracts provide a unique solution to the problem of fluctuating prices. Oil producers are classic examples. They might intend to produce a million barrels of oil to deliver in precisely a year. If the price is $50 for a barrel today, and the producer does not want to risk prices falling lower, it could lock it in. Oil prices have become so volatile that they could be substantially lower or higher a year from now. By selling a futures contract, the producer gives up the opportunity to possibly sell the oil for more in a year. It also eliminates the risk of receiving a lower amount.

Mathematical models actually determine the prices of futures contracts. They consider the present day spot price, time until maturity, risk free return rates, dividends, dividend yields, convenience yields, and storage costs. This might mean with oil prices at $50 that a one year futures contract sells for $53. The producer receives a guarantee for $53 million and will have to provide the 1 million barrels of oil on the exact delivery date. It will obtain this $53 per barrel price despite the spot prices at which the markets are trading on that date.

Futures Exchange

A futures exchange refers to a central clearing marketplace that allows for futures contracts as well as options on such futures contracts to be traded. Thanks to the rapid increase in electronic trading of futures, this term also finds use regarding futures trading activities directly.

There are the two most important futures exchanges in the world today. The biggest in the United States is the Chicago Mercantile Exchange, or CME. This one became established in the last years of the 1890s. In the early days, the only futures contracts available were agricultural products' futures.

This changed rapidly in the 1970s. Currency futures appeared on the major currency pairs after the breakdown of the Breton Woods Agreement. The futures exchanges of today are massive by comparison. They allow for investors to hedge all sorts of financial products and commodities. These range from stock indices and individual stocks to energies, precious and base metals, soft commodities such as orange juice and soybeans, interest rate products, and even credit default swaps.

In today's futures exchange, it is hedging financial instruments and products which create the significant majority of activity in futures markets. Today the futures exchange markets carry an important responsibility for global financial system operations, efficient functioning, and activity. The international nature of this global futures exchange has given rise to the world's first truly international futures market, the ICE Intercontinental Exchange.

ICE is massive and important in not only futures markets. They own and operate 12 different exchanges around the world, including NYSE EuroNext, which controls the famed and venerable New York Stock Exchange and EuroNext exchange (owning the Paris and Dutch stock exchanges, among others). In Europe, this is a serious rival to the historic LSE London Stock Exchange and continental powerhouse the German Deutsche Bourse. The ICE today counts 12,000 listed futures contracts as well as securities. It trades 5.2 million futures contracts every day, as well as $1.8 billion in cash equities every day.

In energies, the Intercontinental Exchange Futures commands almost half of all the traded crude and refined oil futures contracts volume for the entire planet. It is also the location of the most highly liquid market for the European interest rates short term contracts. It controls a wide variety of global benchmarks in agriculture, energies, foreign exchange, and equity indices.

ICE only launched its international futures exchange back in 2000 with the advent of their electronic trading platform. This makes it among the newer futures exchanges in the world, and yet it is a dominant international player still. Their high tech-powered rise increased the access to and transparency of the Over the Counter traded energy markets as well as the new global futures markets exchange they opened shortly thereafter. It was 2001 when they expanded to energy futures with their acquisition of the International Petroleum Exchange.

In 2002, ICE expanded heavily into Europe by opening up their ICE Clear Europe. This represented the first new clearing house in the United Kingdom in a full century. By 2007, the Intercontinental Exchange had cemented its global position in energy trade by acquiring both the NYBOT New York Board of Trade and the Canadian-based Winnipeg Commodity Exchange.

The end result today is an entire ecosystem made up of futures and equities markets, clearing houses throughout the world, listing and data centers and services, and technology-driven solutions which together work to create a full, free, and transparent accessibility to the worldwide futures, energy, derivatives, and capital markets.

Between ICE Futures U.S.'s operations and endeavors within the United States, the futures exchange is enabling and empowering markets which allow for an effective risk management throughout the world economy. Their product offerings and solutions encompass a diverse and broad variety of futures contracts. These span internationally traded equity indexes and futures; credit derivative futures; FX futures; North American oil, power, and natural gas futures; and soft commodities and agriculture futures including sugar, cotton, coffee, and cocoa.

George Soros

George Soros is a Hungarian born multi billionaire investor and philanthropist. In his lifetime he has gone from escaped refugee from the Nazis to twenty-first richest man on earth. Besides making billions of dollars through the investments of the hedge fund he started and still manages, he has contributed generously to various charities throughout the world via his foundation. Soros is considered to be a controversial figure for some of the investments he has undertaken and positions he holds on various global issues.

George Soros was born in Budapest the capital of Hungary in 1930. In the middle of the 1940's, he fled from the Nazis to England where he studied at the famed London School of Economics. After graduating from there in 1952, he sailed to New York in 1956 to begin working for F.M. Mayer, a brokerage firm on Wall Street. He worked for several other firms before starting his own hedge fund that he originally called the Soros Fund in 1973.

He soon renamed this the Quantum Fund and afterwards again the Quantum Fund Endowment. Investors contributed $12 million to this fund that achieved enormous success. With Soros leading the company, it made countless billions for both its investors and Soros himself.

Thanks to this success of this fund and successor fund ventures, Soros showed a net worth amounting to $26 billion as of September 2015 when he was 85 years old. This wealth was high enough to secure for him the spot of twenty-first richest person on earth.

The investment decisions and statements of George Soros have made him a controversial figure over the years. He took on the Bank of England in 1992 in the Black Wednesday U.K. currency crisis and beat it, costing Great Britain billions of dollars. His involvement made the crash so much worse but made he and his investors over a billion dollars in a single day.

He has also authored a number of books on the imminent collapse of worldwide financial markets. Some critics have complained that he manipulated markets to achieve his aims. Soros also criticizes U.S. and Israeli policies and blames them for worldwide anti-Semitism. Besides this,

Soros has attacked the U.S. criminalization of drugs.

On the philanthropic scene, George Soros has been extremely generous and is a leading global figure. He began giving back from his enormous wealth in 1979. By 1984 he had created his Open Society Foundations charitable fund. These foundations fund initiatives on a global scale with the goal of advancing justice, independent media, business development, education, and public health. His foundations boast an activity list that is 500 pages long. Among their work is loaning money to help the Russian university system and setting up New York City after school activities. He has funded the arts and helped places that have suffered from natural disasters. The foundations have also tried to stem the brain drain from Eastern Europe while fighting disease around the world.

Observers either love or dislike George Soros. No one can deny that he is a towering figure in the worlds of currency, finance, and philanthropy. His organizations help to shape public policies and perform enormous humanitarian projects. The author of 12 books has penned works on topics that range from global capitalism to the war on terror. As the head of the Soros Family Fund nowadays, the legendary investor can still move markets with his opinions and positions on markets.

Government Bonds

Government bonds are debt instruments that governments issue to pay for government expenditures. Within the United States, federal government issues include savings bonds, treasury notes, treasury bonds, and TIPS Treasury inflation protected securities. Investors should carefully consider the risks that different countries' governments possess before they invest in their bonds. Among these international government risks are political risk, country risk, interest rate risk, and inflation risk. Governments generally have less credit risk, though not always.

Savings bonds are a type of United States government bonds that the Treasury department sells. They are available in an electronic form. The Treasury offers them directly from their website, or individuals can buy them from the majority of financial institutions and banks. When savings bonds reach maturity, the investors get back the bond's face value along with interest which accrued. These savings bonds may not be redeemed the first year of issue. Any investors who redeem them in their first five years of issue lose three months interest for cashing out too early.

The Treasury of the United States also issues intermediate time frame bonds known as Treasury notes or T-Notes. These notes provide interest payments semiannually at a coupon rate which is fixed. These notes typically are denominated in $1,000 face values. Those with three or two year maturity dates come in $5,000 denominations. Before 1984, T-Notes were callable and gave the Treasury the right to buy them back given specific conditions.

The U.S. government's longest term bonds are Treasury Bonds, or T-Bonds. These have maturity dates ranging from ten to 30 years time. They also provide interest payments on a semiannual basis and come in $1,000 denominated values. These T-bonds are important because they pay for federal budget shortfalls, are a form of monetary policy, and ensure the country is able to regulate its money supply. As all bond issuers, the Treasury department looks at return and risk requirements on the market when it goes to raise capital so that it can be as efficient as possible. This helps to explain the different kinds of Treasury securities and government bonds they offer.

U.S. government bonds have generally been considered to be without risk, which is why they trade so easily in extremely large and liquid markets. The downside to this is that they offer considerably lower returns than do other bonds. TIPS do provide protection against inflation so that any inflation increases will not exceed the interest rate of the bond. The prices of government bonds are based on current interest rates. This means that the fixed rate bonds will decline in value as the interest rates rise, since there is lost opportunity to obtain newer bonds at higher interest rates. Similarly, if interest rates fall, the bond's values will rise.

The federal government is able to control the money supply in part by its issue of the government bonds. If they wish to increase the money supply, they can simply buy back their own bonds. These funds then find their way to a bank and expand the money supply as banks keep small reserves and loan the rest out (in the money multiplier effect). The government is also able to lower the money supply by selling additional bonds which takes money out of circulation. If the government were to retire the funds received from the sale of these bonds, it would reduce the available money supply. More often than not, the U.S. government spends the money.

Hard Currency

Hard currency refers to a type of currency which proves to be generally accepted throughout the globe for payments on services and goods. Such currencies are trusted to be reasonably stable over the short term timeframe. They must be extremely liquid on foreign exchange, or forex (FX), markets. Nations with solid economic performances and highly stable political environments typically issue these.

Because such hard currencies come from economically and politically stable nations, they are greatly respected in settlement of payments and forex trade and markets. Huge multinational transactions commonly become settled in one of the world's main hard currencies. There are a few such currencies. While the U.S. dollar is often referred to as today's ultimate hard currency, a number of other ones exist nowadays. The Euro zone euro, the British pound sterling, the Swiss franc, and the Japanese yen are among these examples.

The phrase is similar to that of reserve currency. The difference is that it is possible to be considered a hard currency while not truly being a reserve currency. The Swiss franc is a classic example of a currency which is most definitely a hard currency but not one of the principle reserve currencies of the world. Markets for the real hard currencies are highly liquid, even when compared to the typically liquid nature of forex trading in general.

A typical means for determining how strong a hard currency actually is revolves around the foreign exchange markets' liquidity. There are eight global currencies which are considered to be by far and away the most heavily traded ones on earth. These are the U.S. dollar (USD), the euro (EUR), British pound sterling (GBP), the Japanese yen (JPY), the Swiss franc (CHF), the Canadian dollar (CAD), the Australian dollar (AUD), and the New Zealand dollar (NZD). Each of these proves to be hard currencies because of their massive liquidity amounts in FX markets. Sometimes the South African Rand (ZAR) is added to this list as a ninth hard currency.

Not all of them are reserve currencies however (as with CHF, CAD, AUD, NZD, and ZAR). The United States dollar is still considered to be the most important reserve currency of the world even today. This is because it settles international trade transactions for between 60 – 70 percent of all international transactions in the world.

Each of these hard currencies earned the confidence and respect of the international business and investment community. This is because they typically do not radically appreciate or depreciate. There are some exceptions to the rule. In 2015, the Swiss franc soared by as much as 40 percent against the euro within hours of the Swiss National Bank abandoning their two year long ceiling versus the euro. Still the Swiss Franc versus both the euro and the U.S. dollar did stabilize within months.

The opposite of a hard currency would be an unstable currency. While the hard currencies are stable in supply and always in demand, weaker unstable currencies come from nations whose finances are in chaos. Argentina and its peso are dramatic examples of unstable currencies. In 2015, the Argentina peso plunged 34.6 percent of its total value versus the dollar. This scared especially foreign investors away from the extremely unattractive currency.

It is interesting to note that currency values primarily derive from the important economic considerations, including a nation's GDP Gross Domestic Product. Part of the reason the U.S. dollar remains so strong is because the country's GDP for 2015 was $17.947 trillion and ranked number one on earth. China came in second that year with a $10.983 trillion economy. India ranked seventh with a $2.091 trillion economy.

Yet neither the Chinese Renminbi nor the Indian rupee enjoys the status of hard currency. It goes to show how the stability of a country's money supply and the policies of its central bank play into which currencies are considered to be hard and which are deemed less stable and less respected internationally.

Hedge Account

A hedge account is an account established with a hedge fund. There are several reasons why a person or business would be interested in setting up a hedge account. These mostly center on the desire for investments that commonly produce higher profits or the wish to hedge, or protect, a business' operations from certain unpredictable and undesirable swings in market prices. Businesses can open up their own hedge accounts in various futures and commodities markets to protect themselves from these business impacting price movements in important related commodities.

A person who is interested in opening a hedge account will have to make application to a hedge fund. Hedge funds are typically restrictive in the types of funds that they will accept from an investor. The investor will have to prove certain income levels or asset base holdings that demonstrate that they are capable of bearing the substantial losses that could result from trades in a hedge account. They must also have liquid cash that they can tie up for long periods of time, since most hedge funds do not allow immediate on demand withdrawals.

Funds that are invested with them could be tied up for a year or longer, and minimum waiting periods apply. Because of all of these reasons, hedge funds are typically looking for people as investors who have in excess of a million dollars of liquid net worth.

Hedge accounts can also be accounts that businesses use to offset the changes in commodities' prices. A company's products may be heavily dependent on prices such as sugar and cocoa if they are a chocolate company, oil and other energy prices if they use energy intensive processes or are shipping companies, or even industrial metals such as copper if they produce wires or cables. Gold and silver mining companies, along with oil producers, routinely hedge their quantities of precious metals and energies that they expect to produce to protect against anticipated declining prices. By locking in the present price for these goods and commodities that they require or will produce later on in the year, they can insulate themselves from price swings that move against them.

This can mean the difference between having to raise prices and risk losing market share or selling goods at a much lower profit margin. Because of this, many major multinational companies around the world routinely protect themselves and their operations through the use of hedge accounts. Some of them even have individuals or departments that oversee these operations.

For a business to set up such a hedge account is not difficult. They only have to open a commodities account with one of the major commodities exchanges, such as the Chicago Mercantile Exchange, the Chicago Board of Trade, New York Mercantile Exchange, or the New York Board of Trade. These accounts can be used by companies for speculating on the price movements of underlying commodities as well, and not only for hedging their operations. In this case, care has to be taken, as the leverage provided by hedge accounts, such as commodities accounts, is enough to bring down a company overnight if they are irresponsible with the trades in the account.

Hedge Fund

A hedge fund is an investment fund which are commonly only open to a specific group of investors. These investors pay a large performance fee each year, commonly a certain percent of their funds under management, to the manager of the hedge fund. Hedge funds are very minimally regulated and are therefore are able to participate in a wide array of investments and investment strategies.

Literally every single hedge fund pursues its own strategy of investing that will establish the kinds of investments that it seeks. Hedge funds commonly go for a wide range of investments in which they may buy or sell short shares and positions. Stocks, commodities, and bonds are some of these asset classes with which they work.

As you would anticipate from the name, hedge funds typically try to offset some of the risks in their portfolios by employing a number of risk hedging strategies. These mostly revolve around the use of derivatives, or financial instruments with values that depend on anticipated price movements in the future of an asset to which they are linked, as well as short selling investments.

Most countries only allow certain types of wealthy and professional investors to open a hedge fund account. Regulators may not heavily oversee the activities of hedge funds, but they do govern who is allowed to participate. As a result, traditional investment funds' rules and regulations mostly do not apply to hedge funds.

Actual net asset values of hedge funds often tally into the many billions of dollars. The funds' gross assets held commonly prove to be massively higher as a result of their using leverage on their money invested. In particular niche markets like distressed debt, high yield ratings, and derivatives trading, hedge funds are the dominant players.

Investors get involved in hedge funds in search of higher than normal market returns. When times are good, many hedge funds yield even twenty percent annual investment returns. The nature of their hedging strategies is supposed to protect them from terrible losses, such as were seen in the financial crisis from 2007-2010.

The hedge fund industry is opaque and difficult to measure accurately. This is partially as a result of the significant expansion of the industry, as well as an inconsistent definition of what makes a hedge fund. Prior to the peak of hedge funds in the summer of 2008, it is believed that hedge funds might have overseen as much as two and a half trillion dollars. The credit crunch hit many hedge funds particularly hard, and their assets under management have declined sharply as a result of both losses, as well as requests for withdrawals by investors. In 2010, it is believed that hedge funds once again represent in excess of two trillion dollars in assets under management.

The largest hedge funds in the world are JP Morgan Chase, with over $53 billion under management; Bridgewater Associates, having more than $43 billion in assets under management; Paulson and Company, with more than $32 billion in assets; Brevan Howard that has greater than $27 billion in assets; and Soros Fund Management, which boasts around $27 billion in assets under management.

Financial Terms Dictionary - Trading Terminology Explained

Hedging

In the world of finance, hedging is the act of putting together a hedge. Hedging involves building up a position in one market whose goal is try to counteract risk from changes in price in another market's position that is the opposite. The ultimate goal is to diminish or eliminate the business or person's possibilities of risk that they wish to avoid. A number of specific vehicles exist to help with hedging. These typically include forward contracts, swaps, insurance policies, options, derivatives, and products sold over the counter. Futures contracts prove to be the most popular version of hedging instruments.

In the 1800's, futures markets open to the public came into existence. These were set up to permit a standardized form of effective, viable, and open hedging of commodity prices in agriculture. In the intervening century, these have grown to include all manners of futures contracts that allow individuals and businesses to hedge precious metals, energy, changes in interest rates, and movements in foreign currencies.

There are countless examples of individuals who might be interested in hedging. Commercial farmers are common types of people who practice hedging. Prices for agricultural crops like wheat change all the time as the demand and supply for them fluctuates. Sometimes these price changes are significant in one direction or the other. With the present prices and crop predictions at harvest time, a commercial farmer might determine that planting wheat for the season is smart.

The problem that he encounters is that these predicted prices are simply forecasts. After the farmer plants his wheat crop, he has tied himself to it for the whole growing season. Should the real price of wheat soar in between the time that the farmer plants and harvests his crop then he might make a great amount of money that he did not count on, yet should the real price decline by the time the harvest is in then the farmer might be ruined completely.

To remove the risk from his wheat crop equation, the farmer can set up a hedge. He does this hedging by selling a certain quantity of futures contracts for wheat. These should be sold at an amount equal to the wheat crop size that he expects when he plants it. In such a way, the commercial farmer fixes his price of wheat at planting time. His hedging contract proves to be a pledge to furnish a particular quantity of wheat bushels to a certain place on a fixed date in time at a guaranteed price. Now the farmer is hedged against changes in the prices of wheat. He does not have to worry anymore about the wheat prices and whether they are falling or rising, since he has been promised a fixed price in his hedging wheat futures contract. The possibility of him being totally ruined by falling wheat prices is completely removed from the realm of possibility. At the same time, he has lost the opportunity of realizing extra money as a result of rising wheat prices when harvest time arrives. These are the upsides and the downsides to hedging; both the positives and the negatives of uncertainty are eliminated.

High Frequency Trading (HFT)

High frequency trading turns out to be a platform for program-based trades. It works with super computers that are able to run huge quantities of trading orders at incredibly rapid speeds. This HFT works with complicated algorithms. These analyze a wide range of markets and then place a number fast-paced orders depending on the conditions in the markets. The secret of the trading algorithms lies in their speed. Those traders who have the quickest trade executions usually make more money than do traders who have slower trade executions.

This high frequency trading has not always been mainstream or even possible. It grew in popularity as some of the exchanges began to provide incentives for corporations that could increase the stock market's liquidity.

As an example, the NYSE New York Stock Exchange works with a number of liquidity providers. These are known as SLPs Supplemental Liquidity Providers. The strive to provide better liquidity and more competition for the exchange and its already existing quotes.

The companies that participate in this program earn either a rebate or a fee when they increase the liquidity. This amount turned out to be $0.0019 in mid 2016 for securities that are listed on the NYSE or NYSE MKT. It may not sound like an enormous amount of money. It adds up to major profits quickly as some of these companies are engaged in millions of transactions on busy days.

The NYSE and other exchanges introduced this SLP program for a specific reason. After Lehman Brothers collapsed back in 2008, liquidity turned into an enormous concern for market participants. The SLP provided the solution to low liquidity. It also made high frequency trading a major part of the stock market in only a few years.

High frequency trading offers some significant benefits to the stock exchanges and financial markets. The most significant one centers on the significantly better liquidity that the programs provide. It has reduced bid ask spreads substantially. Larger spreads are more or less a thing of the past.

Some exchanges tested the benefits by trying to place fees on the HFT. The spreads then increased as fewer trades occurred. The Canadian government started charging fees for high frequency trading on Canadian markets. A study concluded that the end result was 9% higher bid to ask spreads.

There are many who dislike high frequency trading as well. Opponents are harsh in their criticism. Many broker dealers have been eliminated by the computer programs. The human element has been removed from many decisions on the exchanges.

When errors occur, the critics are quick to point out that human interactions could have prevented them. Part of the problem in the speed is that the programs are making decisions in literally thousandths of a second. This can lead to huge moves in the market with no apparent explanation or reason.

The best example of the mistakes that can lead to enormous and scary stock market moves happened on May 6, 2010 during the Flash Crash. The DJIA Dow Jones Industrial Average experienced its biggest drop of all time on an intraday basis. The Dow plunged over 1,000 points and dropped a full 10% in only twenty minutes. It then recovered back much of the loss in the next few hours. When the government investigated the issue, they found an enormous order which had caused the sell off to begin. The HFT computer algorithms did all the rest.

Another criticism concerns large corporate profiting at the expense of the smaller retail investors. The trade off is superior liquidity. Unfortunately, much of this turns out to be phantom liquidity. It is there for the market at one moment and then gone in another. This keeps the traders from benefiting from the liquidity.

High Yield Bonds

High Yield Bonds turn out to be bonds that possess a lower credit rating and higher yield than those corporate, municipal, and sovereign government bonds which are of investment grade. Thanks to the greater risk of them defaulting, such bonds yield a higher return than the bonds which are qualified investment grade issues. Those companies that issue high yielding debt are usually capital intensive companies and startup firms that already possess higher debt ratios. Investors often refer to such bonds as junk bonds.

The two principal corporate rating credit agencies determine the breakdown of what qualifies as a High Yield Bond and what does not. When Moody's rates a bond with lower than a "Baa" rating, or Standard and Poor's (S&P) rates then with an under "BBB" rating, then they become known as junk bonds. At the same time, all of those bonds which enjoy higher ratings than these (or the same rating at least) investors will consider to be investment grade. There are credit ratings that cover such categories as presently in default, or "D." Those kinds of bonds holding "C" ratings and below also have high probabilities for defaulting. In order to compensate the investors who take them on for the significant risks they run of not receiving either their original principal back or accrued interest payments by the maturity date, the yields must be offered at extremely high interest rates.

Despite the negative label of "junk bond," these High Yield Bonds remain popular and heavily bought by global investors. The majority of these investors choose to diversify for safety sake by utilizing either a junk bond ETF exchange traded fund or a High Yield Bonds mutual fund. The spread between the yields on the higher yielding and investment grade types of bonds constantly fluctuates on the markets. The at the time condition of the global and national economies impacts this. Industry-specific and individual corporate events also play a part in the differences between the various kinds of bonds' interest rates.

In general though, High Yield Bonds' investors can count on receiving a good 150 to 300 basis points more in yield as measured against the investment quality bonds in any particular time frame. This is why mutual funds and ETFs make imminent sense as an effective means of gaining exposure to the greater yields without taking on the unnecessary risk of a single issuer's bonds defaulting and costing the investors all or most of their original investing principal.

In the last few years, various central bankers throughout the globe have decided to inject enormous amounts of liquidity into their individual economies so that credit will remain cheaply and easily available. This includes the European Central Bank, the U.S. Federal Reserve, and the Bank of Japan. It has created the side effect of causing borrowing costs to drop and lenders to experience significantly lower returns.

By February of 2016, an incredible $9 trillion in sovereign government debt bonds provided yields of only from zero percent to one percent. Seven trillion of the sovereign bonds delivered negative real yields once adjusted for anticipated levels of inflation. It means that holding such bonds cost investors money, or provided them a real losing return.

In typical economic environments, this would drive intelligent investors to competing markets that provide better return rates. Higher yield bond markets have stayed volatile though. Distressed debts which pay minimally a yield higher than 1,000 basis points greater than a comparably maturing Treasury bond were notably affected. Energy company high yielding debt bond prices collapsed by approximately 20 percent in 2015 as a consequence of the problems in the energy sector which resulted from plummeting energy prices.

High Yield Preferred Stocks

Preferred stocks are a special type of stocks that many companies issue. These types of stocks provide investors with a different level of ownership in a given company. A preferred stock holder obtains a higher priority on the earnings and assets of a company than a common stock holder would enjoy. These preferred stocks also pay a higher dividend that has to be given out before any dividends can be paid to the common stock holders.

As such, they represent a hybrid type of security on the stock markets. They are like common stocks in that they are bought and sold as stocks and represent ownership in a company. These stocks can also trade up and down in price like a common stock. Unlike a common stock, they do not come with any rights to vote for a company board of directors or items on a company ballot at the annual meeting.

They are also like bonds in that they pay a higher dividend that must be paid out unless the company lacks the earnings to pay these holders. In this way preferred stocks have elements of bonds with their fixed rate of dividends. Every preferred stock comes with its own unique details that are set when the company issues the stock.

Preferred stocks are often higher yielding issues. They are most commonly issued by companies that are in industries such as financials, real estate investment trusts, utilities, industrials, and conglomerates. Despite this higher yield that makes them like bonds, they can be traded on the major stock exchanges. They are typically found on exchanges including the NASDAQ and the New York Stock Exchange.

As preferred stocks are a type of equity legally, they show up as equity on any company balance sheet. Both common and preferred stock holders are owners in the company. There are several advantages to preferred stocks that investors like about them.

In the past, individual retail investors were less aware of preferred stocks, but this is changing. Part of the reason they have gained in popularity surrounds market volatility. As common stocks have seen wild price swings in recent years, investors have been looking for more stable instruments in which they can invest.

Preferred stocks fit this need as they tend to be more stable in price than do common stocks. With more baby boomers looking for investments that provide higher yields, this has brought preferred stocks into the spotlight. The retirees gain the advantage of better yields and the opportunity for the price to increase in the issues as well.

Preferred stocks are not new. They have existed from the time when modern day investing began. Institutional investors have known about and invested in them for many decades. Many individual investors did not because they lacked the information they required to select and trade them.

In the past, individuals did not have any lists of preferred stocks from which to pick. The information available was difficult to come up with before the Internet made this kind of information much more readily available. Now there are tools smaller individual investors can find that provide calendar searches for ex-dividend dates.

There are also screening filters that allow individuals to narrow down their search for the best high yielding dividend preferred stocks. Preferred stocks represent another way to diversify an investor's portfolio and earn higher yields on dividends at the same time.

Holdings

Holdings refer to the asset contents in a given portfolio which an entity or individual possesses. Pension funds and mutual funds are good examples of organizations that have holdings. These positions can include all sorts of different investment assets and classes. Among these are stocks, mutual funds, bonds, futures, options, ETF exchange traded funds, and private equity assets.

It is both the kinds and amounts of such holdings in any portfolios that determine how well-diversified the portfolio actually proves to be. Well-diversified portfolios often include various sectors of stocks, bonds from a range of maturities and companies, and a variety of other investments that do not correlate with either stocks or bonds. Alternatively, only a few positions in several stocks that come from only one sector would be indicative of poorly diversified portfolios.

It is actually the mix and amount of various asset classes in any portfolio that will substantially determine what its total rate of return will be. The biggest positions will exert a larger impact on the return of a portfolio than marginal or tinier holdings in such a portfolio will. Many investors make it a practice to closely scrutinize the lists of positions which the world's most successful money managers maintain in an effort to follow their trades.

Such investors try to imitate the trading prowess of these superior results money managers in a variety of ways. It might be the manager has purchased stocks, in which case the imitating investors will try to stake out a similar company position. If these managers sell out of a stake, the investors will similarly sell off their assets in the company. The problem with such a follower strategy is that there is often substantial lag time between that point where the money managers make their moves and when this information becomes public domain knowledge.

There is another variation on the idea of mutual funds, hedge funds, and pension funds. This is the concept of holding companies. Such organizations are groups where the investors organize their positions and assets as an LLC Limited Liability Company. The reasons for this are varied. It might be they wish to decrease their own risk exposure, pool their investment dollars with fellow investors, and/or reduce their taxes as much as possible. Such companies rarely operate their own businesses directly. Instead, they are generally only a vehicle utilized to own various investments and companies.

Probably the best-known example of such an LLC company is the internationally followed Berkshire Hathaway, Inc. This Warren Buffet-dominated Omaha, Nebraska- based corporation originally began as a clothing textiles' manufacturing firm. Over the last numbers of decades, the corporation has solely existed as Warren Buffet's personal vehicle to buy out, maintain, and sell out his numerous and wide-ranging investments in various companies. Among the greatest and most significant positions which Berkshire owns are large stakes in the Coca-Cola Company, Dairy Queen Inc, and their wholly controlled subsidiary GEICO Government Employees Insurance Company.

The simplest way to envision these holdings is to mentally picture a large bucket, which represents the mutual fund. Every rock within the bucket stands for an individual bond or stock position. When analysts add up all of the rocks (as stocks or bonds), this equals the aggregate numbers of all holdings.

Figuring out the best mix of these holdings is the challenge that mutual funds, pension funds, and hedge funds all grapple with on a regular basis. It all comes down to the type of fund which they represent. Those bond funds or index funds would anticipate having many positions. This could mean from hundreds to thousands of different bonds and stocks. With the majority of other funds, too many or too few positions is risky and dangerous. Those funds that hold merely 30 positions would be subject to extreme volatility and single stock risks. If they had 500 to 600 different stocks or bonds then the fund would be as large as many indices like the S&P 500.

Index Funds

Index funds are typically exchange traded funds or mutual funds. Their goal is to reproduce the actual movements of an underlying index for a particular financial market. They do this no matter what is happening in the overall stock markets.

There are several means of tracking such an index. One way of doing this is by purchasing and holding all of the index securities to the same proportion as they are represented in the index. Another way of accomplishing this is by doing a statistical sample of the market and then acquiring securities that are representative of it. A great number of the index funds are based on a computer model that accepts little to no input from people in its decision making of the securities bought and sold. This qualifies as a type of passive management when the index fund is run this way.

These index funds do not have active management. This allows them to benefit from possessing lesser fees and taxes in their accounts that are taxable. The low fees that are charged do come off of the investment returns that are otherwise mostly matching those of the index. Besides this, exactly matching an index is not possible since the sampling and mirroring models of this index will never be one hundred percent right. Such variances between an index performance and that of the fund are referred to as the tracking error, or more conversationally as a jitter.

A wide variety of index funds exist for you to choose from these days. They are offered by a number of different investment managers as well. Among the more typically seen indices are the FTSE 100, the S&P 500, and the Nikkei 225. Other indexes have been created that are so called research indexes for creating asset pricing models. Kenneth French and Eugene Fama created one known as the Three Factor Model. This Fama-French three factor model is actually utilized by Dimensional Fund Advisers to come up with their various index funds. Other, newer indexes have been created that are known as fundamentally based indexes. These find their basis in factors like earnings, dividends, sales, and book values of companies.

The underlying concept for developing index funds comes from the EMH, or efficient market hypothesis. This hypothesis claims that because stock analysts and fund managers are always searching for stocks that will do better than the whole market, this efficient competition among them translates to current information on a company's affairs being swiftly factored into the price of the stock. Because of this, it is generally accepted that knowing which stocks will do better than the over all market in advance is exceedingly hard. Developing a market index then makes sense as the inefficiencies and risks inherent in picking out individual stocks can be simply eliminated through purchasing the index fund itself.

Insider Trading

Insider trading is a generally negative phrase, though it can also refer to a legal activity. The illegal and better known version if it involves a person purchasing or selling a security when they have information that is not publicly available on the stock. The timing involved in such a trade often determines if it is legal or illegal.

If the critical information has not yet been released to the public, then it is not legally allowed. This is because the government determined to level the playing field in investing. Trading securities when investors have special knowledge is not fair to those traders who do not have the ability to access this information.

A person who tips off other individuals is also participating in illegal insider trading. This is the case if the tipster possesses valuable and relevant information that is not available to the public. Fines and jail time can be given to those who pass along illegal insider information. The responsible body for policing this type of illegal trading is the SEC Securities and Exchange Commission. They maintain and enforce rules that protect average investors from the results of illegal insider trading.

Legal insider trading happens all the time. It is not as well known as the illegal version. A legal trade from an insider occurs when company directors buy or sell shares that they fully disclose according to the rules. This occurs every week. The transactions must be electronically turned in to the SEC in a manner that is timely. Not only must they be sent in to the SEC, the company of the person involved must disclose this transaction information on their official website.

Congress passed the Securities Exchange Act of 1934 to address this issue. This first important step pertained to company stock transactions and legal disclosure. Major owners of securities and directors of the company as well had to disclose their positions, any transactions, and any time the ownership changed hands.

Several forms allow corporate insiders to legally disclose their stock affairs. Form 3 permits them to initially file that they have a company stake. Directors use Form 4 to make a disclosure on company stock transactions two days or less after the sale or purchase. They utilize Form 5 for earlier transactions or for transactions that become deferred until later.

It is not only company or corporate directors who are able to be tried and convicted for insider trading. Stock brokers and their clients can also be accused of this crime. Martha Stewart is a classic example of a brokerage client who the courts found guilty for placing insider trades back in 2003.

Martha Stewart received a tip from her Merrill Lynch stockbroker Peter Bacanovic concerning her shares of ImClone, a bio-pharmaceutical company. She used this information to sell her shares. Her broker had obtained this information that the Chief Executive Officer of ImClone Samuel Waksal liquidated all of his position in the corporation.

Waksal learned that the Food and Drug Administration was not going to approve his company's cancer drug Erbitux. After the two sales occurred, the FDA officially and publicly rejected the ImClone treatment drug. This caused a major selloff in the company stock of 16% in a single trading day. Stewart had saved a stock loss of $45,673 by selling out early.

The problem was that her sale had been based on the tip that CEO Waksal had sold all of his shares. This had not been publicly disclosed. Waksal became convicted and received a seven year jail sentence. Martha Steward was also convicted and forced to serve out five months in jail. She also received a number of months of house arrest and then probation.

Intraday

Intraday refers to trades that occur during the normal course of the day. These price movements are especially important for traders who practice short term trading. They attempt to earn profits trading repeatedly throughout the one day trading session. Sometimes the term is utilized to refer to securities which engage in normal trading on the stock exchanges throughout the regular hours' session. This would include ETFs exchange traded funds and company stocks.

On the other hand, investors must purchase mutual funds from dealers directly. Their transactions typically occur after the stock market exchanges close for the day. This happens because the mutual funds must calculate their closing NAV Net Asset Value before they can lock in the buying and selling prices for their fund shares each market day.

Intraday also can be employed to explain a new low or high for a given security. It is always illuminating to consider a real example of such concepts. When dealers or analysts refer to a new Intraday low, they signify that the security touched a new low as compared to its other price points throughout the day in a single trading session. There are many cases where such an intraday low or high is the same as the final closing price for the given security.

Short term traders are always interested in these single day price movements. They watch them carefully with computer power-generated real time charts. This helps them to ascertain the right points to trade in and out in an effort to make money on the short term volatility and movements in the underlying issue stock prices. These shorter term time frame traders generally deploy 60, 30, 15, five, and one minute charts as they are trading in a single session and day. They might employ the five and one minute charts for scalping, while they would utilize the 60 and 30 minute charts for holding periods of a longer several hours.

There are a range of advantages and disadvantages to such Intraday trading. The greatest benefit to it lies in the fact that any unforeseen after market news can not impact the prices of the securities themselves. As an example, consider a surprise earnings report or important economic data release. There are also broker downgrades and upgrades which might

Financial Terms Dictionary - Trading Terminology Explained

happen after the market has closed or before it even opens. By only trading stocks on a throughout the day basis, short term and scalping traders avoid these pitfalls which can cause dramatic price swings and shocks. Intraday trading also permits tighter stop loss orders, greater opportunities for learning, and higher leverage limitations.

Disadvantages in such trading are that there is not always enough time for various stock prices to gain sufficiently in profit. Commission costs are also significantly higher as the traders on a short term basis are often in and out of positions repeatedly throughout he day, raising the costs of trading.

Short term traders are not without their effective strategies that help them to realize profits on an intraday basis. Some of them are range trading in which they work off of resistance and support levels in order to decide sell and buy entry and exit points. There are also scalping trades that seek to earn a large number of profits on minute changes in the price of the securities in question. News-based trading seeks to gain advantage on the increased volatility levels surrounding announced news which may make for interesting and exciting trading opportunities on an intraday basis. Finally, there are high frequency trading strategies. These employ expensive and complicated computer algorithms to take advantage of tiny inefficiencies in the single day trading markets.

Junk Bonds

Junk bonds are almost the same as regular bonds with an important difference. They are lower rated for credit worthiness. This is why in order to understand junk bonds, individuals first must comprehend the basics of traditional bonds.

Like traditional bonds, junk bonds are promises from organizations or companies to pay back the holder the amount of money which they borrow. This amount is known as the principal. Terms of such bonds involve several elements. The maturity date is the time when the borrower will repay the bond holder. There will also be an interest rate that the bond holder receives, or a coupon. Junk bonds are unlike those traditional ones because the credit quality of the issuing organization is lower.

Every kind of bond is rated according to its credit quality. Bonds can all be categorized in one of two types. Investment grade bonds possess medium to low risk. Their credit ratings are commonly in the range of from AAA to BBB. The downside to these bonds is that they do not provide much in the way of interest returns. Their advantage is that they have significantly lower chances of the borrower being unable to make interest payments.

Junk bonds on the other hand offer higher interest yields to their bond holders. Issuers do this because they do not have any other way to finance their needs. With a lower credit rating, they can not borrow capital at a more favorable price. The ratings on such junk bonds are often BB or less from Standard & Poor's or Ba or less by Moody's rating agency. Bond ratings such as these can be considered like a report card for the credit rating of the company in question. Riskier firms receive lower ratings while safe blue-chip companies earn higher ratings.

Junk bonds typically pay an average yield that is from 4% to 6% higher than U.S. Treasury yields. These types of bonds are placed into one of two categories. These are fallen angels and rising stars. Fallen angels bonds used to be considered at an investment grade. They were cut to junk bond level as the company that issued them saw its credit quality decline.

Rising stars are the opposites of fallen angels. This means the rating of the bond has risen. As the underlying issuer's credit quality improves, so does the rating of the bond. Rising stars are often still considered to be junk bonds. They are on track to rise to investment quality.

Junk bonds are risky for more reasons than the chances of not receiving one or more interest payments. There is the possibility of not receiving the original principal back. This type of investing also needs a great amount of skills in analyzing data like special credit. Because of these risk factors and specialized skills that are needed, institutional investors massively dominate the market.

A better way for individuals to become involved with junk bonds is through high yield bond funds. Professionals research and manage the holdings of these funds. The risks associated with a single bond defaulting are greatly reduced. They do this by diversifying into a variety of companies and types of bonds. High yield bond funds often require investors to stay invested for minimally a year or two.

When the yield of junk bonds declines below the typical 4% to 6% spread above Treasuries, investors should be careful. The risk does not become less in these cases. It is that the returns no longer justify the dangers in the junk bonds. Investors also should carefully consider the junk bond default rates. These can be tracked for free on Moody's website.

Leverage

Where business and finance are concerned, leverage pertains to the concept of using investment capital, revenue, or equity to multiply any gains or losses realized. Leverage can be affected in various ways. Among the most popular means of achieving it are through purchasing fixed assets, borrowing money, or utilizing derivatives.

There are several important examples to the use of leverage. With investments, hedge funds work with derivatives to leverage their capital. They could do this by putting up one million dollar cash for their margin and using it to control twenty million dollars of crude oil. They then realize any and all gains or losses achieved by the twenty million dollar crude position.

Businesses may similarly achieve leverage on their revenue by purchasing fixed assets. In so doing, the business would boost its proportion of fixed costs. Any change in revenue would then lead to a greater change in the associated operating income.

Publicly traded corporations are also able to obtain leverage on their stock share holder equity through borrowing money. The greater amount of cash that they borrow, the lower amount of equity capital they will require. This translates to all profits and losses being distributed out to a smaller share holder base, making them proportionately bigger in the end.

There are formulas for the four main types of leverage. Accounting leverage is found by taking all assets and dividing them by all assets minus all liabilities. Notional leverage is found by taking all notional quantities of assets, adding them to all of the notional liabilities, and then dividing the result by equity. To find the economic leverage, the equity volatility has to be divided by the identical assets' unlevered investment volatility. Finally, operating leverage can be calculated through taking the revenue in question and subtracting out the variable cost, then dividing the operating income into the result.

Leverage entails significant benefits and also substantial risks. While it does allow potentially great amounts of money to be made when investments go the way of an individual or organization, it can also involve devastating losses when the investments move against the entity. As an example, a stock investor who purchases stocks with fifty percent margin will double his losses when a stock goes down. Companies that borrow excessively to increase their leverage can experience collapse and bankruptcy in a downturn in business at the same time as a company with less leverage could survive.

Not all uses of leverage entail the same degree of risk. Corporations that borrow money so that they can engage in international expansion, increase their line up of products, or modernize their plants and equipment gain additional diversification. This could provide more than just an offset for the extra risks that result from the leverage. Not all highly leveraged companies are risky either. Public utilities commonly include high levels of debt, but they are generally considered to be less risky than are technology companies that lack leverage.

Liquidity Preference

Liquidity Preference refers to the additional premium which holders of wealth or investors will require in order to trade off cash and cash equivalents in exchange for those assets that are not so liquid. Among these might be government bonds, stocks, or real estate.

It is the basis of a theory in economics known as the liquidity preference theory. The theory goes a step further in suggesting that the investors will want a greater interest rate level on any investments that have longer-dated maturities. This is because such securities will necessarily have a larger amount in time factor and interest rate level risks. The idea states the following: if all else is equal, sensible investors would rather hold cash or similarly liquid assets, given the choice.

There are several good reasons for why investors have such a preference, but one of them is most critical to understanding the motivation behind it. This is that any investments which are quickly liquidated will be far simpler to sell rapidly at full value. It explains why the theory states that shorter term securities' interest rates will generally be less since the investors are giving up a smaller amount of prized liquidity than they would by instead buying into the longer-dated or medium-dated debt securities.

It was the great interwar British economist John Maynard Keynes who first utilized the concept of Liquidity Preference. His understanding of the phrase centered on the important relationship between the amount of funds members of the public would hold and the associated interest rate. Keynes believed that there are only three reasons that consumers hold on to money. They need it for regular transactions. They also have to maintain some on the side in case of unusual and beyond normal budget expectations kinds of unforeseen costs. Finally, they need it for any speculative ventures. Keynes theorized that the amount of speculative cash they kept would have an inverse relationship to the then current interest rates.

The most crucial idea in Keynes' concept holds that when the interest rates are low enough, money supply increases will no longer foster extra investment from the consumers. Instead, the speculative balances of individuals would attract this money. The reason for this would be that the

Financial Terms Dictionary - Trading Terminology Explained

rates of interest were simply too little to persuade cash holders to trade in their cash on hand in lieu of assets that were really far less liquid. The consumers have a feeling that lower interest rates will have to go back up at some point in the coming future. This liquidity preference idea was a cornerstone in Keynes attempts to make sense of the long and painful 1930's decade-long, global depression.

Since the end of the Keynesian era in economics, education, and public policy, the categories which cover liquid assets have necessarily been significantly expanded. The dismal science of economics now connects the demand of consumers for money to a far larger number of different variables. Among these are the many competing additional means of holding wealth and the associated intrinsic yields to them. The interest rate as well as the individuals' income level also plays a part in determining their behaviors ultimately with cash like equivalents.

It is always helpful to consider a real world tangible example to better understand the concept of Liquidity Preference. In the world of debt securities, investors will always require a gradually greater premium (or interest rate) on first medium maturity then longer maturity debt securities than they would on shorter maturity debt securities. In one example, a three year dated Treasury note could pay one percent interest, while the ten year example could pay two percent and the thirty year Treasury bond could offer four percent. For the Treasury bonds' investors to agree to give up their liquidity for longer, they will insist on a greater interest rate return in lieu of tying up their funds for a sometimes substantially longer amount of time.

Margin Call

Margin Call refers to a demand from a broker that the account holding investor (who is utilizing margin) deposit additional funds or securities in order to restore the margin account to a minimum preset maintenance margin level. This could occur with a stock, futures, or commodities margin account. Such margin calls happen as the account value falls to a ratio which that specific brokerage deems unacceptable. Many brokerage houses use their own unique formulas to determine the amount at which they will issue such a call for more funds or securities.

Investors get into this unpleasant position when one or many of their securities they have purchased (utilizing money they borrowed from the brokerage) drops to a specified value point. That is when the call goes out from the broker for more money to restore the account to an acceptable minimum value. Investors will have two choices. They could comply with the request for additional funds and make an urgent deposit. Otherwise, they could sell off some or all of the positions in the account to reduce the need for minimum margin maintenance or raise the account equity position. The third choice of completely disregarding or ignoring the margin call would result in the broker force-selling positions to reduce this maintenance amount required.

Margin calls would not be necessary at all if investors did not buy securities, futures, or commodities with a combination of their own cash plus money they borrow off of the broker. This is why many experts recommend not utilizing such margin accounts unless an investor is a both seasoned and experienced trader.

Investors have equity in these margin-purchased investments. This amount equals the securities market value less the funds they originally borrowed to complete the purchase in the first place. If and when this equity of the account holder drops to lower than the brokerage-set percentage requirement of maintenance margin, then such a margin call becomes issued. Such maintenance margins do vary somewhat significantly from one broker to the next.

The constant is the Federal minimum maintenance margin requirements. These are set at a lowest common requirement of 25 percent, regardless of who the responsible broker is. The brokers can choose to utilize a higher margin maintenance level than this amount, but they can not ever reduce their own limit to less than the 25 percent set by the Feds. Brokers can decide to change their maintenance level higher or lower than their present set one with little to no advance warning or notice, so long as they do not drop it below the government-mandated minimum amount. Raising their margin maintenance requirements may also result in creating a margin call.

Looking at a tangible example helps to clarify the concept and make it more understandable. Investors might purchase $50,000 worth of stocks via a combination of $25,000 of their own funds and through borrowing the balance $25,000 off of the brokerage firm. Assume that this particular broker chooses to utilize the government-set minimum of 25 percent maintenance margin. The investor has no choice but to honor this.

When the investors open the trade, at that point the equity positions of the investments prove to be $25,000 (or $50,000 minus the $25,000 borrowed). This makes the investor equity percentage an even 50 percent (using the $25,000 equity divided by the $50,000 original securities market value). This is twice the required minimum 25 percent margin maintenance.

Yet a week later, our investors suffer a drastic decline in the value of their securities, which precipitously drop to $30,000. The investors' equity is now down to a mere $5,000 (or $30,000 minus the $25,000 borrowed). Yet the brokerage (and government regulations which are the same in this scenario) requires that they keep a minimally $7,500 worth of equity for the account to remain margin-eligible (which is 25 percent of the borrowed amount of $30,000).

It means that there is presently a $2,500 deficit ($7,500 requirement minus the $5,000 actual market value). The broker will then issue a margin call for $2,500 in additional cash to be deposited immediately. Should the investors refuse or take their time, then the broker is legally bound and permitted to sell off some of the securities to reach the minimum $7,500 in account equity value.

Margin Trading

Margin trading is the practice of buying investments on margin. This is accomplished through borrowing money from your broker in order to buy stocks. Another way of understanding margin trading is taking out a loan from your broker to buy greater amounts of stock shares.

Margin trading generally requires a margin account. Margin accounts differ from cash accounts that only allow you to trade with the money that your account contains. Brokers have to get a signature from you in order to open up a new margin account. This could be as an extension of your existing account and account opening forms or as a separate and new agreement. Minimum investments of $2,000 are necessary to open such a margin account. Some brokers insist on larger amounts. Whatever the final margin requirement deposit is, it is called the minimum margin.

After the margin account is up and running, you are able to purchase as much as fifty percent of a stock with margin trading money. The money that you use to buy your part of the stock is called initial margin. Margining up to the full fifty percent is entirely optional. You might borrow only fifteen or twenty percent instead.

Margin trading loans can be held for as long a period as you wish, assuming that you continue to meet the margin obligations. A stock maintenance margin has to be maintained while the loan is outstanding too. This maintenance margin is the lowest account balance that can be held by the account in advance of the broker making you deposit additional funds. If you do not meet this minimum or resulting margin call for extra funds, then the broker has the right to sell your stocks in order to reduce your outstanding loan.

Borrowing money from your broker is not done for the sake of charity. Interest has to be paid on the loan. Also, the marginable securities in the account become tied up as collateral. Unless you pay down the loan, interest charges will be applied to the loan balance. These interest amounts can significantly increase the debt level in the account with time. Higher debt levels in your account lead to still higher interest charges. Because of this, buying stocks on margin is typically utilized only for shorter time frame investments. This is true since the greater amount of time that you hold the margin loan in the investment, the higher a return you will require in order to break even on the margin trade. When you maintain such a margin based investment over a long time frame, it becomes difficult to turn a profit after the expenses are cleared.

It is also important to remember that not every stock qualifies for purchase using margin. The rules pertaining to which stocks can be purchased with margin are set by the Federal Reserve Board. In general though, Initial Public Offerings, penny stocks, or over the counter traded stocks are not allowed to be purchased utilizing margin as a result of the daily volatility and trading risks associated with such kinds of stocks. Besides this, each brokerage can restrict whichever other stocks that they wish.

Mortgage Broker

A mortgage broker is a firm or sole proprietorship that performs a role as an intermediary between banks and businesses or individuals who are looking for mortgage loans. Even though banks have always vended their own mortgage products, mortgage brokers have gradually taken a larger and larger share of the loan originating market as they seek out direct lenders and banks that have the specific products that a customer wants or needs.

Nowadays, sixty-eight percent of all loans begin with mortgage brokers in the United States, making them by far and away the biggest vendors of mortgage products for banks and lenders. The remaining thirty-two percent of loans come from banks own direct marketing efforts and retail branch efforts. Mortgage broker fees are separate from the bank mortgage fees. They are based on the loans' amounts themselves and range from commonly one to three percent of the total loan amount.

Mortgage brokers are mostly regulated in order to make sure that they comply with finance laws and banking rules in the consumer's jurisdiction. This level of regulation does vary per state. Forty-nine of the fifty states have their own laws or boards that regulate mortgage lending within their state's borders. The industry is similarly governed by ten different federal laws that are applied by five federal agencies for enforcement.

Banks find mortgage brokers to be an ideal means of bringing in borrowers who will qualify for a loan. In this way, a mortgage broker acts as a screening agent for a bank. Banks are furthermore able to shift forward a portion of the fraud and foreclosure risks to the loan originators using their contractual legal arrangements with them. In the originating of a loan, a mortgage broker will do the footwork of collecting and processing all of the necessary paper work associated with real estate mortgages.

Mortgage brokers should not be confused with loan officers of a bank. Mortgage brokers are typically state registered and also licensed in order to work as a mortgage broker. This makes them liable personally for any fraud that they commit during the entire life span of the loans in question. Being a mortgage broker comes with professional, legal, and ethical responsibilities that include proper disclosure of mortgage terms to consumers.

Mortgage brokers come with all kinds of experience, as do loan officers, who are employees of banks. While loan officers commonly close more loans than mortgage brokers actually do because of their extensive network of referrals within the bank for which they work, the majority of mortgage brokers make more money than loan officers make. Mortgage brokers generate the lion's share of all loan originations within the country as well.

Mortgage brokers are all represented by the NAMB, which is the acronym for their group the National Association of Mortgage Brokers. The NAMB's mission is to represent the industry of mortgage brokers throughout the U.S. It also offers education, resources to members, and a certification program as well.

Moving Averages

Moving Averages are an indicator that is heavily used in technical analysis. They represent average prices spread out over a period of time. They are more useful because the changes in price action are smoothed out as any random price movements become filtered out.

There are a number of different variations. Two of them prove to be the most commonly used. These are the simple moving average, or SMA, and the exponential moving average, or EMA. A simple moving average is a straight average compiled over a certain number of different time periods. With the Exponential Moving Average, prices that are more recent tend to have a greater amount of weight given to them than prices that are farther back.

Moving Averages are most commonly used to find the direction of the overall trend. They also help to set the levels of resistance and support. Moving averages are also heavily used to create a number of other technical indicators. One of the better known that is based upon the moving averages is the MACD, or Moving Average Convergence Divergence.

Moving Averages tend to be lagging indicators themselves. This is because programs and charts derived them from historical prices. They are useful even despite this lagging nature. The longer a time frame that an individual considers with a moving average, the bigger the lag will be. For example, 200 day moving averages would lag significantly more than 100 day moving averages and even more than 20 day moving averages.

Different Moving Average time frames are employed depending on the trading needs. Investors who are practicing short term trading will be most interested in shorter time-frame Moving Averages. Investors who pursue long term trading will find longer time frame moving averages to be more helpful.

Many different traders and investors find the 200 Day Moving Average to be a useful and significant benchmark and tool. When there are breaks to the top or bottom it sends major trading signals.

For example, if a 200 day moving average acting as a support were convincingly broken, then the underlying security would likely continue moving down. Conversely, if the same important moving average was functioning as a resistance point, then a break of this average to the topside would likely signal the instrument would continue moving up significantly.

Moving Averages deliver a variety of critical signals for trading by themselves. When two of them cross, it can be even more significant. Moving Averages that are going up demonstrate that the instrument or security is trending higher as part of an uptrend. A Moving Average that declined would show the security to be trending lower and involved in a downtrend.

A bullish crossover is another confirmation of movement to the upside. This happens as a shorter time frame Moving Average crosses over and above another Moving Average that is longer term. Similarly, a bearish crossover signals that there is more momentum to the downside. It happens as the shorter time frame Moving Average makes the cross beneath a Moving Average which is longer term.

Another important usage surrounds supports and resistances. When stocks or other securities are trending up, moving averages function as supports. A shorter term uptrend would look to 20 Day Simple MAs. These are a part of Bollinger Band indicators as an example. The longer term uptrend often looks for support at the popular 200 Day Moving Average.

Conversely when securities trend downwards, these moving averages act as resistances. An interesting point about 200 Day Moving Averages is that they are so widely followed that they work in many cases either as support or resistance simply because so many people watch and give them significance.

Financial Terms Dictionary - Trading Terminology Explained

Mt. Gox

Until 2014, Mt. Gox used to be the largest bitcoin exchange operator in the history of virtual digital currency and its poster boy bitcoin. The Japanese-based company arose in July of 2010. By the year 2013, it had grown to dominate the bitcoin exchange market by handling an astonishing 70 percent of all bitcoin transaction in the world.

In less than a year later in February of 2014, the company was forced to suspend stock trading, close down its exchange service and website, and to file for bankruptcy protection known as civil rehabilitation. The courts began looking for a buyer of the stricken exchange at this point. By April of 2014, the firm had started official liquidation procedures under the auspices of a court-appointed bankruptcy trustee.

This is when the news, which was only unconfirmed rumors before, emerged that nearly 850,000 bitcoins which belonged to company customers had been missing and probably stolen. The value of said bitcoins at this point proved to be $450 million. The good news for account holders is that fully 200,000 of the supposedly stolen coins were found. In the beginning it was unclear whether the coins had been fraudulently mishandled, stolen, mismanaged, or some combination of all of them. By April of 2015, WizSec produced evidence which showed that the majority of the missing digital currency units were actually stolen right out of the Mt. Gox hot wallet gradually and over several years. This theft began consistently in 2011.

The company initially grew out of a fantasy gaming community project. Its humble origins dated back to late 2006. Programmer Jed McCaleb famous for his games and apps Stellar, Ripple, Overnet 1, and eDonkey2000, came up with the idea to develop a website for the players of Magic: The Gathering Online. This would enable them to trade various cards like stocks, which already traded online. He bought the domain name mtgox.com as an acronym for Magic: The Gathering Online eXchange. When the developer lost interest in what he assumed would never be a profitable project, he later sold it off to investor-developers who had visions for its platform as a bitcoin exchange.

By 2013, the site was by far and away the largest bitcoin exchange operator in all the world, dealing in 70 percent of the global bitcoin trade. By May in 2013, Mt. Gox was trading an impressive 150,000 of the digital currency units each day, as demonstrated by the Bitcoin volume charts.

It was only one month later that suddenly Mt. Gox suspended all client withdrawals in U.S. dollars. Tokyo's Mizuho Bank which handled their U.S. transfers began pressuring them to close out the account from this moment. Transactions were restored on July 4, but there were consistent problems through the rest of the summer and fall.

Wired Magazine broke the story in November of 2013 that Mt. Gox clients suffered from several weeks to even months of delays when they attempted to cash out their bitcoins for other currencies or take out bitcoins in the forms of withdrawals. The article claimed the company was "effectively frozen out of the U.S. banking system because of its regulatory problems." By February of 2014, client complaints had mounted regarding the long delays in withdrawal processing. February 7 saw the final halting of all bitcoin withdrawals by the company.

The news just continued to grow worse from this point. February 23 witnessed the resignation of CEO Mark Karpeles from the Bitcoin Foundation. The next day, Mt. Gox had suspended all trades. Its website went dark a few hours later and never came back online. A leaked document on the company's crisis management insisted that the company had become insolvent after the loss of 744,408 bitcoins in a theft that had been ongoing and undetected for literally years.

At this point, six of the other major bitcoin exchange operators issued a joint press release asserting that they had no connection with the fallen former giant of the industry. The last communication from the company came out on February 25 when they reported that all of their transactions had been closed out until further notice thanks to recent reports and their impacts on the operations of the firm.

Net Asset Value

The Net Asset Value refers to a mutual fund and its per share value. It is also known by its acronym NAV. Exchange traded funds, or ETFs, can also be referenced by the NAV. These values which the companies themselves compute for investors only provide a snap shot of the NAV at a particular time and date. In either security type, the fund's per share dollar value arises from the aggregate value of every security within its portfolio minus any liabilities the fund may owe. Finally this is expressed over the total number of outstanding shares in order to arrive at the shares' ultimate NAV.

Where mutual funds are concerned, the Net Asset Value is derived one time every trading day. They utilize the closing market prices for every security within the fund's holdings in order to determine this. Once this is done, the fund is able to settle all sell and buy orders which are outstanding on the shares. These prices will be set by the NAV of the mutual fund in question for the value per the trade date. Investors will always be required to wait to the next day in order to obtain their actual trade-in or trade-out price.

Because mutual funds do pay out nearly all their capital gains and income, such NAV changes are never the optimal gauge for the performance of the given fund. Instead these are better determined by looking at the yearly aggregate return, or total return.

With ETFs, these are actually closed end types of funds. This means that they actually trade more like stocks do. The shares of these Exchange Traded Funds therefore constantly trade at the market value. It might be a literal value which is higher than the NAV. This would be trading at a premium to the Net Asset Value. It could similarly trade under the NAV. This would mean the prices were trading at a discount to the NAV.

With these ETFs, the Net Asset Value becomes computed once at the markets' close so that the fund can correctly report the ETF values. During the day however, these are figured differently than the mutual fund computations. This is because the ETFs will compile the during-the-day NAV in real time at numerous points in every minute of the trading day.

It is helpful to consider an example of how the mutual funds compute their Net Asset Value calculations. The formula is actually very straightforward. It is simply that the NAV is equal to the mutual fund's assets less its liabilities with the difference divided by the total number of shares outstanding. The assets in the case of mutual funds include cash equivalents and cash, accrued income, and receivables. The main portion of their assets commonly are their investments, which will be priced per the end of the day closing values. Liabilities equate to the complete longer-term and shorter-term money owed, along with each accrued expense. Among these expenses will be utilities, salaries of the staff of the fund, and various operational costs for running such a fund.

Consider that the fictitious Diamond Stocks Mutual Fund counted $200 million in investments, figured utilizing the end of day closing prices of all their assets. Besides this, it has $14 million in cash equivalents and cash and another $8 million in receivables in total. The daily accrued income amounts to $150,000. Besides this, Diamond Stocks owes $26 million in its shorter-term liabilities and has $4 million of longer-term liabilities. The daily accrued expenses amount to $20,000. With 10 million outstanding shares, the net asset value would equate to $19.21 in the case of the Diamond Stocks Mutual Fund.

New York Mercantile Exchange (NYMEX)

The New York Mercantile Exchange proves to be the biggest physical commodity exchange for futures buying, selling, and trading in the world. Since they merged, it is comprised of both the NYMEX Division and the COMEX Division. At NYMEX, traders are able to trade platinum, palladium, and energy markets.

COMEX is where they trade FTSE 100 index options as well as silver, gold, and copper futures. NYMEX still keeps a place for the open outcry system where traders shout and make hand gestures to indicate their purchases. This operates only during the day time. After normal business hours, the electronic trading system takes over for the night.

The NYMEX origins go back to an association of Manhattan dairy merchants. In 1872, a group of them came together and formed the Butter and Cheese Exchange of New York. Once eggs joined the various dairy businesses handled on the exchange, they changed the name to Butter, Cheese, and Egg Exchange. By 1882 they had added canned goods, dried fruits, and poultry to the offerings. The name received its final change to reflect the broader product offerings as the New York Mercantile Exchange at this time.

Though COMEX Commodities Exchange and NYMEX used to be separately owned and run exchanges, they merged together to become two divisions of the NYMEX Holdings, Inc. back in 1994. They listed on the New York Stock Exchange on November 17, 2006 trading under the NMX ticker symbol.

In March of 2008, the CME Group of Chicago committed to a conclusive agreement to buy NYMEX holdings for $11.2 billion combination in cash and stock offerings. In August of 2008 the deal finished and NYMEX and COMEX began to function as DCM Designated Contract Markets for the CME Group. They joined sister exchanges the Chicago Board of Trade and Chicago Mercantile Exchange as part of the four DCMs.

In 2006, the New York Mercantile Exchange became almost entirely electronically traded. NYMEX keeps a smaller venue operating for those traders who prefer to engage in the open outcry historic and sentimental form of trading. There they utilize complicated hand signals and shouting while standing on a physical trading floor to buy and sell. The hand signal system is being preserved by a project published on the subject.

NYMEX's headquarters is found in the Battery Park City area of Manhattan in Brookfield Place. They also maintain offices around the world in such cities as Washington D.C., Boston, San Francisco, Atlanta, London, Dubai, and Tokyo. The options and futures traded here on precious metals and energy commodities have developed into important tools for companies that are seeking to mitigate their risk through hedging their own positions. Because these various instruments are traded so easily and liquidly, companies are able to discern future prices and to hedge their future needs. This is why NYMEX has grown to become such a critical part of global activities in hedging and trading environments.

Today the NYMEX manages literally billions of dollars in metals, energy carrier, and other commodities that companies and traders sell and buy every day for delivery in the future. This is handled on either the physical trading floor or the electronic trading system by computers.

These prices on the exchange and its numerous transactions become the basis of pricing for individuals and companies who purchase commodities around the globe. The Commodity Futures Trading Commissions agency of the U.S. government actually regulates the NYMEX floor. Trading on the exchange is performed by independent brokers sent by specific companies.

New York Stock Exchange (NYSE)

The NYSE is the acronym for the world's largest stock exchange, the New York Stock Exchange. With a market capitalization of companies listed on it totaling at $11.92 trillion dollars in August 2010, it also possessed an average day trading value of around $153 billion in 2008. By market capitalization, the NYSE has no rivals for size.

The New York Stock Exchange is owned and operated by the NYSE Euronext company. This outfit came into being in 2007 when the NYSE merged with the completely electronic Euronext stock exchange. Four rooms make up the trading floor of the NYSE that is found at 11 Wall Street. Its main building is found at 18 Broad Street on the corners of Wall Street and Exchange Place. This building became a National Historic Landmark back in 1978, along with its sister 11 Wall Street Building.

Occasionally known as "the Big Board," the New York Stock Exchange allows for sellers and buyers of stocks to exchange shares in all of the companies that are listed for public trading. Its trading hours prove to be 9:30 AM to 4:00 PM on Monday to Friday. Holidays are spelled out in advance by the exchange itself.

The NYSE has always operated as an in person trading floor since its inception in 1792. Today, this works in an auction format that is ongoing. Floor traders here are able to make stock transactions for investors. They simply gather together surrounding the particular company post where there is a specialist broker working as auctioneer in open outcry format to get buyers and sellers together and to oversee the auction itself. This specialist works directly for the company that is an NYSE member and not the exchange itself. These specialists will commit their own money to assist the trades about ten percent of the time. Naturally, they also give out information that serves to bring together sellers and buyers.

In 1995, NYSE began making the automation transition for the auctions. This started with hand held computers that were wireless. Like this, traders were capable of executing and getting orders electronically. This ended a 203 year tradition of paper based trades.

From January 24 of 2007, most every stock on the NYSE is able to be traded on the electronic Hybrid Market. With this ability to send in customer orders for electronic confirmation immediately, orders can also be sent to the floor for auction market trade. More than eighty-two percent of the NYSE order volume came to the floor electronically in only the first three months of that first year.

Only those who own one of 1,366 actual seats on the exchange are permitted to trade shares directly on the exchange. Such seats are sold for enormous sums. The highest price paid for one amounted to $4 million in the tail end of the 1990's. The highest price ever paid adjusted for inflation proved to be $625,000 in 1929, which would amount to more than six million dollars in terms of 2010 dollars. Since the exchange became a public company, the seats have been instead sold in one year licenses.

Nikkei 225

The Nikkei is an abbreviation for Japan's foremost, best known, and most respected stock index of Japanese companies. Its full name is the Nikkei 225 Stock Average. This index is price weighted and made up of the top 225 industry leading companies which investors trade on the Tokyo Stock Exchange. The United States equivalent of this Nikkei is the Dow Jones Industrial Average.

This stock index originally came into existence as the Nikkei Dow Jones Stock Average. Investors knew it by this name during the years 1975 to 1985. Today's Nikkei 225 carries the name of the Japan Economic Newspaper "Nihon Keizai Shimbun" which is generally referred to as Nikkei. This newspaper is the sponsor for the index and its calculation. There has been a calculation of this index going back to September of 1950. There are many well known firms that make up this index. Some of the most recognized are Toyota Motor Corporation, Sony Corporation, and Canon Inc.

The Nikkei 225 proves to be Asia's oldest stock index in existence. The country founded it in its industrialization and reconstruction efforts that followed the end of World War II. Stocks which make it up are not ranked by market capitalization like in the majority of such indices around the world. Instead they are ranked and listed based on their share prices. The denominations of every stock's value are in Japanese yen. Each September the Nikkei's make up undergoes review so that necessary changes can be made effective for October.

The actual Tokyo Stock Exchange began operating in 1878. This exchange received a major boost in the heat of World War II when the Japanese government decided to merge Tokyo's Stock Exchange with five other exchanges to make a single, unified national Japanese Stock Exchange. This pan-Japanese exchange had to be shut down in August of 1945 towards the conclusion of the war. It finally opened again on May 16 in 1949 as part of the new legislation the Securities Exchange Act.

An enormous asset bubble engulfed Japan during the late 1980s. The government bore responsibility for this as they employed both monetary and fiscal stimulus programs to attempt to offset the nation's currency led recession. The yen had risen 50% in the beginning of the decade. From 1985 to 1989, both land and stock prices tripled in value. When the bubble reached its peak, Tokyo's Stock Exchange comprised an astonishing 60 percent of all capitalization for global stock exchanges.

This bubble exploded in 1990. That year alone the Nikkei 225 Index dropped by a third. This economic and stock market stagnation continued for decades so that in the midst of the Great Recession in October 2008, the Nikkei's value had dropped below 7,000. This represented an astonishing plunge of over 80 percent from the high set back in December of 1989. The government worked to re-inflate the index powerfully from June 2012 to June 2015 as it rose 150 percent. The government's economic stimulus programs coupled with efforts of the Bank of Japan assisted in this asset appreciation. Even at these loftier levels, this still proved to be almost 50 percent under the high set in 1989.

Investors who wish to invest in the index may not buy it directly. A few different ETF Exchange Traded Funds track its performance. These include the Japan iShares Nikkei 225 by Blackrock and the Nikkei 225 Exchange Traded Fund by Nomura Asset Management. Investors can trade the index via ETFs in dollars on the New York Stock Exchange by purchasing or selling shares of the Nikkei 225 Index ETF by Maxis.

Option Spreads

Option spreads are option combinations which have traders combining two different options contracts with varied strikes but identical expiration dates. They do this in a strategy to limit their overall risk. The idea behind these option spreads is relatively simple, but the possible effects of some spread constructs can become slightly more complicated.

Reducing the concept of option spreads to their most intuitive elements involves the discussion of the two legs, or option contracts, which comprise the spread itself. Putting on two legs refers to traders combining as an example a call option purchase with one which they sell at the same time. In other words, the traders who enter this strategy will take on both sides of the market when they make options spreads. It will either be in buying the one and selling the other, or selling the one and buying the other option contract.

The idea behind buying and simultaneously selling two options with the same expiration but different strikes is that this action reduces the risk. When traders sell a call and also buy a call, they are less exposed to a fall in the market or the option premium time decay thanks to the option which they sold, for which they received a premium. The net cost of the spread is therefore less than that of simply buying a call.

Another way of looking at this maneuver is that the cost of the one call is subsidized by the sale price of the one which the traders sell. The one sold is further out of the money than the one bought, which reduces the cost of the overall spread options. This effectively limits aggregate risk, exposure to the relentless time decay factor, and the penalty for the price movement potential to the downside.

Consider a real world example. If HSBC bank stock is trading at $53 per share and traders believe that the stock price will rise in the short term, they might decide to put on a bull call spread. They might construct this spread by buying a $55 strike price call at the same time as they sell a $60 strike price call. The expiration date in this example is irrelevant so long as the two call contracts have the same expiration date. In this example, the traders pay $500 for the $55 strike call and receive $250 for the $60 strike price call. The net cost of the spread position is $250 then.

In this example, the maximum risk is limited to the $250 net cost of the spread. Instead of having a $500 risk from only buying the single $55 strike price call, risk is reduced in this case by half for also selling the $60 strike price call. The trade off for this lowered risk is a reduced maximum potential profit. The reason is that as the stock price reaches $60 per share, the spread owners realize their maximum profit point. This is $500 gross realized for a $250 maximum net profit (maximum $500 gross proceeds minus the $250 spread cost). Even if the stock price were to rise to $65 per share, it would not change the profit possibility, since the sold call with a strike at $60 means that the spread owners can not capture any additional gains in the price of the stock beyond the strike price which they already sold.

If the price of the stock moves against the spread owners, they can not lose any more money than the maximum $250 net cost of the spread, regardless of how low the underlying stock price moves against them. This makes these bull call and bull put spreads very popular with options traders, since they are effective at reducing risk while still allowing for large profit potentials.

Options

Options are contracts on stocks, indexes, currencies, commodities, or debt instruments. There are two principle types. These are call options and put options. Call options give holders the ability to purchase a set amount of the underlying instrument for a specific price in a certain amount of time. This specific price is known as the strike price. Put options grant holders the ability to sell the exact amount of the underlying instrument at a fixed price in a given period of time.

With options on stocks, the set amount of the underlying shares that calls and puts cover are typically 100 shares. Option contracts have two parties to them. The first are the sellers who are also known as writers of the option. The buyers are the holders of the option.

Option values are made up of two components. These are intrinsic value and time value. Intrinsic value is the amount that the option is in the money. For an option to be in the money, the stock price must be higher than the strike price for calls. For puts, the stock price has to be lower than the strike price. The value that is left after subtracting intrinsic value is the option's time value. When an option has no intrinsic value, one hundred percent of its value is time value.

Investors can buy and sell options until they run out of time. At this point, they expire either with some intrinsic value or worthless. They can also be exercised. When an option is exercised, the seller must transfer the underlying shares to the holder of the option. When the instrument is not able to be transferred over, then the parties settle in cash instead.

Investors like this financial tool because they give buyers peace of mind. The most an option holder is able to lose is the total price that they paid when they bought the contract. If options are not exercised or sold within the given time frame, then they expire. An option that expires worthless does not involve any exchange of shares or cash.

Buyers and sellers have different potential profits with options. Profit potential is limitless for the buyers. For the sellers, the profit is limited to the price which they receive for the contract. Sellers have unlimited loss potential unless they own the underlying shares or instrument. When a seller of an option holds the underlying instrument, the option is covered.

There are two main reasons that investors buy options. These can be to gain leverage or to obtain protection. The leverage benefit means that the option holder can control a larger amount of equity for a much smaller price than it costs to actually buy the shares. This exposes the buyer to a far smaller potential loss.

Options provide protection to investors who own the shares that underlie the contract. While the owners of the option hold the contract, they gain protection against adverse price movements in their shares. This is because the contract provides the ability to obtain the stock at a certain price during the option's contract time-frame. In this case, the cost of the option is the premium that the owner pays.

There are several downsides to options. The trading costs for options are higher than with buying the underlying shares of the stock or other instrument. This is because the spread between the bid and ask is higher for options. Option commissions also cost more than do stock commissions.

Option trading is more complicated than stock trading too. Options also have to be watched more closely than do stocks generally. The time involved to trade and maintain option strategies can be significant.

Over The Counter (OTC)

OTC is the acronym for Over the Counter. In the business and financial world, Over the Counter trading is also known as trading off of the exchange. Such OTC trading goes on when financial instruments of various kinds, including stocks, commodities, bonds, or derivatives, are traded literally between the buying and selling party themselves, without having an exchange in the middle of the transaction.

Over the Counter trading can be said to be the opposite of exchange trading. Exchange trading happens in facilities or over electronic market places that are specially created for the trading of these instruments. Stock exchanges and futures exchanges are the places that exchange trading takes place and Over the Counter trading does not.

Within the United States, Over the Counter stock trading is done via market makers who ensure that there are markets in both Pink Sheet and OTCBB, or bulletin boards, securities. They do this through the utilization of quotation services that are between dealers, like Pink Quote, run by the Pink OTC Markets, and OTC Bulletin Board for the OTCBB. While Over the Counter stocks typically do not either list or trade on any form of stock exchange, stocks that are listed on exchanges may be traded on the third market over the counter.

OTCBB quoted stocks have to follow the reporting rules as set out by the United States SEC, or Securities and Exchange Commission, regulatory body. Pink Sheet stocks are not governed by such reporting requirements. Still other stocks that are traded as OTCQX meet different disclosure guidelines that they are permitted to work under in the OTC Pink sheet markets.

OTC can also relate to contracts created between two entities. In these contracts, the two parties concur on the way that a specific trade will be settled at a certain future point. These typically come from investment banks and go out to their own clients. Good examples of these types of OTC arrangements are swaps and forwards. Such contracts are typically arranged over the phone or via computer. Derivative OTC contracts fall under the governance of an agreement provided by the International Swaps and Derivatives Association. This type of OTC market is sometimes called the Fourth Market.

In the Financial Crisis of 2007-2010, many of these OTC derivative contracts created and wreaked havoc in international financial markets specifically because they were traded over the counter, and no one exactly knew what risk and credit were entailed in the contracts that totaled in the tens of trillions of dollars and were made between mysterious partners. To address this critical problem, the NYMEX, or New York Mercantile Exchange, set up a mechanism for clearing many of the most frequently traded energy derivatives that were previously traded only OTC. Now, many of these customers can simply hand over the trade to the exchange's clearing house ClearPort. This removes the dangers associated with both performance and credit risk that were previously seen in these OTC transactions. Other exchanges are endeavoring to do the same thing to try to take derivatives and credit default swap contracts away from the shadowy world of Over the Counter trading. The G20, or Group of Twenty Industrialized and Industrializing nations, is considering ways of rewarding parties for bringing such OTC derivative transactions onto regulated exchanges as well.

Penny Stocks

Penny stocks are those securities that usually trade for comparatively lower prices, off of the big stock exchanges, and with smaller market capitalizations. Many analysts and investors look at these securities as higher in risk and extremely speculative. This is because they feature significant bid and ask spreads, less liquidity, smaller followings, and lesser capitalization and disclosure requirements. Many of these smaller stocks trade on the pink sheets or OTC Bulletin Board in what is known as the "over the counter market."

Penny stocks used to be those which traded for under a dollar, but thanks to the SEC this is no longer the case. The SEC altered the definition so that all stock shares which trade for less than $5 are now considered to be a penny stock. These companies have fewer listing requirements, regulations, and filings which govern them.

It is important to remember that penny stocks best suit investors who can stand more risk. They come with greater amounts of volatility which can lead to steep losses or possibly greater returns. The lower volumes and greater amounts of risk are why the moves in these stocks can be staggering. These companies struggle with fewer resources and less cash, but sometimes achieve breakthroughs that can catapult their share prices higher. It is safer to trade or invest in penny stocks which are listed on the NASDAQ or the AMEX American Stock Exchange because these exchanges more vigorously regulate their constituent companies.

Four factors make these micro cap stocks so much riskier than traditional blue chip stocks. The information which the public has access to is usually lacking. It is harder to make well informed decisions on companies that do not provide sufficient information. Other information that is offered on such micro cap stocks can come from less than reputable sources.

Another feature that makes penny stocks so risky is that they do not have a common set of minimum standards. Neither the pink sheets nor the OTCBB require these companies to live up to minimum requirements to stay listed. They will have to file certain documents in a timely manner with the OTCBB, but not with the pink sheets. These standards traditionally offer a safety cushion that helps to protect investors. They are a benchmark for other smaller companies to achieve.

A third difficulty with these micro cap stocks is they lack history. A great number of such companies could be nearing bankruptcy or recently founded. This means that their track records are either non existent or poor at best. A lack of historical data compounds the difficulty of assessing a company's future and their stock's near and long term possibilities.

A final danger with penny stocks is their lack of liquidity. This creates two problems. An investor may not be able to sell out of the stock at an acceptable price. With low liquidity, there may be no buyer available at any price. Lower liquidity also leads to the possibility for traders to manipulate the prices of the stocks themselves. They can purchase enormous quantities of the issue, promote it themselves, and then sell it at higher prices to other investors who become stuck with it. This is called a pump and dump strategy.

Pivotal Points

Pivotal Points refers to a system for predicting stock price movements that Jesse Livermore created and developed. Time Magazine described him as the most incomparable living American trader of his day. In the 1920's, he used the system to amass a fortune that at its peak valued $100 million. As a share of the U.S. GDP of the time, this amounts to $14 billion in current dollars as measured against today's GDP.

This represented the first time that any investor had documented using Pivotal Points. Livermore famously wrote about it in his book, Reminiscences of a Stock Operator. These Pivotal Points are so useful because more than 90 years after Jesse created them investors still utilize and teach them.

Pivotal Points are the levels at which stock prices find support and resistance. In fact they are the primary levels of both support and resistance, depending on whether they are higher or lower than the price of the stock. Because of the importance of these Pivotal Points, they are the levels where the greatest price movement generally happens. There may be other resistance and support levels. Other levels are less important than the pivotal ones.

There are two principal ways that Pivotal Points are utilized today as they were in the 1920's when Livermore first created them. In the first case, investors can employ them to decide what the general market trend is. Market trend is important because it tells investors which way the market is generally moving.

Should the Pivotal Point price be broken to the upside, then the stock or market proves to be bullish. If instead the Pivotal Point is broken in a downward movement, then an individual investor considers the case to be bearish for the stock or market.

A second way to utilize the Pivotal Points is as a price level for either entering or exiting a trade. Finding the right level to open a position or close out an existing one is critical. Investors can place buy limit orders based on the Pivotal Point resistance level breaking. They might also use the Pivotal Point support level as their stop loss to exit a trade should this critical support line fail.

Nowadays it is easy to figure up Pivotal Points. Computer programs and charting software can find the levels easily. When Jesse first created them, these points had to be manually figured out with no more than a calculator, pencils, and paper. There are a number of formulas that can be used to determine them. Jesse Livermore made his own charts by hand. He looked for the levels where the stocks tended to bounce several times to find them.

Many traders today consider Pivotal Points to be shorter term use indicators. Because a number of investors use them for a single day trading, they have to recalculate them every day. Despite this fact, even day trading Pivotal Points is considered to be helpful. This is because a person can quickly calculate up important levels where there will be significant price movement.

Preferred Stock

Preferred stock is referred to as preference shares or preferred shares as well. Preferred stock is the name used for a particular equity security which exhibits both characteristics of a stock equity as well as an instrument of debt. Because of this, preferred stocks are commonly deemed to be hybrid types of instruments. In the claims on a company's assets in the event of default or bankruptcy, preferred stocks prove to be higher ranking than mere common stocks, yet subordinated to bonds.

Preferred stocks have a number of interesting properties. They typically come with a dividend that is often fixed. They also enjoy preference versus common stocks where dividend payments are concerned and at any liquidation of the company's assets. A downside to preferred stocks is that they do not include voting rights as do common stock shares. Some preferred stocks offer convertible features that turn them into common shares of stock at a certain time. There are preferred stocks that may be called in early at the wishes of the issuing company. All terms for a preferred stock are listed out specifically in the Certificate of Designation.

Since preferred stocks are somewhat like bonds, the big credit rating companies all rate them for quality of credit. Preferred stocks generally garner lower ratings than do bonds, as the dividends of preferred stocks are not guaranteed as are bonds' interest payments. Preferred stocks are also subordinated to all of the creditors, making them less secure.

Dividends are a key feature of preferred stocks and the main motivating factor in acquiring them. Preferred stocks come with dividend payment preference over other shares. While this does not guarantee that the stated dividends will be paid, the company has to pay such dividends to the preferred share holders before they are allowed to issue any common stock shares' dividends.

These dividends for preferred stocks might be either noncumulative or cumulative. Cumulative preferred stocks mandate that companies who neglect to cover stated dividends up to the full rate must cover them fully at a later date. In each passing dividend time frame, the dividends continue to accumulate. This might be on an annual, semi annual, or quarterly basis.

Dividends that are not paid on time are labeled dividends that have passed. These passed dividends for cumulative stocks are called dividends that are in arrears. If a stock does not possess these cumulative features, then it is called a straight preferred stock, or a noncumulative dividend stock. With these types of non cumulative preferred stocks, the dividends that become passed simply vanish for good if they are not paid on time.

Besides these preferred stock features, they have various other rights. Some types of preferred shares do include a particular group of voting rights for the approval of unusual events like the ability to issue and sell extra shares, to approve the company to be sold, or even to choose the board of directors' members. In general, preferred stocks do not have voting rights. Many preferred shares also come with a liquidation value that states what sum of money was put into the issuing corporation as the shares became issued.

Prime Brokerage

A prime brokerage refers to a particular category of different financial services which a number of brokerages provide to their important clients. Services they deliver under this umbrella cover a number of different types. Among these are leveraged trade orders, loaning of securities, and cash management assistance. The majority of the bigger brokerages offer such prime broker services. This includes Goldman Sachs, Morgan Stanley, and Paine Webber.

The demand for such prime brokerage services originally came from the hedge funds. These special investment pools often place enormous trades. Because of this fact, they require particular attention from the major brokerages. These prime brokerages are also called prime brokers sometimes. They are usually comprised of enormous financial institutions. They tend to have business transactions with similarly large financial institutions as well as the hedge funds.

Prime brokers and their services are not mutually exclusive. While these financial services broker companies provide a wide range of such services, the clients do not have to participate in all or even most of them. The large clients have the choice to receive some of their financial services at other institutions that best suite their needs.

There are many such prime brokerage services the broker dealer may deliver to its best clientele. Whichever brokers are assigned to these important accounts will be expected to offer services as settling agent and gratuitous financing for leveraged trades. They could provide assets custody and even everyday account statement preparation. These prime brokers have the advantage of enjoying substantial and varied resources that smaller to medium-sized financial and brokerage institutions simply can not match within their own operations. This means that the prime brokers deliver a means for many of the bigger and more important financial institutions to "outsource" a range and host of their administrative investment activities so that they can instead concentrate their best efforts on strategy and on their investment goals and returns.

As an example, there may even be concierge types of services offered by the prime broker. There are a wide range of such highly specialized offerings the broker might include in an effort to keep their largest, most important clients satisfied. Among these are cash financing, securities financing, capital introduction, and even risk management services. There are also services that go above and beyond what would be expected of a typical broker. These could include the ability to sublease space within their offices and to obtain free access to other benefits based within their facilities. These are non- traditional services, and participation in them is completely voluntary for any client.

Some of these services require the hedge fund or other important client to post collateral. This is especially the case where brokerage securities are lent out to the customer. In this way, the prime brokerage is able to reduce its risk it takes on and also to obtain faster recourse to funds should they be required.

The truth is that the overwhelming majority of such clients of the prime brokerage will be comprised of bigger financial institutions, funds like hedge funds, and bigger private investors. It is true that hedge funds and money managers are some of the most important clients which attain the minimum qualifications to participate. Others who might meet the threshold for participation in the program include a range of professional investors and those who engage in arbitrage. Hedge funds know all too well that the level of these prime broker services will often play a substantial part in the success or failure of their fund.

Among the more common kinds of clientele that participate in and attain the standards for prime broker services are commercial banks and pension funds. Both of these groups will typically handle enormous quantities of money which they must invest. They also have in common that they lack the in-house resources to adequately invest and maintain such large dollar investments by themselves.

Proprietary Trading

Proprietary Trading refers to a type of trading in which the bank or other financial institution invests its own funds for its own benefit. They do this instead of investing the money of and for their clients and gaining a commission fee for trading for their customers. Such trading happens as a firm makes the choice to engage in market profiteering instead of existing on the tiny commissions which they realize for taking and processing others' trades.

Those banks and companies which pursue such proprietary trading feel certain they enjoy some from of competitive advantage. It is this which provides them with the confidence in their own abilities to make outsized returns versus other traditional investors.

Proprietary trading is actually a dangerous and risky type of trading. Rather than safely carrying out the orders of their clients and collecting their fair commissions, the bank traders take on real positions using the capital of the company. In other words, they will enjoy the entire profit or suffer from the brunt of the full loss of such a position. These firms will do this entirely electronically to boost their speed of execution. They will employ the firms' own leverage in order to multiply the size of their positions as well as the hoped for returns or actually realized losses which they incur.

This actually occurs because the company's own trading desk at these huge financial institutions decides they can do it for themselves. These companies are typically investment banks or brokerage firms. They will then utilize their own corporate balance sheet and capital of the company in order to make transactions in the financial or stock markets. Such trades are commonly speculative. The products in which they trade are commonly complicated and dangerous investment vehicles such as derivatives and credit default swaps.

Naturally these financial companies receive benefits from proprietary trading on their own behalf. The biggest one is that they often do enjoy higher profits, at least until a financial crisis hits like with the one in 2007-2009 that nearly overthrew most of the American, British, and continental European banking system financial institutions. With these proprietary trades, the brokerage firm or investment bank gets to keep all of the investment gains which they realize from their investments.

A second benefit which these large financial firms enjoy is that they will be capable of inventorying an impressive array of securities. It allows them to offer their speculative inventory directly to their clients who could not have obtained it any other way. It also helps the institutions to be well-supplied with securities in the event of illiquid or declining markets when it is more difficult to buy such securities on the free markets.

The last benefit pertains to the second one. With such proprietary trading, financial firms can evolve into an important market maker. They gain the ability to offer liquidity for a particular security or even range of securities through dealing in such investments. They can realize profitable spreads and fees when acting in this capacity.

The ugly truth is that this proprietary trading has led to enormous losses for the investment banks in particular. Thanks to the likes of such one time investment banking firms as Merrill Lynch, Bear Stearns, Lehman Brothers, and others engaging in such dangerously over-leveraged proprietary trading schemes before the outbreak of the financial crisis, they nearly brought down the entire financial system.

The Lehman Brothers moment refers to the point where the company failed completely. All other investment banks began to crater at this point. Bear Stearns ceased to be a going concern. Merrill Lynch the one-time largest investment bank and brokerage had to be bought out by Bank of America in order to survive. Both Morgan Stanley and Goldman Sachs, the only remaining two of the big five, were forced to change into traditional banks, backstopped by the FDIC, This helped them to stave off total collapse at the height of the Global Financial Crisis of 2008/2009.

Because of these unmitigated disasters, the Dodd-Frank Legislation and Volcker Rules were passed. These made it increasingly more difficult to engage in such trading for a financial firms' own benefits and with their leveraged balance sheets and company capital.

Put Option

Put options are financial contracts that are entered into by two parties, the buyer of the option and the seller, or writer, of the option. They are generally called simply puts. A purchaser is able to establish a long position in a put option by buying the right to actually sell the instrument that underlies the put.

This is done at a particular price called the strike price and is only valid with the options' seller for a certain amount of time. Should you as the buyer of the option choose to exercise your rights, then the seller has to purchase the associated instrument off of you at the price that was set in advance, whatever the present market price proves to be. In consideration for the buyer gaining this option, you pay an option premium amount to the seller of the option.

Put options are a form of insurance against loss. This is because they offer a guaranteed price and purchaser for a given amount of time for an associated instrument. Put option sellers also benefit when they obtain profits for selling you options that you do not choose to exercise. Options are almost never exercised if the instrument's market value stays above the strike price within the put option contract time frame.

You as a buyer of a put option also have the ability to make money. This is done by selling the associated instrument for a higher price and buying back the position for a significantly lower market price. When an option is not sold or exercised, it expires worthless, representing a total loss of the premium paid for it.

When you purchase a put, you do so with the idea that the associated asset price will decline by the expiration date. The other reason for taking on such a put option is to safe guard a position that you own in the asset or security. Purchasing a put option provides an advantage as compared to selling a stock short. The most that you can lose with a put option is the money that you have paid for it, while those who sell short have an unlimited loss potential. The downside to a put is that the gain potential is restricted to a certain amount. This turns out to be the strike price of the option minus the spot price of the associated asset and the premium that you pay for the option.

A seller or writer of a put feels confident that the associated asset price will go up or remain the same but not decline. Sellers of puts engage in this activity in order to collect premiums. A writer of a put has a limited loss equal to the strike price of the put minus the spot price and the premium that has already been obtained. Put options can similarly be utilized to reduce a risk in the option seller's investment portfolio. They can be part of complicated strategies called option spreads.

A put option that is not covered by owning the underlying security or asset is referred to as a naked put. In these types of put scenarios, the investor might hope to build up a position in the stock that underlies the options so long as they can get a cheap enough price. If you the buyer do not exercise these options, then the seller of the put gets to keep the premium that you paid for the option, representing a profit to the seller.

Should the associated stock's actual price be lower than the strike price of the option when the expiration date comes, then you as a buyer have the ability to exercise the put option in question. This makes the seller of the put option purchase the associated stock at the strike price of the option. You as a buyer would profit to the amount of the difference found between the market price of the stock and the strike price of the option. Yet, should the price of the stock prove to be higher than the strike price of the option on the expiration day, this option becomes worthless. The loss to the owner of the option is restricted to the money that you paid for it, which then becomes the profit to the put option seller.

Reserve Currency

Reserve currency proves to be that particular currency which central banks (and sometimes important international financial institutions) hold. They keep such currency so that they are able to have an influence on their own country's exchange rate or to pay down their debt obligations which are international in nature. A substantial number of global commodities remain priced according to the reserve currency. This includes such heavyweight items as gold and oil. Nations require this currency to acquire these commodity goods.

There is an advantage to keeping quantities of a reserve currency. It allows nations or international companies to reduce their risk of changing exchange rates. The purchaser that possesses the currency reserve will not be forced to exchange their own currency to be able to complete the purchase. Since the last years of World War II in 1944, the American dollar has enjoyed the status of being the principle reserve currency which other countries use globally. This has caused other nations to carefully watch the monetary policy the U.S. pursues to make certain their reserve values do not suffer too much from inflation and currency debasement.

The second reserve currency of the world is the euro used by countries of the euro zone. Countries also can use the SDR Special Drawing Rights created by the International Monetary Fund to settle some international obligations, making it a third currency reserve. Increasingly, nations like China and Russia are trying to shift other nations away from the U.S. dollar as their currency reserve. China is going about this by signing currency exchange swap agreements with as many countries' central banks as it can to settle in Chinese Yuan.

The U.S. originally gained its status as dominant reserve currency because it came out of World War II as the globe's main economic power. This had enormous impacts on the economy of the world. In the immediate aftermath of the war, the U.S. GDP comprised 50% of global output. This made it inevitable that its currency the dollar would emerge as the world's currency reserve as happened in 1944. After this event, a number of other nations decided to peg their exchange rates up to the dollar. The dollar had the backing of gold in those days, making it comparatively stable. This pegging move helped other nations to stabilize their own volatile currencies.

Financial Terms Dictionary - Trading Terminology Explained

In those early decades, the world as a whole gained advantages from such a stable and strong dollar currency. The U.S. benefited significantly and prospered as it enjoyed the most favorable exchange rate for the dollar. America began to undermine this arrangement when it printed extra dollars. The currency reserve had gold backing it, but the U.S. was able to get around this by issuing dollars that its Treasury debt backed. In time the gold which backed the dollars became less valuable as the dollars multiplied to finance U.S. deficit spending. Other nations' dollar currency reserves' value began to decline along with the gold value of paper U.S. dollars.

This eventually had to come to an end. With the U.S. printing and flooding markets with huge quantities of paper dollars to pay for the Vietnam War and Great Society spending, other countries became wary. They started converting their dollar reserves for the gold backing them. This central bank run on the American gold became so severe that President Nixon had no choice but to de-link the dollar from gold and float dollars against other currencies.

This led to the present day system of floating exchange rates. Gold skyrocketed as the dollar commenced its multi decade decline in value which has seen gold prices reach as high as over $1,900 USD per ounce. The dollar still remains the dominant currency reserve mostly because other nations had built up such large amounts of it and U.S. dollar denominated Treasuries.

Revenue Bonds

Revenue Bonds are municipal bonds. Their payments on principal and interest come from a special project's revenue. This could be from a highway toll, toll bridge, or area stadium receipts. Whatever the specific project may be, its revenues are what support the underlying bond issues.

These revenue bonds are utilized to finance projects which will eventually produce income for the issuing authority. Generally any government agency or even government fund which they run like a business will be able to issue these types of bonds. Such bonds stand in contrast to those competing types called general obligation bonds, or GO bonds.

General obligation bonds may be paid back by drawing on a number of different tax sources. Those investors who purchase such GO bonds are relying on the "full faith and credit' by which the municipality promises to repay them with any means necessary. This makes the revenue bond issues riskier. They only can promise the revenues from a particular project. Because of this fact, the revenue bonds pay a higher interest rate than do the GO bonds.

Municipalities structure revenue bonds in a particular way. They possess maturity dates of from 20 to 30 years most of the time. The issuers offer them in standard $5,000 even increments or amounts. There are a number of these bonds which include maturity dates that stagger. This means their maturities will not be on the same day and year. Bond aficionados call these serial bonds.

A toll road is a classic example of such revenue bonds. A municipality might issue this in order to pay to construct a new toll road. The revenue which would secure this issue would be the tolls they collect in the future from those drivers who utilize the road. The construction expenses will have to be covered before the bond holders are completely paid off at maturity.

These revenue bonds became popular because the issuing authorities' debt limits are set by legislation. They may only borrow so much money according to the laws. These types of bonds allow them to side step the legal debt limit restrictions so that they can build new improvements within their jurisdiction.

This also means that government groups which rely only on only tax dollars can not issue such bonds. Public schools are one example of this. They would not be able to pay off a revenue bond since they would not have any income off of a specific project.

These revenue bonds should not be confused with combination bonds. The combination ones are usually municipal bonds with two sources of financial backing. On the one hand, they enjoy revenue off of an existing or a future project. At the same time, they are covered by the full faith and credit of the issuing municipality or agency. This makes them a true combination of both revenue and general obligation bonds. Naturally, these types of bonds are deemed to be considerably safer. Such lower perceived risk results in the agency paying a lesser interest rate than they would have to give investors on comparable revenue or even general obligation bonds.

It is helpful to consider a real world example of a revenue bond. The MTA Metropolitan Transportation Authority of New York chose to float Green Bonds back in February of 2016. MTA announced it will put this $500 million in total proceeds towards covering the costs of renewal projects on infrastructure. This includes upgrades to their various railroads. The bonds were issued by the Transportation Revenue Bond of the MTA. They received backing from the income of the MTA transportation service. This income comes from two sources, subsidies which the State of New York provides and operating revenues of the agency.

Reverse Split

A reverse split is also known as a reverse stock split. Reverse splits are used to reduce the total outstanding number of a given company's shares. This action boosts the value of its stock and the resulting earnings per share. Not everything concerning a stock changes in a reverse stock split. One thing that remains the same is the market capitalization. Market capitalization refers to the value price of the total outstanding number of shares.

A reverse split works by a certain process. In this scenario, a company involved will actually cancel out the presently existing shares for every share holder. They will replace these with a smaller number of new shares. These new shares will be issued in an exact proportion to your original stake in the company.

Such a reverse split proves to be the exact opposite of a stock split. Reverse splits can also be called stock merges, since they literally reduce the total number of outstanding shares and proportionally increase the price per share. Companies commonly issue the reverse split shares according to an easy to understand ratio. You might receive one new share for every two old shares, or possibly four new shares for every old five ones that you owned.

Looking at an example of the way that a reverse stock split actually works is helpful. Say that a company in which you own stock shares decided to affect a one for ten reverse split. If you had one thousand shares of the company, then you would only own one hundred shares of the resulting issue. This would not change the value of the shares that you held though, as the price of the shares would increase by ten times. If the shares had been worth only four dollars per share, now they would be valued at forty dollars per share.

There are several reasons why companies choose to do a reverse split of their stock shares. They might feel that the actual price per share of their stock is so low that it is not appealing to new investors. Some institutions are only allowed to buy shares that trade at a certain minimum value, such as five dollars per share or higher. Reverse stock splits can also be used to reduce the number of share holders, since they can force smaller shareholders to be cashed out, which means that they no longer possess any shares of the company. In this case, you would receive the value of your shares in cash.

There is a negative connotation associated with engaging in reverse stock splits. Because of this reason, they are not done lightly by companies. A company might find that its share price has declined so precipitously that it becomes in danger of having its shares de-listed from the stock exchange. They could quickly boost the share price with the reverse split. Stocks that have undergone a reverse split will usually have the letter D added to the end of their symbol tickers.

A board of directors for a given company is allowed to perform a reverse split without consulting with its share holders to obtain their approval. The Securities and Exchange Commission also does not have any say over such reverse stock splits. They are instead regulated by a state's corporate laws and the company's own articles of incorporation, along with the company's by laws.

Securities Markets

Securities Markets refer to either literal physical or virtual online places for traders and investors to buy and sell securities. These markets have been dramatically changing in the last several decades in order to best meet the requirements and wishes of investors and traders alike. Traders must have such markets which are easy to access, highly liquid, and that levy the most competitive transaction costs possible. These three core needs of traders have combined to create several different kinds of market structures around the globe. Among these are markets which are order driven, quote driven, hybrid, and brokered.

Many Securities Markets are order driven. With these markets, the sellers and buyers on the exchanges match directly up, typically using a computer system. The middle man is eliminated in such a market structure. This makes them the opposite of markets which are quote driven. Price discovery is accomplished thanks to the traders' limit orders on every security. The majority of such order-based markets utilize an auction system. Naturally sellers will be seeking the highest possible price while buyers are on the hunt for the best possible bargain. When they match, execution of trades happens.

The two kinds of such markets are the continuous auction and the call auction markets. The greatest advantage to this style of market is the massive quantities of investors and traders who will offer to sell and buy a security. This means that prices are competitive and provides superior prices for all traders. It does have a downside. When a security has only a few members trading, then liquidity is often weak. The TSX Toronto Stock Exchange of Canada represents a market that is order driven.

Securities Markets which are quote driven are also referred to as dealer markets. In such market structures, the sellers and buyers have a transacting middle man in between them in the form of a dealer or market maker. It is up to the market makers to provide the ask and bid quotes on stocks for which they are willing to sell and purchase shares. These market makers have exclusivity in their market functions (many times) and receive special privileges. Among these are low to no exchange fees, specific order book and order flow information, and the unique ability to post the stock quotes. Such markets are most common with OTC over the counter markets like the NASDAQ and London's SEAQ, the FOREX market, and the bond markets. Nowadays NASDAQ has become more of a hybrid type with elements of order-driven structures in place.

The greatest advantage to such quote-driven securities markets appears when stocks or markets are illiquid. Dealers are able to boost the traders' liquidity with their intervention, as they often keep a security inventory on hand. They get to enjoy the spread between the bids and ask as a compensation for this accommodation.

Hybrid markets are also popular structures with many Securities Markets. They are sometimes called mixed markets. The NYSE New York Stock Exchange is a well-known example of this category. Naturally this system will utilize characteristics from the two order-driven and quote-driven arrangements. When they have low liquidity periods, these markets are able to fall back on the dealer-provided liquidity to improve transactions.

A final type of Securities Markets is the brokered markets. Brokers represent middle men who engage in discovering counterparties for any trade. As customers request of a broker to help them complete an order, the brokers will go through their extensive networks in an effort to locate an appropriately matching client. These types of markets are mainly for those securities which do not have a traditional public market. Illiquid and unique securities fall into this category. Where huge block trades of highly illiquid stocks or bonds are concerned, brokered markets are employed. Direct real estate is another classic example of such a brokered type of market. Real estate brokers are the ones who fill the service of matching up a unique seller and interested buyer in this case.

Selling Short

Selling short, or short selling, is a strategy used in trading stocks. In the selling short process, you borrow the shares of the stock in question from your stock broker. You then turn around and sell the stock shares borrowed for a certain price that the market offers. Your hope is that the price of the stock will drop, so that you can buy back the stock shares for a lesser amount. This creates a profit for your transaction. The practice is buying low and selling high done in the reverse order.

If the price of the stock drops, then this process of short selling makes you money. The down side to it is that when the price of the stock instead rises, then you lose money. Detractors of selling short claim that you can subject yourself to an unlimited amount of risk, since stock prices could rise without stopping. This means that you could potentially lose more than the amount of money that you invest if a given stock that you sold short took off and ran away without you closing out the transaction. Profits are limited by the distance of the stock price to zero, since a share's price can never decline below zero.

Such selling short trades are closed out by repurchasing the shares that you sold short earlier. When it is time to close out the transaction by buying back the shares, this is called covering. The other names for this process are buy to cover or simply cover.

There are risks involved in selling short stocks. The biggest risk is that the stock could go up indefinitely. For example, you might sell short ten shares of IBM's stock at $100 per share. This means that you have put a thousand dollars into the trade. If the stock later declined to ninety, then you would realize a gain of one hundred dollars. If instead it rose to $130 before you covered it, then you would lose three hundred dollars. While the lowest that the IBM shares might decline is to zero, potentially making you as much as one thousand dollars in profits, they could also rise to three hundred dollars, losing you two thousand dollars.

Short sellers can also fall victim to a short squeeze. As the stock price that you have shorted rises, some investors who shorted it will choose to limit their losses by buying the stock back. Still other investors may have no choice but to buy back the shares in order to satisfy any margin calls on their declining valued position. All of this buying back to cover creates a bigger increase in the price of the stock. The final outcome is a large move up in the price of the stock that creates significant losses for those who continue to be short the stock.

Shareholders

Shareholders are companies, people, or institutions which own minimally a single share of the stock in a given company. They can also be referred to as stockholders. These stockholders are not only investors, but also the owners of the corporation. As owners, they gain the advantageous results from the firm's success. This can translate into higher stock prices, dividend payouts, or hopefully both. Should the corporation not perform well, the stock holders can similarly lose value in their investments as the stock price goes down.

There is a difference between shareholders and owners of partnerships and sole proprietorships. The stakeholders in corporations do not experience personal liability for the financial and debt obligations of the corporation. Should the company in question fail, creditors can not attempt to secure payments or assets from the stockholders as they might be able to do from owners of entities which are privately held.

Corporations with shareholders have another important difference from other structures of businesses. They depend on their executive management and board of directors to handle the day to day operations. This means that the stock holders do not have much control over the daily operations of the company.

Shareholders may not have much involvement in the company's decisions, but they still have important rights. These are specified by the corporation's bylaws and charter. One of these is the right to go through the company records and financial books. Another is to sue the company for officer and director committed mistakes. Even common stock holders have the right to vote on important corporate decisions like whether to agree to a potential merger or on the makeup of the board of directors.

Shareholders have what may be their most important right when a company goes into liquidation through dissolution or bankruptcy. They have the rights to regain a representative amount of the recovered proceeds. They are in line after the secured debt holders including bondholders, preferred stock holders, and creditors, all of whom have precedence over the common stockholders.

Stock holders have several other rights which they enjoy. They receive a part of dividends which their company announces. They also gain the privilege to attend in person the annual meeting of the corporation. Here they are able to learn more regarding the performance of the firm. They can also choose to sit in on the meeting using a conference call. If these common stock holders are not able to or interested in going to the annual meeting, they can instead choose to vote through the mail or online using a vote by proxy. All of these rights which belong to preferred and common shareholders are detailed in the corporate governance policy.

A great number of corporations elect to create two classes of stock. These are common and preferred shares. The majority of stock holders purchase and hold common stocks since they are more of them and they are less expensive than preferred shares. Unlike preferred stock holders who are due to receive dividends every quarter, common shareholders must wait on the board of directors to decide if and when they will be paid a dividend in a given quarter. The directors must decide if this is an appropriate way to utilize the corporation's funds.

Preferred stockholders lack the voting rights of common shareholders. They do receive higher dividends on a more frequent basis. Their payments have to be paid at least yearly and their dividends are also guaranteed. For investors more interested in creating a reliable annual income from investments, preferred shares can be a very helpful tool.

Special Drawing Rights (SDR)

Special Drawing Rights are currency units of the International Monetary Fund. These units were originally worth .888671 grams of gold and $1 when they were initially created under the gold standard in 1969. In 1973 the pegged currency system set up at the Bretton Woods conference collapsed.

The IMF then re-defined these SDRs as a basket of the major world reserve currencies. Until October 1, 2016, SDR baskets are comprised of U.S. dollars, euros, British pounds, and Japanese yen. On October 1 this definition will be broadened to add in the Chinese renminibi. The IMF created these unique currency units in order to supplement the existing currency reserves of countries who are members.

Every day the IMF figures up the SDR value and puts it up on their website. The value is a composition of its various parts. They figure the value as measured in U.S. dollars by adding up the value of each currency in the basket in dollars. To do this, they utilize the noon time exchange rates from the London market fixing.

Every five years, the IMF has an Executive Board meeting to review the components of the Special Drawing Rights. They have the ability to hold this meeting earlier should financial circumstances call for it. The idea is to make certain that the basket continuously mirrors how important various currencies included are in the financial and trading systems of the world. The review that ended in November of 2015 decided that the Chinese renminbi currency had become freely usable enough to include as the basket's fifth currency alongside the dollar, euro, British pound, and Japanese yen.

They also adopted a new method for determining how much of each reserve currency will make up an SDR. Equal weighting is now being given to the exports of the currency issuing nation and a composite financial indicator. With the financial indicator, each of the components is being given an equal weighting. It is based on the reserves in the currency held by other countries, the amount of foreign exchange turnover for that currency, and the total of international debt securities and bank liabilities which are held in that currency.

Until October of 2016, the Special Drawing Rights components are U.S. dollars at 41.9%, euros at 37.4%, British pounds at 11.3%, and Japanese yen at 9.4%. As of October 1, 2016 the new SDRs are instead comprised of U.S. dollars at 41.73%, euros at 30.93%, Chinese renminbi at 10.92%, Japanese yen at 8.33%, and British pounds at 8.09%. This represents the new SDR value in a change more significant than any made in decades. The next scheduled review for the SDR is set to occur on September 30 of 2021.

Special Drawing Rights can be given out to member states of the IMF as a proportion of their IMF quotas. This gives every member an international reserve asset that will not cost them anything. Charges are made on allocations and then utilized to cover any interest owed on SDR holdings. Member countries that do not utilize their holdings which are allocated do not pay since any charges equate to the interest they receive. Members whose holdings become greater than what they are allocated receive interest on the extra ones.

SDRs today are only used in limited capacity as reserve assets. Their main purpose is to function as the account unit of the IMF and a few international organizations. The SDR is not actually a claim against the IMF or a true currency. Instead it represents a possible claim against the IMF members and their currencies.

Statistical Arbitrage

Statistical arbitrage turns out to be a scenario where a disparity in price exists between the natural price of an asset, or its inherent value, and the current market price. There are traders who specialize in arbitrage situations who will try to gain advantage from this fairly unusual situation of disparity hoping to profit from it as it naturally corrects. Some traders believe that statistical arbitrage will always yield a profit, at least on a paper trade basis. The reality is that in actual trading, unforeseen events and a limitation in investing resources could easily interfere with their capability of making money efficiently enough to be worth doing.

Statistical arbitrage is used in contrast to the generic form of arbitrage to distinguish its differences. The statistical variety relates to the actual techniques utilized in gaining advantage from the disparity that exists in two markets. With generic arbitrage, it could be that a stock price is higher in the stock market of one country than another where it is listed. In theory, traders could guarantee themselves profits simply by purchasing the stock on the cheaper exchange and simultaneously selling it on the dearer listed one. The guarantee depends on how high the transaction costs and currency conversion costs will be. There is also a considerable risk that the two divergent prices may correct themselves naturally before the traders are able to both buy and sell the security on the different exchanges.

This statistical arbitrage is a bit different from general arbitrage. In the statistical variant, such asset disparity is not simply between two or more markets. Instead it has to do with the price of an asset currently and the underlying value of the same asset. A company security proves to be a good example to contemplate. The market price will be decided by the interaction between traders in the form of supply and demand. The stock also possesses an intrinsic value which is derived from the dividends it declares to its investors and how this relates to competing investments. There may be variance in the market price because of temporary effects and external factors, as with relevant industry-specific bad or good news.

Those traders who engage in statistical arbitrage operate under the assumption that eventually the price of the asset will go back to its correct underlying value. Because of the disparity, they anticipate that the price in the future will change, and then they position accordingly to profit. In normal circumstances, these traders might consider and employ literally hundreds of different stocks at once so that they are able to effectively reduce their overall risks of an unforeseen event stopping the stock from going back up to its normal price in a fast enough time frame so that the trader makes money on the deal.

There is another meaning for statistical arbitrage. There might be a type of imbalance from the values that would typically be anticipated. Casino games like roulette are the classic example of this. Because half the spaces are red and the other half are black, players betting on red will win double their stakes should they be right. The wheel also contains a 0 that does not pay anything. This means that the chances of correctly ascertaining the color are actually just under one out of two. This house advantage is a disparity that could also be considered to be a statistical form of advantage. There is no way for the players to benefit from this, but casinos make a fortune off of it on a regular basis.

Stock Broker

Stock brokers are professionals who are both licensed and registered with the Financial Industry Regulatory Authority or FINRA. In general, stockbrokers work for a broker dealer or a stock brokerage firm. Stock brokers are not to be confused with financial advisors or financial planners, who perform many different services for their clients.

Stock brokers have a primary responsibility. Their job is to purchase and sell stocks, bonds, mutual funds, and other related investments on behalf of their clients. These clients can be retail investor individuals or institutional clients. Institutions as clients refer to not for profit companies, universities and colleges, foundations, and other similar groups.

Stock brokers trade stocks for their clients over a stock exchange or sometimes an over the counter market. Among the larger and better known stock exchanges are the New York Stock Exchange and NASDAQ. They are compensated for these trades with commissions or fees that the trader pays. These fees range widely from one type of stock broker to another. Online stock brokers offer the lowest commissions to their clients. These types of brokers usually charge under $15 per trade.

There are a variety of names for stock brokers in the industry. These various titles refer to different licenses the brokers may hold, the various services they deliver to their clients, and the kinds of securities which they trade. Stockbroker is an older designation for these individuals who are now more commonly referred to as brokers, reps, registered reps, or financial advisors.

Not all of these titles refer to exactly the same type of professional. The scope of a financial advisor or financial planner is generally much broader than that of a stock broker. A stock broker would primarily handle the trades in and out of given securities. Financial advisors and planners look at the entire picture of a person's investments and future goals to come up with a comprehensive investment and financial plan for the individual.

The requirements to become a stock broker vary. In the U.S., these professionals usually need to hold a bachelor's degree. The brokerage firms are preferably looking for applicants who have a business degree in a subject such as finance, economics, accounting, or a related field. Those applicants who possess master's degrees in business or finance receive preferential hiring treatment. Because they are in greater demand, they are able to command higher salaries than applicants who only hold bachelor's degrees.

Once a stockbroker candidate is selected, they must be sponsored by the brokerage that hired them. They can only take the exams required by the stock market industry if they have the sponsorship of such a brokerage firm. There are a variety of exams that are available to stock broker candidates. American stock brokers have to take and successfully pass the Series 7 exam, as well as the Series 63 exam or the Series 66 exam. Once they have completed such exams, they can be registered with the Financial Industry Regulatory Authority. At this point, the candidate is officially a registered representative, or stockbroker.

In the past, a stock broker was a professional that only wealthy investors and individuals could afford. They were able to access stocks and other investments through these brokers. Minimum account sizes kept out smaller investors generally.

Thanks to the Internet, access to the markets broadened considerably. Discount brokerage firms and discount stock brokers proliferated. These allow for individual investors to trade stocks and other investments for low and reasonable fees with much smaller minimum account sizes. They do not offer personal advice to their clients. Thanks to these changes that technology empowered, most any individual is able to invest in the markets today.

Stock Split

Stock splits occur when corporations decide to expand the number of underlying shares in the company. They do this by setting out a ratio for the stock split. They might say that for every one share of stock, there will now be two, which would double your existing shares. This would be called a two to one stock split.

If you had one hundred shares of the stock before the split that were trading at twenty dollars per share, then you would possess fifty shares of the stock trading at ten dollars each share after the split occurred. The value of the total shares owned does not change as a result of a stock split, only the amounts of shares that you possess and the per share price of the stock in question. In either case, they would still be worth two thousand dollars.

Companies mostly engage in stock splits because of a liquidity motivation. There are many companies that feel that more expensive stocks keep investors from buying them. By splitting the shares, the price of the shares declines proportionally. They hope that this will result in a scenario where greater quantities of shares of the stock are then purchased and sold. The downside to this argument is that the higher volume of the shares traded could cause larger drops and increases in the price of the stock, which leads to greater volatility in the share prices.

While numerous investors believe that stock splits are beneficial, there is no real evidence to support this feeling. Stocks do not automatically rise back to the price that they maintained in advance of the split. The extra shares do not result in greater amounts of dividends being realized by the investors either, since each share then represents proportionally smaller earnings, assets, and dividends of the company involved in the split.

While most companies go through stock splits as the price rises, a select few have steadfastly refused to do so. Berkshire Hathaway proves to be the most famous case of this. In the 1960's, it traded at only $8 each share. In recent decades, you have seen its value jump up to $150,000 per share. The Washington Post has also seen its non splitting shares trade upwards of six hundred dollars each. The shareholder base of both companies has remained consistent and stable as a result of not splitting the stock shares.

Stocks

Stocks are financial instruments that are issued by publicly traded corporations. These shares of stocks prove to be the tiniest portion of ownership that you can acquire in a company. Even by owning a single share of a company's stock you are a small part owner of the firm.

Owning shares of stock gives you the privilege of voting for the underlying company's board of directors, along with other critical issues that the company is considering. Should a company decide to distribute earnings to share holders as dividends, then you will get a portion of them.

With the ownership of stock, your liability in the company is only limited to the value of your shares. This means that should a company lose a lawsuit and be forced to pay an enormous fine or judgment, then you can not be made to contribute to it. The company's creditors also can not pursue you if the company runs into financial trouble and goes bankrupt.

Two different types of stock shares exist. These are common shares and preferred shares. The vast majority of shares that are issued are common stock shares. These are the shares that members of the public hold most of the time. They come with full voting rights and also the possibility of receiving dividends that the company pays out.

Preferred stocks come with fewer voting rights but give preferential treatment for dividend payment. Preferred stock issues are paid out before common share dividends. Companies that offer preferred stock typically pay dividends on both classes of shares anyway. Preferred stocks also have a higher claim on the assets of a company if it fails.

Liquidity is a feature of stocks that should always be considered. Common stock shares are almost always more liquid than are preferred shares. Large companies offer the greatest amount of liquidity in the trading of their stocks. Because of the depth of the stock markets, you are able to purchase and sell the shares of practically all companies that are publicly traded at any time that the exchanges are working.

When you purchase a stock, you are looking for two different kinds of gains. Cash flow or passive income with stocks comes from the dividends that they declare and pay out. Capital gains appreciation is realized when you buy a stock at a lower price than the price that you get when you later sell it. While cash flow dividends are smaller payments that are realized on a generally quarterly basis, capital gains turn out to be larger one time returns made when you sell the underlying stock shares investment. At this point, you would no longer own the stock and you would have to purchase another stock in order to work towards cash flow gains from dividends, as well as other possible capital gains.

Straddle

A straddle is a a type of option strategy which is designed to assist traders in succeeding in markets that are either neutral or aggressively breaking out to one side or the other. While there are other similar result strategies that are both sophisticated and extremely complex like iron butterflies and iron condors, straddles are among the least difficult to grasp such strategies that accomplish the same results without the difficulty and confusion. Executing such a strategy only needs the person to buy or sell a single call and put at the same time.

In the universe of these straddle options, there are two types. These are long and short straddles. To put either one on, the option trader must obtain or sell an equivalent number of put and call contracts that both have the exact same expiration dates and identical strike prices.

A long straddle involves buying a put and call at this identical expiration date and strike price. It increases in value by gaining from a change in market price that drives the contracts' volatilities higher. So long as the market price moves solidly in one direction or another, this type of long straddle position will allow the holder to profit.

Conversely a short straddle needs a trader selling both a call and a put simultaneously at the identical expiration date and strike price in order for it to be activated. When the individual sells these option contracts, he or she collects a premium for profit. Traders will thrive in a market that has very little market change or volatility. Profit opportunity is solely based upon the market not moving convincingly in either the upward or downward direction. When the market begins to thrust either up or down, then the received premium becomes in danger.

When markets begin to move sideways, traders may be unclear which direction they will break out towards. This is where the long straddle comes in handy. It allows for traders to profit if the market moves convincingly in either direction. In purchasing both a call and a put, they are able to cash in on the moves of the market whichever direction it takes. The call captures the upside when the market goes up, while the put gains significantly when the market falls.

There are some drawbacks to this long strategy of straddles. The strategy is expensive to put on, there is a risk of total loss of premiums paid, and there can be a lack of volatility. The cost can be reduced by purchasing out of the money options instead of at the money options. Risk of loss is a serious factor in this trade. All of the money paid out on the straddle is at risk if the market does not move convincingly in one direction or the other.

The goal is to attempt to exit faster from the losing side of the straddle while taking as high a gain as possible from the winning side of it in order to maximize returns and turn a profit. Should the losses on the option grow faster than the gains on it, or if the market does not move sufficiently to one side or the other, then the trader will lose on the strategy potentially all of the money they paid for the it. Finally, if the market does not gain in volatility or move in one convincing direction, then both the call and put options contracts will decline in value each day until eventually the options expire worthless and all premiums paid become a total loss.

Conversely the short straddle has a characteristic that is both its greatest strength and weakness at once. The traders sell the puts and calls equivalently instead of paying for them. It is the premiums received which generate any and all income and profits from the strategy. The downside to this upfront income and potential profit is that traders assume an unlimited risk to obtain this premium at the beginning of the trade. So long as the market remains basically level, the short straddle position is safe and the premiums they obtained the traders will eventually capture. Every day the market stays steady, the options contracts lose more of their time and volatility value, gradually accruing the received premiums to the benefit of the option seller.

Should the market choose a single direction though, the traders must pay not only for the losses which build up, but they must return the received premium which they gained upfront. The only way to bail out of this strategy and cut the potentially limitless losses lies in repurchasing back the very options they sold for a loss. They can do this in a profitable point as well to lock in a portion of the profits. Eventually, the options will expire and whatever premium value they obtained is the maximum profit, if the market did not move against them in one direction or the other.

Strangle

A strangle is a strategy in which traders buy or sell calls and puts which are very slightly out of the money at the same time. They must have the same expiration dates but typically have different strike prices. The long version of this strategy provides a limited amount of risk and unlimited profit potential.

It makes money if the traders are convinced that the stock or index which underlies the options contracts will move aggressively to one side or the other and experience substantial volatility in the short term. A long strangle is also known as a debit spread, since the traders pay out a net debit in order to establish the trade.

It is possible to realize huge gains using this type of long strangle option strategy. For this to happen, the underlying security has to experience a powerful move either upward or downward by the date of expiration. The formula for determining profit on such a trade is as follows: Profit is gained when the underlying instrument's price is greater than the strike price for the long call plus the net premium paid or the price of the underlying security is less than the strike price of the long put minus the net premium they paid. The profit amount actually equals the price of the underlying instrument minus the long call strike price (and minus the net premium paid), or the strike price for the long put minus the underlying price (and minus the net premium they paid).

The risk is also limited in this strategy to the total premiums the traders pay. The highest possible loss on a long strangle option is realized if the underlying issue trades between the strike prices of the options which were purchased on final expiration day. On that date, the two options will be worthless and expire as such. The options traders at this point suffer total loss on all premiums paid to open the trade at the beginning. Another way to say this is that the maximum loss equals the total premiums paid plus commissions paid.

The breakeven points are two. The upper side breakeven point equals the long call strike price plus the net premium paid. The lower side breakeven point equals the long put strike price minus the net premium they paid.

The opposite strategy to this long strangle is known as a short strangle. Short strangles such as these are employed by traders when they do not believe there will be much movement associated with the given underlying security, stock, or index. The traders receive a premium, which represents the ultimately maximum potential profit, when they open this trade. They also receive a net credit when they enter into the sales of the two call and put option contracts. This is why these are referred to as net credit spreads.

While maximum gains for a short strangle are limited to the total net premiums received, the potential losses are unlimited. This is because the traders are on the hook for a limitless amount of decline or increase in the underlying security price. In the end, the only such protection traders of short strangles have is the amount of premium which they receive in the form of a net credit upfront at the beginning of the trade. It is possible to cut potential losses ahead of the option contracts' expiration date by buying back the call and put at the then going market rate. Similarly, they can realize their paper gains earlier than expiration date by simply closing out the trade through a purchase back of both calls and puts for the fair market prices.

Swing Trading

Swing trading refers to a wide range of shorter time frame trading strategies used in the stock market. Once a purview of only wealthy or professional full time traders this form of trading has become far more broad-based and accessible to regular investors. This is thanks to the vast proliferation over the past few years of the Internet revolution, an explosion in information and charting capabilities, and a range of affordable, efficient and fast online trading platforms.

Those who practice swing trading try to realize gains in a financial instrument such as stocks by holding them for from only overnight to even several weeks. The majority of swing traders will employ a technical analysis to consider various stocks that might offer shorter term momentum in price. It is possible that such traders will also use intrinsic fundamental analysis of the stocks alongside their analysis of patterns and trends in the price.

Because swing trading requires speed and availability to execute these types of trades, the majority of those traders or investors who utilize it are day traders or those who work from home. The institutional traders work with enormous sizes which prohibit them from quietly entering and exiting stock trades. It is the individual lone-wolf trader who can take advantage of these shorter-term movements in the prices of stocks. They have the advantage of not having to go head to head against the large investors of the trading business.

The ultimate hope for swing trading (which differentiates it from pure day trading) is that the trader will be able to realize a more substantial move in the price than the intraday trader can manage. This is because the swing trader takes for granted bigger ranges in the price and movement. With this in mind the traders who practice it must use careful cash management and stop loss orders in an effort to reduce their loss potential. Swing traders are utilizing charts with longer time frames ranging from 15 minutes through hourly to even daily and weekly charts.

Many swing traders confine their efforts to an ETF exchange traded fund or a particular stock when they engage in these relatively shorter-timeframe trading periods. It is rare for them to hold on to their stocks for more than three to four weeks. It separates these traders from the buy and hold or longer-term timeframe investors. Such investors could conceivably maintain a given investment for several years and into decades when the company is performing well.

Swing traders are not all using the identical trading strategies either. A great number of them will employ mean-reversion techniques. This is simply a complicated way of saying that they wish to purchase their stocks at lower prices and hope for a move in the direction to sell them later at higher prices. There are also traders who seek out momentum play stocks which are already moving ahead sharply. They ascribe to the concept that a winning stock will continue to act like a winning stock. This is the reason that they buy at high price points hoping to sell the stocks for even greater price levels.

Other swing trading strategies revolve around earnings release plays. They might place a short term trading bet that they company will outperform Wall Street's expectations. They could similarly sell the ones that they believe will under-perform the consensus view with their earnings.

Some swing traders employ still more sophisticated and complex strategies using macroeconomic concepts as part of their formulating ideas. They may hold that a given economic data release will come out higher or lower than the general consensus forecast. They could make a market position in an effort to benefit from such a result. When they do this, traders must be correct not only regarding the economic data release, but also concerning the impacts such news will have on their chosen asset in question.

Trade Credit

Trade credit refers to special financing terms which are many times given to a business by a supplier. This situation arises when a business buys supplies or goods and the financial officer or owner of the vendor agrees to provide either all or half of the purchased order on credit. In the case of half on credit, the balance half would become payable on delivery of the merchandise to the business.

When businesses receive a half order trade credit, they have several possibilities for paying for the balance on delivery. If they have ample resources, they can simply pay with cash. Otherwise, they can borrow the money to pay for the other balance on the inventory. This is why such credit remains among the most critical means of lowering the amount of working capital smaller businesses especially require. It is even more common and necessary with retail operations.

Suppliers normally extend such trade credit to a purchasing business once they have been a regular client for anywhere from 30 days, to 60 days, to 90 days. This trade credit has the advantage of being interest free. An example of this concept helps to make it clearer. Perhaps a supplier ships the Great Sweater Company knitted hats. The bill might normally be due within thirty days. Since Great Sweater Company enjoys these special credit terms, they would have an additional 30 days to cover the cost of the knitted hats which the vendor supplied.

When companies first start a new business, it is difficult to obtain such credit from the suppliers and vendors. In fact they will initially require each order to be paid by either check or cash on delivery. This will be the case until the new business demonstrates that it can successfully pay its bill in a timely fashion. It is a common practice in the business world. For those startups that need to raise money to make the operations work in the early days, it is important for them to be able to negotiate some form of this credit with their suppliers. It becomes easier earlier if the business owner can provide a well-developed financial plan.

It is important for businesses to properly utilize this trade terms credit. When they become trapped in the mentality of it being a necessary means of permanently financing the operations, then the business is in trouble.

Instead it should be viewed as a useful source of funding for covering shorter term and smaller needs. This credit is not really a longer term solution to the funding problem.

For businesses who do not avoid this trap, they often times become heavily committed to working with the supplier who generously extends such trade credit terms. The end result of this is that the business is not able to choose a more aggressively competitive supplier that provides better prices, more timely deliveries, and/or a higher quality product because they do not offer such generous credit terms for their buyers. There is a trade off for everything in business.

It is important to realize that trade credit is rarely free. Every supplier may have its own terms. Yet most of them will provide a significant cash discount for those businesses that pay their invoices in 10 days or less. The same as cash price may be for 30 days. By waiting for the 30 days to pay the invoice, it is costing the business the two percent discount. If a business chose to do this for 12 months a year, it would mean the merchandise was costing an additional 24 percent versus the price of paying the 10 days same as cash terms.

When a business pays after the 30 days credit expires, most vendors charge from one to two percent interest in penalties. By being late for a year, this could cost an additional from 12 to 24 percent. This is why effectively utilizing trade credit means that a business will need to plan intelligently ahead so it does not lose cash discounts consistently or pay late fee penalties needlessly. Little details like this separate successful businesses from ones which fail.

Financial Terms Dictionary - Trading Terminology Explained

Trade Deficit

Trade deficits are unfavorable balances of trade. With a trade deficit, a greater valued amount of goods and services are being imported than are simultaneously being exported. This stands in contrast to trade surpluses that occur when a larger amount of goods and services are exported by a nation than are imported in return. Trade deficits are also called trade gaps.

These trade deficits and trade surpluses are a part of the balance of trade, or net exports, which proves to be the total difference between imports' and exports' tangible value within a country's economy during a particular time frame. The balance of trade results from the relationship of the country's exports and imports.

Economists have held varying opinions on how negative or non important that trade deficits might be. Some have said that issuing paper money not backed by anything other than faith and credit of a government in exchange for valuable produced goods is not a bad thing. Professor Milton Freedom, the founder of monetarism, is one of the main proponents of this particular point of view. He felt that what would likely happen is that high exports would raise the U.S. currency value, while high imports would lower the U.S. dollar value.

Friedeman said that the worst case scenario for running trade imbalances would be that easily and inexpensively printed U.S. dollars would leave the country in order to pay for the excess imports versus exports. Friedman claimed that this produced the same result as if the country that earned the dollars through exports simply set them on fire and did not send them back to America. His policies became influential in the late 1970's and early years of the 1980's.

Other influential investors and businessmen have made opposite arguments. Warren Buffet is perhaps the greatest investor in American history. He claims that the constant U.S. trade deficit proves to be the biggest financial threat facing the national economy. He says that it is worse than the enormous annual national budget deficit and consumer debt levels together.

Buffet has said that other countries in the world own three trillion dollars more of America than we own of their countries. This investment imbalance has only increased since Buffet made these arguments nearly five years ago. Buffet and his followers are so worried about the imbalanced trade deficit that they have suggested instituting import certificates as an answer to the American problem and to bring balanced trade back to the country.

Trade Barriers

Trade barriers are those restrictions to free international and bilateral trade which governments throw up in an effort to protect domestic industries and businesses. These government created restrictions often take a number of different forms. Among them are tariffs, import quotas, import licenses, subsidies, embargoes, voluntary export restraints, local product requirements, currency devaluations, and outright trade restrictions. Whatever forms the barriers to trade actually take, they generally work off of similar principles. The idea is that a heavy cost be imposed on trade which increases the cost of the traded (and especially imported) goods, services, and capital. When two or more countries continuously employ barriers to trade one against the other, a trade war often becomes the end result.

The majority of economists mostly concur with the idea that such economic barriers are harmful to both countries which impose them and those which experience their direct consequences. They lower all around economic efficiency and harm or distort national comparative advantages. Free trade is the concept of removing all such trade barriers besides those which are considered mission critical to national security. The truth is that even the biggest champions of free trade in the modern world, such as the United States and Great Britain, engage in subsidies of favorite industries like steel and agriculture as they deem it to be expedient for these critical domestic industries' long term survival.

While there are many different types of trade barriers which countries can erect, the most typically utilized ones are tariffs, subsidies, duties, quotas, and trade embargoes. While the concept of free trade is a popular catch phrase in the post-modern world, the reality on the ground is that no country fully practices such free trade. In fact, all countries are guilty of employing some types of trade barriers for their own exclusive benefit and those of their industries and companies.

Tariffs are probably the most common type of barrier to trade. This means that a company places taxes on certain goods which are imported into the nation via its ports, railroads, or airports. Though it is unusual, tariffs could also be placed on national exports. Tariffs throughout history have always been an important government revenue source. They were easy to enforce and collect since ships had to come in through the closely government monitored ports.

Subsidies are yet another typical kind of barrier to trade. They are generally set up to safeguard and encourage important domestic industries and companies. They can also be utilized to ensure that important critical goods and services are available at a price which residents can afford. It often makes the imports uncompetitive as a byproduct. Food crops are often heavily subsidized so that the population can comfortably afford a consistent food supply at prices they can manage. Steel is another product that often benefits from heavy subsidies. This is because many nations deem domestic steel supplies to be vital to their national economic interests. Steel supplies which are domestically available are essential in wartime when shipping lanes may be interdicted.

Probably the most extreme version of trade barriers is embargoes. These more or less outlaw the export or import of any goods or services with a particular nation. This is typically enacted to punish an offending country or to cause them to make radical internal political changes as a result of the pain of a weakening economy. Throughout much of human history, embargoes were war tactics and led to the outbreak of official war. Today these barriers to trade are not a cause of wars.

There are several important trade bodies globally today which work to reduce and eliminate barriers to trade of different countries. The broadest and most effective of these is the WTO World Trade Organization which enacts and enforces stringent rules on member states regarding the legality of tariffs and other trade barriers. This has driven some countries and economic blocks to employ other trade barriers than tariffs. The EU simply bans the importation of most any generically modified product. This outlaw bans the overwhelming majority of American food products in practice. The WTO has gotten wise to this tactic and begun to investigate these types of barriers too.

Financial Terms Dictionary - Trading Terminology Explained

Trading Blocks

Trading Blocks are pacts between various countries typically having a common geographical area. They form them for protections against non-member nations' imports. These trading agreements are also a type of economic integration that has more and more impacted the global trade patterns and trends. A few different kinds of trading groups like these exist today.

Preferential Trade Areas are the first and probably most common form. These PTA's occur when countries of a common geographical area decide to eliminate or at least reduce the tariff barriers that exist on certain goods which they import from other nations in the PTA. This represents the first small but critical step in the development of full scale trading blocks.

The next logical progression in the trading agreements development is to form a Free Trade Area. If two or still more nations within the region concur on eliminating or at least reducing the barriers to all trade on every good imported from the other members, they establish this second step in the chain.

The third step forward is to establish a Customs Union. This means that all trade barriers and tariffs between the group members are canceled, and a unified external tariff policy against non members is placed. It allows the member states to negotiate trading deals with third parties as a single more powerful trading block. They can enter agreements this way with other trading blocks or even the World Trade Organization if they wish.

Full economic integration begins to occur if the members of the trading block continue down the path towards its eventual logical conclusion. This leads them to a common market, the first major leap into economic integration. Member nations are now trading freely in every area of economics and resources, not only physical goods. It entails all services, labor, capital, and goods barriers being eliminated.

They also work to reduce and finally eliminate any non-tariff barriers. The common markets are only truly successful when all micro economic policies and other rules are brought into harmony as well. These include anti-competition laws and anti-monopoly regulations. Some trading blocks at this stage also begin to implement key industry common policies, like the EU's Common Fisheries Policy and Common Agricultural Policy.

There are numerous advantages to members of a trading block once they are fully formulate and established in practice. Free trade within the block allows member states to specialize in areas of production in which they have the greatest comparative or absolute advantages. Trade increases between key members as they have improved access to one another's national markets. Trade creation is the inevitable result. It refers to the phenomenon that free trade creates as more expensive domestic producers are outcompeted by more economically efficient and less expensive imports from other trading blocks members.

Lower priced imports also mean a greater consumption effect and higher demand. Economies of scale allow the producers in these nations to benefit and apply the savings to lower pricing for their customers. More jobs are often created because of the higher and growing trade between the block members. Finally, companies within the block may have to be more efficient against their own block rivals, yet they do gain effective economic protection against less expensive imports out of non-block member based corporations. The EU shoe industry is a good example of this. They are economically protected by tariffs on cheaper shoe imports from Vietnam and China.

There are some significant disadvantages of these trading blocks too. Trading blocks usually distort global trade by reducing the benefits of global specialization and comparative advantages of the world as a whole. Those producers which are less efficient than global competitors will be shielded from the outside of block more efficient ones. Trade is diverted away from the most efficient producing companies which are only guilty of being based outside of the trading block area.

Turtle Trading System

The Turtle Trading System proved to be a classic system that followed trends. It works by trading on breakouts much like those used in the Donchian Dual Channel System. In this particular method of trading, two breakout figures are important.

The first is a longer 55 day channel breakout point to enter the trade. The second one is a shorter 20 day channel breakout point to exit the position. If the prior trade turned out to be a losing one, then the system employs a dual length method of entering the trade using the shorter 20 day chancel breakout entry point. Stop losses in the Turtle system are set based upon the ATR Average True Range.

This system at first proved to be a secret. In the late 1970s and early 1980s, bits and pieces of classical successful trading systems pioneered by legendary traders Richard Donchian, Jesse Livermore, and Darvas were taken and cleverly combined into what became known as the Secret Turtles Trading System and Rules.

It was Richard Dennis who actually took the new system and created a challenge and test. He wanted to prove that regular individual people could become successful traders if only they had a successful system to follow in trading stocks. He created a class of 14 individuals in 1983 to put this to the test.

Richard Dennis gathered together these 14 regular people who had no stocks or commodities trading experience before joining his mentorship program. He taught them and trained them in the rules of the highly secretive system and program. The class of new traders was then given individual actual dollar accounts so they could trade.

For the next year they traded according to the Turtles Trading Breakout System to prove the point that any people could make money trading if they had the right instructions and a proven system to devotedly follow. At the end of that first year, the experiment demonstrated that the 14 traders had returns which averaged 80%.

Years later after the experiment and program had ended, one of the first

Turtles revealed the secrets of the system. Curtis Faith proved to be an original 1983 class Turtle Trader and he unveiled the now not so secret Turtle Trading Rules to Wall Street and general investors on his site www.OriginalTurtles.org. This is how it came out that the system utilized trend following in its proven approach.

It was this website that at last shared the rules of the Turtles Trading System with the world. The rules fell under four main sections of theories for highly profitable trading. The first one was position sizing. This taught would be traders how to know the right amount to buy and sell in a particular trade.

The second set of rules pertained to entry points. They showed traders the best way to know how to time trades. They taught the method for knowing when and at what price level to get into the trade in the first place.

The third group of instructions gave details on how to set stop loss levels. No mater how many successful trades the system provides, it must manage its losses. No system is right all of the time. This is why it is critical to have price levels at which to takes losses and exit out of a losing position.

Finally the system had a section of rules on profitable exit points. Winning positions could not be left to run forever. A point came when it was the optimal time for traders to take their profits. These rules set out the right price levels to cash out of winning positions. Both stop loss and profitable exit points were based on formulas that worked off of the Average True Range.

Unit Trust Fund

A Unit Trust Fund is effectively a vehicle in which individuals can invest their money. Investors can sink their funds into these investments using a range of financial service providers. These include an investment management company, a stock broker, and even sometimes a local or larger bank. These Unit Trust Funds are essentially a large pooled reserve of capital. They permit assortments of investors to combine their liquid assets to invest them. All of the investments together amount to the aggregate assets of a fund.

It is generally the case that such a Unit Trust Fund will have the legal structure like a mutual fund but which is unincorporated. They permit the funds to contain these shared assets and ensure that all profits become dispersed directly back to the individual unit share owners rather than reinvesting them. Such an investment fund becomes established under the auspices of a trust deed. Each investor is literally a member of the trust fund beneficiaries.

A Unit Trust Fund's success comes down to how experienced and professional a management company which runs it actually proves to be. The managers are allowed to invest in a wide range of investments. Some of the most typical of these include mortgages, securities such as stocks and bonds, real estate property, and cash equivalents such as CDs and money market funds.

The Unit Trust concept is widely utilized in Great Britain and a number of former British colonies and current day British territories. Among these are Jersey and Guernsey of the British Channel Islands, the Isle of Man, Ireland, Fiji, Australia, New Zealand, Singapore, Malaysia, South Africa, Kenya, and Namibia. Within the United Kingdom at least, unit trusts are interchangeable with the phrase mutual fund, though they are quite different from the American versions of mutual funds.

With regards to the assets of a Unit Trust Fund and their value, this can be expressed by taking the price per unit and multiplying it times the amount of units. Naturally there will be expenses taken off of this figure before it is considered final. Some of these expenses include management fees, trading transaction fees, and other relevant costs.

It is the unit trust fund managers who manage the trust in order to realize the greatest potential returns and profits. Trustees will be assigned in order to make certain the manager of the fund is properly pursuing the various objectives and goals of the Unit Trust Fund. Ultimately these managers work for the unit holders who have all rights to the assets of the trust in question. In between the stakeholders in the trust and the manager of the fund in question are the registrars. These middlemen are merely a type of liaison standing in between the two parties. They carry out a number of administrative duties.

These unit trust funds turn out to be open-ended in nature. This means that as new or existing investors add additional money to the trust, then more units will be created at the unit buying price that is current. Similarly, as holders sell their units for cash, an equivalent amount of the fund assets will be sold off at the present selling price per unit.

The income of the fund managers is realized by the bid and offer spread. This represents the difference between the price of buying the units and the price of selling them. This spread will vary from one moment to another and be based on the types of assets the fund manages. It might be merely a couple of basis points for those assets which can be liquidated expeditiously and simply, as with government sovereign bonds. The spread could be even five percent or still higher for assets which are more difficult to buy or sell. Real estate properties are examples of less liquid assets that take longer to transact.

Wilshire 5000 Index

The Wilshire 5000 Index is also called the Total Stock Market Index. The reason for this impressive sounding name is that its ultimate goal is to track the aggregate returns of most ever publicly traded stock that is based in the United States and trades over one of the major American stock market exchanges. This index is not necessarily the most famous one in the investing universe though. The truth is that despite this fact, it remains the biggest market index on earth, when it is measured by actual market value.

The Wilshire 5000 Index is actually a misnomer. There are not only 5,000 firms within the index as many incorrectly suppose. Instead, there are over 6,700 individual companies' stocks within it. The number of firms actually changes all the time. When the Index was first created, it actually had only 5,000 composite companies. As more business have been created and traded publically on the major three U.S. exchanges since the Wilshire's inception, this has necessarily required that they add more net numbers of companies in order to keep up with their objective of representing all major American corporations.

In order to be a candidate for inclusion in the Wilshire 5000 Index, there are three criteria which the firms must meet. They have to be headquartered domestically within the United States. They must also trade actively over one of the significant stocks exchanges in America. Finally, their pricing data has to be easily accessible to both members of the general public and the American investing community.

The Wilshire index actually does not evenly weight all of its constituent members, as is typical with other market cap weighted indices as well. In fact, they provide a greater weighting to firms that are more highly valued and an underweighting to those companies which possess a lesser firm value. The ticker symbol for The Wilshire 5000 Index proves to be TMWX. The index is famous for its efforts to track the all around American stock markets' performance.

Some publically traded United States' based corporations are routinely excluded from any inclusion in The Wilshire 5000 Index. Among these are the stocks which trade over the OTC BB Over the Counter Bulletin Board platform and system. This includes the stocks from micro cap companies and those which are valued as penny stocks. All companies which trade on the NASDAQ, American Stock Exchanges, and NYSE New York Stock Exchanges are typically included. It is what makes the Wilshire index the most truly diverse of all American indices anywhere.

Those larger companies which are a part of the Wilshire index have a greater weighting and will thus have greater impact on the movements of the underlying index.

With the Wilshire 5000 Index, the 500 biggest firms command over 70 percent of the total value of the index. This actually means that it is an economic performance measurement of only American companies, the largest 500 of which dominate the up and down movement of the index.

It is important for investors to realize that the ETFs, index funds, and other mutual funds based on the Wilshire 5000 have a unique expense characteristic. The costs of maintaining a passive portfolio of over 6,700 different stocks which are constantly changing naturally will be higher than for a index fund that has only 30 or even 500 composite constituent corporations within it, as in the Dow Jones 30 companies' index or the S&P 500 composite index. Despite this fact, the fees do not amount to a much higher percentage wise difference for investments in the Wilshire 5000 Index.

XAU Precious Metals Index

The XAU precious metals index proves to be a stock shares index which trades on the United States' based Philadelphia Stock Exchange. This index is comprised of 29 different precious metals mining firms. Though there are 29 participants in the index, the index is heavily dominated by only the three largest of them. These three overwhelming players are mega-gold mining companies Barrack-Placer, Newmont Mining, and Anglo Gold Ashanti. Between the three of them, they represent over half of the entire index.

As of May 5, 2017, the 29 companies comprising the XAU precious metals index were as follows: Agnico Eagle Mines Limited, Anglo Gold Ashanti Limited, Barrick Gold Corporation, Coeur Mining Incorporated, Compania de Minas Buenaventura, El Dorado Gold Corporation, First Majestic Silver Corporation, Freeport-McMoran Incorporated, Gold Fields Limited, Gold Resource Corporation, Goldcorp Incorporated, Harmony Gold Mining Company Limited, Hecla Mining Company, Iamgold Corporation, Kinross Gold Corporation, McEwen Mining, New Gold Incorporated, Newmont Mining Corporation, Nova Gold Resources Incorporated, Pan American Silver Corporation, Primero Mining Corporation, Rand Gold Resources Limited, Royal Gold Incorporated, Sandstorm Gold Limited, Sea Bridge Gold, Silver Standard Resources Incorporated, Silver Wheaton Corporation, Still Water Mining, and Yamana Gold Incorporated.

Back in 2006, the Philadelphia Stock Exchange expanded its XAU precious metals index and grew the exposure beyond the traditional North American, British, South African, and Australian based miners to include significant exposure to Eastern Europe, South America, and Russia. They did this by adding in another four mid cap and small cap companies that had gold mining properties in those three parts of the world. At the same time, Placer Dome was acquired by Barrick Gold and became removed from the index.

The four new companies which they added to this important precious metals index were Royal Gold Incorporated, Rand Gold Resources Limited, Couer D' Alene Mines Corporation, and Bema Gold Corporation. Bema Gold Corporation was later acquired by Kinross Gold Corporation and subsequently became delisted from the XAU precious metals index. It is not terribly surprising that Canadian Bema Gold Corporation was taken over, as even in the heyday of rising gold prices back in 2005, Bema proved to be an anomaly in the gold mining world as it represented one of the only gold companies on earth to lose money in the booming gold price days of the mid 2000's.

The development of adding additional gold mining company exposure to Russia, Eastern Europe, South America, and Australia came about because of geographical leadership changes in both the gold and silver mining industries. The XAU precious metals index has long been the most closely studied and heavily watched bell weather of gold mining company shares. It outperformed the overall stock markets in the first five years of the new millennium, and managed to triple in market cap and overall share pricing from 2001 to 2005.

The Philadelphia Stock Exchange allows trading of the XAU precious metals index every Monday through Friday from 9:30am until 4pm local Philadelphia time. This index has only one serious rival in the world of gold mining companies' indices. This is the HUI Index listed as the AMEX Gold BUGS Index. The two indices represent the world's most closely followed precious metals composites.

There has occasionally been some confusion with the name XAU precious metals index. This is because XAU also denotes a single ounce of gold. Thanks to the ISO 4217 currency standard, the symbol became representative of the yellow metal itself.

Xetra

The Xetra is a Frankfurt, Germany based trading system. What makes it so significant is that it is a completely electronic platform for trading German stocks. The Deutsche Borse first launched this platform for handling the stock trades back in 1997. This system provides broad order depth and greater flexibility for viewing the German markets. Traders can watch and access trading in German stocks, bonds, funds, commodities contracts, and warrants on the Xetra system.

The system has proven itself well enough to be adapted by other stock exchanges throughout Europe and the world since it began operating. The creators of Xetra originated it for the Frankfurt stock exchange. Since then, it has spread to other national stock exchanges in Vienna, Austria; Dublin, Ireland; and Shanghai, China.

Part of the success of Xetra lay in its relatively early launch. As such, it became among the first of the great electronic and global trading systems. Making German capital markets more accessible for foreigners and their investment proved to be one of its key benefits. Xetra has expanded to handle over 90% of all of the stock trades for the Frankfurt Stock Exchange.

The Frankfurt Stock Exchange represents Germany's largest trading exchange. Also known as the FRA, it is based in Frankfurt. Deutsche Borse owns and operates Xetra and the Frankfort Stock Exchange along with all of Germany's other trading exchanges. Thanks in part to the success of the Xetra, this exchange represents one of the most efficient and biggest facilities for trading markets on earth. It is also among the oldest stock exchanges around the globe.

The Frankfurt Exchange handles practically all of Germany's trading. It also manages a significant portion of all trading in the whole of Europe. The FRA makes a large portion of its profits from the Xetra trading system. The many foreign investors flowing in because of Xetra are responsible for a significant share of the profits. FRA is open each day of the week from 9:30am till 5:30pm.

There are a number of important stock indices based on the Frankfurt Stock Exchange and run by Xetra. Among these are the DAX, the Eurostoxx 50 and the VDAX. Xetra DAX is Germany's equivalent of the Dow Jones Industrial Average in America and the Financial Times Stock Exchange 100 in London. This blue chip index of their stock market exchange contains the 30 most important German companies that are traded on the FRA.

Deutsche Borse states that the performance of these companies is measured according to market capitalization and order book volume. All of the prices from the DAX are taken off of the Xetra trading system. While the DAX is an important index with its 30 Prime Standard companies represented, this does not equate to the strength of the whole German economy.

Prime Standard companies listed on the Xetra DAX and other important Frankfurt exchanges such as SDAX, MDAX, and TecDAX have to attain international transparency standards. This means they have to use international accounting standards as with US-GAAP or IAS. Their quarterly reports and ad hoc disclosure must be in German as well as in English. They must hold minimally one analyst conference every year. Finally, these companies must publish a financial calendar.

Xetra computes the DAX index values once every second. It has done this since the technology began managing all electronic functions for the DAX on January 1, 2006. After the Xetra closes each weekday, the DAX index keeps trading under the name L-DAX. These prices are based on the FRA trading venue floor trades and continue until 5:45pm. At this point, the L/E-DAX Index picks up trading until 8pm.

Trade Balance

Trade balances are used to describe the difference between the value of goods and services that are exported versus those that are imported into a country. Countries might have positive trade balances, where they export a greater value than they import. They might also have negative trade balances, or trade deficits, when they import a larger value of goods and services than they export.

Positive trade balances create cash stockpiles and investment surpluses. Nations like Singapore, South Korea, Taiwan, and most of the Gulf Oil states like Saudi Arabia, Kuwait, and the United Arab Emirates continuously run positive trade balances. Negative trade balances create currency outflows or government debt that must be issued and sold domestically or exported as payment for the extra imports. Countries like the United States and Great Britain commonly run negative trade balances.

Positive trade balances are beneficial and constructive to a nation. They can be run forever in theory, so long as other countries continue to purchase their goods and services at high levels. Negative trade balances, or trade deficits, are harmful to a country over long periods of time. They can not be carried on forever, since eventually the negative trade balance running countries will reach a point that they have spent all of their money covering the imports or issued an amount of debt that finally becomes unsustainable and undesirable to investors any longer.

The United States' trade balance specifically refers to the differences between the value of American goods and service exports versus goods and services imported into the United States. This trade balance proves to be among the largest Balance of Payment components. America's Balance of Payments is constantly pressuring the U.S. dollar's value. These deficits minimally bring down the value of the currency for a country that continuously runs them.

Trade balances are reported in the United States and other advanced economies. The problem with such reports is they commonly come out some time after the data is current. This means that most of the information contained within such trade balance reports has already been anticipated and affected the markets. The Foreign Exchange markets do move based on these trade balance reports though, since trade balance data helps to form or support foreign currency trends. To this FOREX market, the Trade Balance report has proven historically to be among the most significant released from the United States.

Trade Associations

Trade Associations refer to those groups which offer a means for businesses in a certain industry or segment to interact in a way that benefits all parties concerned. Such an organization will be funded by member company contributions. These associations typically work to promote the industry's image to the public.

It might also deliver a single voice in the form of a government legislative lobby. They interact with government officials on issues which will affect the industry itself. Besides such critical functions as these, associations have other roles. These could include a way for the organization to educate the consumers of the general public on the main products and concerns of its particular industry.

Much of the time such industry trade associations will be established as not for profit organizations. This allows companies which associate in the same segment to cooperate together on those issues which affect them all in common. It is also true that these organizations are particularly useful for safeguarding an industry's integrity. This is because they commonly establish behavior standards which all member companies have to honor in order to maintain a good standing record.

Those companies or groups which refuse to live up to the standards the group develops and enforces in common suffer from the consequences. The leaders of the trade association might eventually choose to expel the business from the trade association for continued misbehavior. This would cost the offending company a serious amount of credibility before not only the industry, but also buying customers of the general public.

It is these trade associations which typically maintain all necessary means to ensure the industry's undivided voice will be heard by the law makers in a given nation or jurisdiction. This is why many participating member corporations choose to operate through the trade association in order to encourage industry-friendly legislation which will best help their industry segment to succeed. Similarly, this association could choose to lobby against any legislation that they feel will harm their collective best interests and those of their industry as a whole.

It is true that a number of businesses will elect to back marketing plans and public relations campaigns on their own to increase the exposure of their products and name brand with the relevant consumers. The beauty of a trade association such as this is that it will similarly endeavor to create interest through making members of the public aware and educating them on the industry in general and also the various products it offers. They will not concentrate their efforts on the goods for sale by a given member company. Instead, they will back publicity and marketing or advertising campaigns which lead customers to buy and consume the given industry's goods they produce in general.

This starts with offering the public facts and figures which consumers can easily understand and appreciate. The idea behind such education efforts of the trade association is that it will make it easier for the marketing efforts of the individual companies within the industry to have maximum impact. Besides lobbying, educating, and marketing, these trade associations frequently act as conference sponsors for their member businesses to attend.

Such a conference's purpose and offerings typically center on boosting the industry's overall practical performance. They do this through delivering useful information that every conference participant is able to grasp and remember. Members then take home this information to the other members of their firm and share it with those who could not attend the conference. Practically every business or trade association will sponsor at least one or more of these forms of gatherings or conferences once every year.

Trade Agreement

A Trade Agreement refers to a contract agreed upon and signed into force of law. These are made between two (or sometimes more) different countries regarding their trading relationship. It is entirely possible for such agreements to be either multilateral or merely bilateral. Multilateral trade agreements are those which exist with more than two nations.

In the majority of cases, international trade itself becomes regulated by a variety of one sided barriers. Among these different sorts of barriers are non-tariff barriers, tariffs, and restrictions on trade. A Trade Agreement is a way to lower such discouraging to trade barriers and restrictions. The generally held belief is that they will provide advantages which include more trade for all parties concerned.

It may come as a surprise to many that it is very complicated to successfully conclude a major Trade Agreement. The reasons for this are varied. There will always be coalitions of groups which do not want overseas competition to increase because of greater tariff-removed trade. Non-economic barriers to trade are also widespread in the world today. Some of them exist because of national security concerns. Still other government issues on trade concern the wish to protect a local culture and way of life from foreign "corruption," as was the case with Communist Eastern Europe and the former Soviet Union empire.

There are typically three principle elements which one Trade Agreement will often have in common with another. These are the reciprocity rules, treatment of non-tariff barriers, and a clause for most favored trading nation. Reciprocity rules must be a part of any kind of a trade agreement. All parties in the deal must each benefit from this type of arrangement or there will not be any incentive to enact it in the first place. For any such agreement to happen, all sides must assume that they receive minimally as much as they will lose from the deal. Simply put, if Britain drops tariffs on Australian beef, then they will rightly expect Australia to drop tariffs on British London high street fashions.

The second idea, a common treatment of non-tariff barriers is a clause that becomes necessary in such a Trade Agreement. The reason for this is one nation may slyly decide to put up other barriers to trade in place of the tariffs they agreed to reduce or eliminate. As an example, they might institute sales or excise taxes on certain goods, quotas, so-called health requirements, specific license requirements, voluntary restrictions on imports, and also outright prohibitions on certain goods. Rather than attempt to spell out and make illegal any kind of non-tariff regulation, the treaty parties must sign off on a clause that they will provide the same kind of treatment to their trading nation's businesses and goods as they would to those of their own country. Steel is one such industry example where this has occurred in the past.

Finally, there is the most favored trading nation clause. It mandates that one or more nations in the treaty must consent to not lowering barriers additionally on a non-participating country. It means that if Britain and Australia sign a reduced tariff agreement on beef, and then Britain agrees to a still lower tariff on beef with New Zealand, then Australia will automatically receive the same lower tariff on beef as New Zealand now enjoys.

Examples of several sweeping multilateral trade agreements do exist in the modern world. Two of the largest, best known, and most successful prove to be the European Free Trade Association from 1995 and the North American Free Trade Agreement (NAFTA) from 1993. Both of these deals became more possible because of the rules established by the World Trade Organization.

Stock Buybacks

Stock buybacks occur when companies repurchase their own company shares from the markets. They are sometimes called share repurchases. A buyback is like a company choosing to invest in itself, since it is actually employing its own cash reserve to purchase its own stock.

Companies may not be shareholders in themselves, which means that their shares are absorbed back into the company. This has a net effect of decreasing the quantities of stock share which are outstanding. This also increases the size of each owner's stake in the company as there are not as many shares and claims on the company's earnings.

There are two means in which stock buybacks occur. They can be done via tender offers or open market purchases. In a tender offer, all shareholders receive such a tender offer from the company to submit some or all of their shares by a specific deadline. Such an offer divulges the quantities of shares which the company wishes to buy back as well as the price range they are agreeable to offer.

These tenders are nearly always at premium prices versus the current market level. Investors who are interested in participating will let the company know how many shares they wish to sell them at the price they will take. The company involved in the share repurchase would then put together the right combinations so that it could purchase the shares it wants for the lowest price.

Companies can also enter the open markets to engage in stock buybacks. They do this precisely as individual investors by buying shares at the going market price. The difference between the company and an individual investor doing this is that the market sees a company repurchasing its own shares as a significantly positive action. This generally leads to the stock prices rising quickly.

A company management will state that the share repurchase is their best option for deploying the firm's excess capital at that given point in time. The management of a firm is supposed to be interested in maximizing the returns for their stake holders. These stock buybacks do usually boost the value of shareholders. There are other motives for company managements buying back shares. They may believe that the stock market has overly discounted the prices of its stock shares.

Stock prices can decline from many different causes. These might be that earnings were less than anticipated, the economy is poor, or there are negative rumors surrounding the company. Firms that pay out millions of dollars to invest in their own shares show that the company management feels the market has punished their share prices unfairly with the discount. This is always seen positively.

Stock buybacks can also create better fundamentals for a company's balance sheet. Since the repurchased shares become either cancelled or treasury stock, this lowers the number of outstanding shares as a result. This decreases the balance sheet assets as the cash is spent. With fewer assets on the balance sheet, the return on assets ROA goes up in the process. Return on equity ROE also grows as the outstanding equity is reduced. The markets generally prefer higher ROAs and ROEs. Managements that do share buybacks just to boost their balance sheet fundamentals are looked at negatively and as problematic.

Stock Market Index

A stock market index refers to a collection of stocks which are combined together to create a bellwether for a group of similar companies in the market. The idea is to present an index which tracks a certain sector, market, currency, commodity, bond, or other type of financial asset.

Stocks which are collected in such an index are put into a so-called basket. An example of this is easy to understand. A person who wished to invest in the DJIA Dow Jones Industrial Average index would buy into the shares of the index basket that represented the 30 component companies. This means that the investor would then own 30 different companies' stock shares.

The idea behind indices is that they track the underlying assets or market. The XAU Gold and Precious Metals Index is comprised of those companies which mine precious metals including gold. Purchasing shares in this index means that an investor has the benefit of exposure to the entire gold mining sector. They achieve this without having to acquire shares in all of the gold mining firms of the globe. It is accomplished because shares in XAU represent all of the gold mining shares in the form of the entire industry.

These indices were fashioned to imitate particular markets. This does not mean they will ever be accurate all of the time nor even 100 percent at any given point. This is because there are a wide range of factors that can change the market course which indices will not always capture with perfection immediately.

Not every stock market index is liquid. This means that it could be hard to get in and out of some index-based positions. It is also the case for some stock company securities too. Because of these problems, there are alternatives to a stock market index. These are called ETF Exchange Traded Funds. Such ETFs have the advantage of being constructed in order to imitate an index. This is done in the same way that indices imitate stock markets and various other assets. The ETF has the advantages of being immediately ready for trade and a pre-arranged package. This makes an ETF a true mini portfolio available for an affordable price with reasonable fees (especially as compared to mutual funds).

Financial Terms Dictionary - Trading Terminology Explained

There are many stock market indices that are well-known throughout the world. The most famous of these is surely the DJIA Dow Jones Industrial Average. This 30 stock company index trades every day on the NASDAQ and NYSE New York Stock Exchange. The component companies of this most famous of indices on the planet include such internationally respected giants as the Walt Disney Company, General Electric Company, Microsoft Corporation, McDonald's, and Exxon Mobile Corporation.

Another internationally followed index is the S&P 500. It measures the values of 500 of the large cap stocks of the United States. The NASDAQ Composite index follows the fortunes of fully 4,000 different company stocks as they trade daily. Yet another stock market index often called the total market index is the Wilshire 5000. While somewhat less famous than the other three, this index of indices follows the performance of every publicly traded corporation which is headquartered within the U.S. The four indices mentioned here address the daily progress of the large American companies. A competing index the Russell 2000 follows the performance of an impressive 2,000 smaller corporations of the U.S. markets.

The market index values are called points. This means that if the London FTSE 100 rose 150 points in a single day that the value increased versus the prior day's close to that point. It means that the total net gains of all the composite companies collectively increased by a net of 150 points.

Indices such as these assist investors by helping them to keep tabs on the health of various industries in which they may have interests or capital invested. If the DJIA continues to drop repeatedly for a period of many weeks or a month, investors could reasonably conclude at least some of the companies within the underlying index have run into serious trouble. This would be a prescient warning to evaluate the portfolio and perhaps liquidate some of the holdings in favor of other ones which were performing better.

Short Squeeze

A short squeeze relates to a scenario where a traded stock or commodity which has been heavily shorted suddenly moves aggressively higher without advance warning. This creates a self-fulfilling prophecy in which the short sellers feel so painful a loss that they are forced to close out their shorted positions. They actually increase the upward momentum and pressure on the stock by doing so. Such short squeezes give the impression that short sellers have no choice but to abandon their own short positions at a significant loss typically.

These are often triggered by sudden positive news announcements or company developments which give the idea that a stock may be beginning a turnaround in its fortunes. It could be this is only a temporary effect, yet not many short sellers are able to afford to hold losses which are running away limitlessly on them. In these cases, they stop the proverbial bleeding by closing them out, even though this means booking the so- far only paper losses.

When the stock begins to rise astronomically and quickly, the trend becomes self- reinforcing many times as the short sellers all trip over each other in their stampede towards the proverbial exit doors. When stocks go up 15 percent in only a single trading session, the short sale holders will often have not choice but to sell out and cover these loss-making positions via buying back the stock. When sufficient quantities of short sellers all do this at once, the stock price rises even more.

There are two practical means of determining which stocks are at greatest risk of falling victim to a short squeeze. The tools are short interest and short interest ratio. With short interest, this refers to the aggregate shares which are short sold as a percentage of all outstanding shares. Short interest ratio proves to be the actual numbers of shares that are sold short divided using the average daily trading volume of the stock in question.

Considering a hypothetical example helps to understand this concept better. A biotech company Britex possesses a drug which is a participant in advanced FDA clinical trials for treating skin cancer. Investors may be highly skeptical about whether or not such a drug will really work effectively and without dangerous and unacceptable side effects. Because of their doubts, 10 million shares of the Britex stock out of their total 50 million shares may have been short sold. This means that the short interest on Britex stock proves to be 20 percent. As the daily trading volume averages approximately a million shares, the SIR would be five. This SIR conveys that it would require five trading days for the short sellers to be capable of purchasing back all of their shares which they have sold short.

It could be that the enormous short interest has caused the price of the stock to drop from $15 to around $5 per share in advance of the clinical trial results. If the results were successful as the announcement came out that it treated skin cancer effectively, Britex stock would gap massively up on the news results. It could rise to more than $8 because speculators will simply pour into the stock. Short sellers would then be desperate to cover their short positions as soon as possible. The short squeeze in Britex shares would then be on in full force. This could press the stock to significantly higher levels because of the rapid unwinding of the short positions.

Those investors who are contrarians seek out stocks that are overly shorted exactly because a serious risk of short squeeze exists. They can build up massive long positions in such heavily shorted securities when they determine that the odds of success are much greater than what the short interest implies. They are taking on a calculated risk and hoping for a tremendous risk to reward potential payoff when the stock is only trading for a few dollars per share. They assume risk only limited to the price of the long positions, since the stock can not drop below zero. The potential for profit is in theory limitless.

Treasury Bonds

Treasury Bonds are also called T-Bonds. These financial instruments prove to be government debt issued by the United States federal government at a fixed rate of interest. Such debt securities come with maturity dates of longer than 10 years. The T-bonds offer interest payments twice per year. Because they are federal debt instruments, their earned income may only be taxed by the federal level authorities of the Internal Revenue Service. Though nothing is really risk free in the investing world, investors generally consider these bonds to be virtually without risk, since they are issued by the United States federal government. Investors perceive them to have a minimal amount of default risk.

Such Treasury Bonds turn out to be among the four kinds of Department of Treasury issued debt. They employ all of these to finance the runaway spending activities of the Federal Government. In these four debt types are the T-bills, Treasury notes, T-bonds, and TIPS Treasury Inflation Protected Securities. Each of these different debt securities is different according to both their coupon payments and their varying maturities.

Despite this, every one of them are the benchmarks for their particular fixed income categories. This is because they are American government backed, almost free of risk, and guaranteed by the revenues and tax base of the United States Treasury. In theory the Treasury can always levy higher taxes to make sure the interest and principles are repaid on these financial instruments. As they are all the lowest returns in their investment category, they are also deemed to be benchmarks for the various fixed income types of investments.

Such Treasury Bonds come standard issued with maturities which vary from 10 years to as long as 30 years. Their denominations start at $1,000 minimums. Each coupon interest payment pays out on a semi-annual basis. The bonds themselves sell via an auction system. The most of them that investors can purchase is $5 million when the bid proves to be non-competitive or as much as a full 35 percent of the entire issues when the bids turn out to be competitive.

It is important to understand what a competitive bid actually is. These types of bids declare that the bidder will accept a certain minimum interest rate bid. These become accepted according to the comparison versus the bond's set rate. With noncompetitive bids, bidders are guaranteed to receive the bonds so long as they will take them at the pre-set interest rate. Once the bonds have been auctioned off, the buyers may sell them off via the secondary market.

Investors call the active market for Treasury bonds re-sales the secondary market. Thanks to this enormous market, T-bonds and T-bills are extremely liquid. It means they can be easily resold on a constant continuous basis. It is this secondary market that causes the T-bonds' prices to gyrate considerably in the markets. This is why both yield rates and current auction rates for the T-bonds determine their prices via the secondary market.

As with all other kinds of standard bonds, these Treasury bonds will experience declining prices as the rates at auction increase. Conversely, the bonds will experience rising prices when the auction rates decrease. The reason for this inverse relationship is that the future cash flows of such bonds becomes discounted according to the higher rate.

T-bonds are also important because they are part of the yield curve for the fixed income markets. As one of the four principal investments which the American federal government offers, they make up this yield curve. The curve is critical because it pictorially displays the range of maturity yields. It is typically sloping upward since lower maturities provide lower rates than do the farther out maturity varieties. There are cases though when the farther out maturities experience peak demand. This causes the yield curve to become inverted. In such a scenario, the farther out maturities will have lower rates than the closer dated maturities.

Treasury Bills

Treasury Bills prove to be among the largest category of United States issued Treasuries. They are also called T-Bills for short. Treasury Bills have maturities of a year or less. They never pay investors interest before they mature, making them somewhat like zero coupon bonds. The government instead sells Treasury Bills at a face value discount, which causes there to be a positive yield to maturity. Numerous economists and ratings agency consider Treasury bills to be the lowest risk investments that American and foreign investors can purchase.

T-bills come issued with varying maturity dates. These typical forms of weekly Treasuries can have four week maturity dates, thirteen week maturity dates, twenty-six week maturity dates, and fifty-two week maturity dates. Every week, the government runs single price auctions for its Treasury bills. The quantity of thirteen week and twenty-six week Treasury bills available for purchase at auction are actually announced every Thursday. They are then offered on Monday and issued on the next Thursday.

Four week T-bill quantities get announced Mondays for next day auctions. The bills become issued on Thursday. Fifty-two week bills become announced only on the fourth Thursday, to be auctioned the following Tuesday and issued that Thursday. Associated purchase orders have to be received before 11 AM on Monday auctions at Treasury Direct. Minimum purchases for these T-bills are a reasonable $100, marked down from the former $1,000 minimum. The Treasury redeems T-bills that mature every Thursday. The biggest buyers of T-bills prove to be financial institutions such as banks, and primary dealers in particular. These Treasuries in their individual issue all get one of a kind CUSIP numbers.

Sometimes the Treasury cash balances are lower than usual. At these times, the Treasury often opts to sell CMB's, or cash management bills. They sell these in much the same way as T-bills, at auction with a discount. Their main difference lies in their irregular amounts and shorter terms of fewer than twenty-one days. They also possess different week days for auction, issue, and maturity. As these CMB's mature on the identical week day as typical T-bills, commonly Thursdays, they are termed on cycle. When they instead reach maturity on another day, they are known as off

Financial Terms Dictionary - Trading Terminology Explained

cycle.

Treasury bills are regularly sold on the secondary market too. Here, they are both quoted and sold via annual discount percentages, known as a basis. The secondary market trades these T-bills heavily.

The Treasury has modernized its means of offering T-bills to investors recently. Treasury Direct is their means of selling T-bills over the Internet, so that funds can be taken out and then deposited straight to the individuals' bank accounts. This permits investors to make better rates of interest on their savings than with simple bank account interest.

Wall Street

Wall Street is a physical street that is seven blocks long and runs from Broadway to the New York East River. It lies to the south of the Manhattan borough of New York City. The street is incredibly significant because it has played host to a number of the most important financial entities in the United States.

The city originally got its name because of an earthen built wall that Dutch Settlers of the city erected in 1653 to ward off an anticipated invasion of the English. The street's importance grew so rapidly that before the Civil War in America this was already known as the nation's sole financial capital. In the district of Wall Street there are many important buildings and headquarters.

The street contains the Federal Reserve Bank, the New York Stock Exchange, the International Commodity, Cocoa, Sugar, Coffee, and Cotton Exchanges, and the NYSE Amex Equities. There are also numerous municipal and government bond dealers, investment banks, trust companies, and insurance and utilities' headquarters located here. A great number of the major American brokerage firms have their headquarters in this financial district.

Because of Wall Street, New York City is sometimes called the most important financial center in the world as well as the greatest and most powerful city economically. Investors find the two biggest stock exchanges in the world as measured by market capitalization here in the NASDAQ and the New York Stock Exchange. A few other significant exchanges also make or made their headquarters here. These are the New York Board of Trade, The New York Mercantile Exchange, and the one time American Stock Exchange.

In the 2000's there were seven major Wall Street firms here. These included Lehman Brothers, Merrill Lunch, Morgan Stanley, Goldman Sachs, Citigroup Inc, JP Morgan Chase, and Bear Stearns. Several of these companies failed outright or had to be sold at urgently distressed prices to rival financial companies in the Great Recession that ran from 2008-2010. Lehman Brothers had to file for bankruptcy in 2008. The U.S. government made JP Morgan Chase buy Bear Stearns. The Treasury and the Federal

Reserve then forced Bank of America to purchase Merrill Lynch.

The catastrophic collapse of this many major financial firms dramatically downsized Wall Street with massive re-structuring. It proved to be especially severe for the economies of New York City and the surrounding states. This was because the financial industry in New York produced nearly a quarter of all income in the city. It also amounted to about 10% of all tax revenue for the city and 20% of taxes for the state of New York. City and state government revenues and budgets suffered dramatically from this loss of revenue for years. The Boston Consulting Group estimated in 2009 that as many as 65,000 jobs were permanently gone as a result of the financial crisis.

This city and financial center has grown to become a global symbol for investment and high finance. Movies have been made about it including two with the same title Wall Street and its sequel Wall Street: Money Never Sleeps. The financial district has become a part of modern mythology in many ways starting back in the 1800s.

The street emerged as a hated symbol of the greedy robber barons who took advantage of workers and farmers to the populists of the 19th century. When times were good it represented the way to get rich quick. Following such terrible stock market crashes as 1929 and 2008 the street looked like the home of financial manipulators who could crush major international companies and even derail the economies of entire nations.

iShares

iShares prove to be a group of ETF's, or exchange traded funds, that are run by BlackRock. The very first iShares were called WEBS, or World Equity Benchmark Shares. They were later renamed iShares.

Today iShares are traded on stock exchanges the world over. This iShares proves to be the biggest ETF issues in both the United States and the world as a whole. Most every iShares fund actually tracks the performance of either a stock market index or a bond market index. The London Stock Exchange, the New York Stock Exchange, the American Stock Exchange, the Toronto Stock Exchange, the Hong Kong Stock Exchange, and the Australian Securities Exchange, along with various other Asian and European stock markets, all trade listed iShares funds.

There are hundreds of iShares issued funds. While many of them cover large and small indexes in the United States and internationally, others deal with specialized sectors or commodities. Naturally they have funds on an enormous variety of indexes, like the Dow Jones, NYSE Composite, and the Russell 3000 in the United States markets. These cover large cap, small cap, and mid cap indexes of stocks ranked according to their dollar amounts of market capitalization.

iShares also has funds that cover a wide variety of sectors, ranging from energy funds and industrial funds, to financials funds and health care funds, to consumer staples and discretionary funds, to materials funds and technology funds, to telecommunications funds and utilities funds. Besides this, they also offer a good variety of real estate index funds for both international and United States real estate.

The iShares listed funds cover a wide range of developed and developing international indexes, such as China, India, Brazil, Peru, Chile, Israel, Indonesia, Mexico, South Korea, Taiwan, Turkey, Poland, Japan, and emerging market index funds. Beyond this, they offer index funds for all of the various major regions of the world, including Africa and Middle East funds, the Americas funds, European funds, and Asian funds.

They count various global sectors of index funds in their stable too, such as a nuclear energy index fund, a global clean energy index fund, and a global timber and forestry index fund. Where bonds are concerned, iShares provides a good variety of index funds based on treasuries, government credit, corporate credit, municipal bonds, mortgages, and global bonds.

They have specialty index funds like dividend stocks funds and socially responsible corporation funds. Finally, in the category of commodities, iShares offers two especially popular funds, the Gold Trust fund that trades under the symbol of IAU, and the Silver Trust fund, that trades as SLV.

iShares originally arose as a collaboration between investment bank Morgan Stanley and fund manager Barclays Global Investors in the 1990's. By the year 2000, Barclays decided to launch a major expansion of the ETF market. To this effect, they started up and marketed more than forty new funds that they branded under the name of iShares. The other funds that Morgan Stanley and Barclays had launched as WEBS were soon renamed iShares as part of the broader effort.

Quota Effects

Quota Effects refer to the economic consequences of a government body imposing an import quota in a national economy. Such import quotas are the legal limitations on the quantities of specific imports that companies are allowed to bring into a given nation. As an example, the United Kingdom might decide to restrict the quantities of Japanese cars that may be imported to 1 million vehicles each year.

The simple answer to the question on effects this causes in a specific country which enforces them is that they will lower foreign imports to the benefit of domestic producers and suppliers. At the same time, this causes more complicated, unintended, and undesirable side effects. Consumers will pay higher prices for their goods, the overall economic well being of the nation may decline, and nations which have been targeted with the import quotas may choose to retaliate with quotas of their own on the imposing nation's exports.

Rising prices occur as Quota Effects come into play. It is always helpful to consider a concrete and real world example of this concept. If a nation which is a major sugar producer controls around 55 percent of the entire market, they may decide to impose sugar import quotas. This would cause the aggregate available supply of sugar in the domestic market to decrease. Additional demand for sugar would lead to sugar prices rising. The purchasing power of consumers in this nation would suffer. It may be that the domestic sugar producers are able to increase production and meet the demand. If not, the prices will stay high so long as the import quotas are in place. Demand destruction (loss of demand because prices are simply too high) may occur as well.

Increases in domestic production can also be positive Quota Effects. The national producers will have the opportunity to fill the gap of foreign sugar producers and suppliers. If the quotas have reduced the individual sugar imports from four pounds per individual to two pounds, then domestic producers of sugar will need to boost their inputs, production, and labor participation hours in order to fill in the missing two pounds of sugar per consumer. This is particularly beneficial for those domestic industry producers who have the factory capacity and employee numbers to expand their production. They only thing they might be lacking is the incentive to produce additional sugar as the foreign imports of the good are cheaper than what they can additionally produce.

Import quotas such as these also have dramatic and typically negative consequences for the large international multi-nation corporations. These companies have high priority on their international production and trade capabilities. Only the domestic consumption within their nations would not be enough to meet their production and sales targets. Look at General Motors as a classic example of this fact. For the year 2008, they produced around seven million vehicles in total which they sold. Yet a mere three million of such sales occurred within the United States. Had one of their major international country buyers chosen to impose an import quota on American cars, then they would have been forced to rapidly develop an alternative market for the cars, or to reduce production and the resulting income and profits alongside it.

The primary reason that countries resort to such import quotas is that they wish to safeguard one of their important industries from free market failure against the major international MNC players. This is the same thing as putting failing industries on government assistance to keep them going. What many economists believe is that countries should allow their failing industries to disappear and try to focus instead on ones at which they have a competitive and comparative advantage. As an example, the United States is unable to directly compete with China for clothing articles production. The U.S. should instead focus its efforts on maintaining its effective market domination in the computer software development business.

Repurchase Agreements

Repurchase agreements refer to types of short term time borrowing. It is the government securities dealers who engage in them. The appropriate dealer will first sell such government securities to institutional investors or financial institution investors. They usually do this for overnight. After this, they will purchase them back the next day.

Those parties who sell the security and agree to subsequently buy it back in the near future are involved in such a transaction as a repo. The opposite end of the transaction parties who buy the security and consent to sell it back in the near future are engaging in a reverse repurchase agreement.

Economists and analysts consider repurchase agreements to be money market instruments. They are typically utilized to raise shorter time frame capital. In these arrangements, the buyer functions as the short term time frame lender. The seller carries on like the shorter term borrower. The collateral is the security itself. In this way, both entities involved in the transaction meet their goals to secure liquidity and funding.

Repurchase agreements typically rank as safe forms of investments. This is because the security being traded is also collateral. It also helps to explain why the majority of such agreements have Treasury bonds as their security. Besides this, the United States Federal Reserve uses these types of agreements themselves. They deploy them to control the amount of bank reserves and the overall money supply. Individual investors like these agreements for financing debt security purchases. In any case, the repurchase agreement is always and only a shorter term investment. The term or rate refers to the maturity period of the repo in question.

Even though they are many similarities between these agreements and interest paying loans which are short term in nature, repurchase agreements are different. They represent true purchases. Yet the buyers keep such instruments only temporarily. This is why both accounting and taxing authorities treat them as loans. Those agreements which specify their maturity date represent term agreements. In the majority of cases, these agreements will reach maturity either the next week or alternatively the following day.

Other Repurchase agreements are open ones. This is because they do not have a maturity date specified by and in the contract. It means the sellers or buyers can complete the terms of the agreement and then renew them or instead choose to terminate them. Almost all such open arrangements will wind down in from one to two years.

Three different kinds of repurchase agreements exist. The first is called a specialized delivery repo. These financial transactions mandate that the agreements and maturities must have a guarantee of bonds. Such an agreement is uncommon.

There are also the held in custody repos. With these, sellers get cash for the security sale. They still keep it within a custody account on behalf of the purchaser. Such an arrangement is still less common than the specialized delivery repos. This is because there is a chance that the seller could declare bankruptcy, leaving the borrower unable to access the collateral as a result.

The most common kind of repurchase agreement is the third party repo agreement. Such arrangements involve either banks or clearing agents which act as intermediaries of the transaction between sellers and buyers. They safeguard each party's interest this way. By taking possession of the securities involved, they make certain that the seller will obtain cash when the agreement commences and the purchaser will transfer over the funds for the seller and also make delivery of the securities when maturity occurs. Such arrangements as these make up more than 90 percent of the total repo market. In 2016, this market contained around $1.8 trillion.

Risk Arbitrage

Risk arbitrage is also known as statistical arbitrage. It is different from pure arbitrage as it involves risk or speculation. It is also far more accessible to retail traders than real arbitrage. Because of the reasonably high probability that risk arbitrage offers traders, experts generally consider it to be playing the odds. Despite the risk involved, this form of arbitrage has grown to be among the most practiced type by retail traders. Three main types of this arbitrage exist, liquidation, merger and acquisition, and pairs trading arbitrage.

Liquidation arbitrage is a kind that involves determining the liquidation value of a business' assets. If a company possesses a book value of $100 per share and trades at $70 per share, it falls under this type. If the company determines it will liquidate, there would be an opportunity to make $30 per share on the dissolution of the company. When bigger companies practice this they buy companies whose parts are worth more than the whole of the company. They then sell off the various parts or assets to make money.

Merger and acquisition arbitrage remain the most practiced form of the strategy. The goal is to find a company that is undervalued at its current share price. If it is selected by another company as a takeover target, then it presents opportunity. The offer for this target will raise the company share price to near this level. The earlier investors get in on such a prospect, the more they are likely to profit from it.

If the merger does not go on as planned, the share prices will probably drop. Speed is the necessary factor to make this type of arbitrage work. Traders who practice this type usually receive streaming market news and trade on Level II trading. When a merger deal is announced, these traders attempt to buy in before everyone else does.

An example of this type of a deal would be a company trading at $40 which received a takeover bid for $50. The share price will rapidly rise towards $50 but not reach it until the merger actually closes. It might move to $48 per share. Those who get in on it immediately have a chance to make as much as $10 per share, or a 25% return. Others who buy in at $48 only have a $2 per share arbitrage opportunity for 4%. So long as the takeover happens as planned, both parties will make their returns. If it fails in the end for some reason, they will both likely take losses. The amount they lose depends on the price they paid and how far the stock falls back down on the failed acquisition.

Pairs trading arbitrage may be less common than the other two but it is especially useful in sideways trading markets. The idea is that investors find stock pairs which trade at a high correlation. They could be unrelated or related so long as their historical trading chart demonstrates that they trade in near tandem. Usually pairs with the greatest likelihood of success turn out to be larger stocks competing in the same industry.

The goal is to wait until one of these pairs has a price divergence in the 5% to 7% range. The variance also needs to last for some significant amount of time like two or three trading days. Investors then buy the cheaper stock long and sell the more expensive one short.

The last step is to wait for the prices to approach each other again. Once the prices are back in line, this type of arbitrage closes the trade and pockets the percentages they were apart initially. If the investor both bought the one long and sold the other short, then the gains can be twice the percentage the pair was apart.

Russell 2000 Index

The Russell 2000 Index represents a British-based American stock market index which measures the actual price performance of around 2,000 small cap companies located in the United States. It is actually a portion of the far larger capitalized Russell 3000 Index, comprised of the 3,000 largest American stocks. The Russell 2000 still equates to the major benchmark for the United States' based small cap stocks today.

The way these two indices work is that the complete index is the Russell 3000. The lower capitalized 2,000 stocks in this 3000 Index are the ones comprising the Russell 2000 Index itself. FTSE Russell is the subsidiary company of the world renowned London Stock Exchange Group, based in the United Kingdom, which created and maintains the popular benchmarking index.

Without a doubt or real rival, the Russell 2000 Index proves to be the most frequently relied upon benchmark for the various families of mutual funds that present themselves in their prospectuses as small cap funds. Conversely, with large cap stock-based mutual funds, they rely on the S&P 500 index. It means that this Russell 2000 is easily the most frequently and universally referenced measurement for the aggregate performance in the mid cap to small cap company space and their corporate stock prices. Though it is the bottom 2,000 issues in the Russell 3000 Index, the market capitalization weighting of the 2,000 bottom stocks only turns out to be a mere eight percent of the overall market cap within the all around Russell 3000 Index.

The ticker symbol for the Russell 2000 is ^RUT on most platforms and trading systems. Per March 31st of 2017, the market capitalization weighted average for companies in the Russell 2000 remains about $2.3 billion, while the median market cap proves to be approximately $809 million. The biggest company in this popular market index has a market cap amounting to nearly $13.3 billion. The index first traded higher than the 1,000 point mark between May 21st and May 22nd in 2013.

A similar but not serious rival to this small cap behemoth index is the S&P 600, produced by Standard & Poor's. It is far less frequently sourced and cited, as are other competitors maintained by various rival financial providers.

One unique breakdown of the Russell 3000 and Russell 2000 indices is for a special sub index called the Russell 3000 Growth Index. Included in this special index are companies which demonstrate greater than average levels of growth. This is why this growth index is utilized as a best measurement gauge of the American growth segment stocks. In order to be included in the Russell 3000 Growth Index, they must demonstrate higher forecast earnings and greater price to book values.

The company Russell Investments has a precise procedure for determining these various indices component stocks. They screen the biggest 3,000 common stocks in the United States to form the Russell 3000 Index. The biggest 1,000 companies screened are named composite members of the Russell 1000 Index, while the subsequent 2,000 companies become members of the Russell 2000 Index. Russell Investments has strict rules on those issues which can not be included in their indices. They may not be either foreign stocks or ADR American Depository Receipts. They also can not be components of the BB bulletin board stocks or OTC pink sheet stocks.

It is interesting to note that investors who like this Russell 2000 Index have a number of options in both exchange traded funds as well as mutual funds that do their best to replicate its real performance. None of them match it perfectly though. This is because there are trading costs and expenses involved in acquiring the various 2,000 component companies, stock selection market cap imbalances, and changes to the index's constituent companies which are difficult to replicate with precision. Investors can not directly invest in the index itself, or any stock market index for that matter.

S&P 500 Index

The S&P 500 Index refers to a world famous American stock market index. It is comprised of 500 stocks today which analysts and investors view to be the leading indicator for American stocks and equities. They call this the mirror of the large cap world performance. Economists are the ones who select the components of the S&P 500.

The S&P 500 Index itself proves to be weighted based on market value. It is among the three most significant benchmarks of the American stock markets along with the Dow Jones Industrial Average and the NASDAQ Composite. There are also various other lesser known S&P indices which focus on either mid cap firms or small cap companies which boast lower market capitalizations of from $300 million to $2 billion. A wide range of investment products exist that trade on the S&P 500. Among these are both ETF exchange traded funds and index funds in which investors can speculate or invest.

Most investors consider the S&P 500 Index to be the most crucially accurate measurement of the large cap American equities performance. It is true that this index only concentrates on the bigger capitalized portion of the stock markets. Yet it is deemed to be representative of the overall market simply because it covers a substantial part of the entire U.S. stock market value.

It is the S&P Index Committee that picks out the 500 constituents of this index. This committee is comprised of a team made up of economists and analysts who work for Standard & Poor's. The professionals in this group contemplate a number of different characteristics when they decide on the 500 constituent companies that make up the index. Some of the most important considerations are liquidity, market size, and grouping of their industry.

In recent years, the S&P 500 Index has become so widely followed and popular that it has surpassed the DJIA Dow Jones Industrial Average as the preferred benchmark metric of United States' stocks. Part of the reason for its inevitable success is that the S&P 500 includes an impressive and more representative 500 different American firms versus the only 30 companies in the Dow Jones Industrials.

Besides this, another major difference exists between the two popular indices. While the S&P 500 employs a market capitalization methodology that delivers greater weight to bigger companies, DJIA utilizes a different price weighting procedure that provides greater weight to stocks which are more costly by price. Many economists and investors consider the market cap weighting method to be more true to life of the way the market itself functions.

It is difficult for individual investors to personally duplicate the S&P 500 alone. This is because the portfolio would require for them to purchase stocks from fully 500 individual companies in set quantities in order to replicate the methodology for the index. This is why it is so much easier for investors to simply buy into one of the good S&P 500 products. Some of these are the SPDR S&P 500 ETF, the Vanguard S&P 500 ETF, and the iShares S&P 500 Index ETF.

There are other S&P indices in the S&P 500 Index family. The 500 index is also a member of the S&P Global 1200 family. Besides this, there are the popular indices including the S&P Small Cap 600 Index with its smaller capitalization firms, the S&P Mid Cap 400 Index with its mid cap corporations, and the composite of the three S&P 500, 600, and 400 indices--- the S&P Composite 1500 Index.

The original name of the S&P 500 Index was the Composite Index. This arose in 1923 to track a small group of American stocks. Standard & Poor's expanded the index in 1926 to 90 stocks and finally to the present 500 in 1957.

Financial Terms Dictionary - Trading Terminology Explained

Securities and Exchange Commission (SEC)

The SEC is the acronym for the Securities and Exchange Commission. This Federal government agency actually governs the buying and selling of stock securities and other types of related investments. The SEC also works to safe guard investors against impropriety and fraud. They encourage the development of the market with the end goal of keeping America in the first place as the world's leading economic giant.

The Securities and Exchange Commission came into existence in 1934. The stock market crash in 1929 prompted a tremendous regulatory response where the national government observed that it had to oversee and monitor investments within the U.S. The SEC is headquartered today in Washington D.C. Its staff is comprised of five commissioners who are appointed, as well as the personnel working in eleven different regional offices throughout the country. They work together to create, amend, and enforce the laws that regulate investments in the country.

The SEC has various critical missions. Among the most significant one is their role in ensuring that the markets are transparent. To do this, they significantly regulate securities trading within the U.S. Companies are required to turn in a variety of legal financial documents during the year so that investors may obtain a true picture of the total financial health of the firm in question.

The documents are kept on file in a database that is available to the public. Anyone who is interested is allowed to inspect them by logging on to the SEC's website and working through their system of electronic documentation. The SEC has great powers that it exercises in enforcing the rules. It is able to mandate company audits if it has suspicions of illegal behavior. Those it finds in violation of its rules may be brought by the SEC to court.

In keeping with the SEC's mandate to help safe guard investors, they monitor the trading of stocks and the individuals responsible for selling them. This means that exchanges, their dealers, and all stock brokers are required to work through the Securities and Exchange Commission. They can be subjected to inspection from time to time to be certain that they are properly taking care of their customers. Consumers have the right to report practices that are unfair to the SEC directly. If you are an investor, you ought to avail yourself of the SEC's wide range of documents on the various publicly traded corporations that they keep in their database on their website.

The SEC additionally governs companies that are interested in undergoing Initial Public Offerings in order to become public companies. Such interested firms have to file a significant quantity of documents with them first. To help them accomplish this, the SEC engages a big staff. Their document database includes regulations and directions for filing such documents. Consultation help is available if companies run into difficulties.

The SEC also promotes education. If you are an investor who wants to learn more about safe investing, then simply go to their website. They have workshops and publications on the site to help all investors. This is in addition to all of the companies' documents kept on file there.

Printed in Great Britain
by Amazon